建築パース

新戦力マスター

Mastering New Architectural Rendering Techniques

Foreword

まえがき

今までのパースに関する出版物は、作品集的なものに多くの比重がおかれていました。作品集的なパース書が、専門家にとって、イメージ的なデザイン分野で大きな意味があったことに由来していたからでしょう。
しかし、多くの読者のなかには、パース画製作の教科書的な技法書を切望していた方も少なくなく、特に、初心者や学生にとっては、作品集的なものよりも、その製作技法に関心が強かったように思われます。現に、彼らの本棚には何冊ものパース書で埋められていることがそれを物語っています。
本書は、初心者から専門家であるプロに至るまで、理解しやすく、教科的手法で実例を示しながら、パース画の着色手順を解説した技法書であります。
また、過去に購入された書物も無駄になることがないように配慮し、他書にはなかった内容に重点をおき、技術書にありがちな難解な技法なども、極力、簡略化してあります。
特に、見習者が体得しなければならない隠れたポイントや注意事項を中心に、最小限の画材と用具で、着色手順だけでなく、色づくりから筆づかいに至るまで細かく説明しました。
是非、解説文を一字一字ていねいに読み進め実習してみてください。つまずいても、それなりに進み、最後のページまで読み終えた後で復習してみてください。きっと、パース画着色に自信がわいてくるはずです。
初心者は、第２章は流し読みですまし、第３章の「表現の実際」から練習してください。本書の巻末に、うまく描けなかった場合のチェックポイントと注意事項を実例で示してあるほか、質疑応答の添削サービスも設けてありますので確信をもって練習してください。
本書は、読者の手助けを念頭に、初心者にはあくまでも教科書的に、他方、専門家やプロの方にはパース辞典としての役割を果せるようにまとめてあります。
この書を踏み台にして、よりよいパース画の完成を目指して利用されることを望みます。
本書の目的はその点にあり、著者としては、微力ではありますがそれを希望してやみません。

松原弘晃

In retrospect, most of the publications which have addressed the subject of perspectives to date have tended to place substantial weight on serving as collections of actual works.
This trend can be attributed to the fact that such collection weighted perspective writings are of major significance to professionals in view of their work in the field of image design.
Among the more general audience, however, there are many readers who yearn for publications which take a textbook-like approach to perspective drawing technique. Especially strong interest is believed to exist for such production technique writings, rather the work collections, among the ranks of beginners and students of the discipline. The presence of large numbers of perspective books on the bookshelves of these persons is solid testimony that this belief is based on true.
This volume is a technical text which uses a curriculum-like approach to present actual examples, while examining the coloring sequence of perspective drawings. It is structured to facilitate ready understanding and use at all levels, from the novice to the expert professional.
Close consideration has also been taken to prevent the books purchased to date from going to waste, with the focus of this text placed on areas which have not been covered in these other volumes. In addition, formidable techniques, which are so prone to appear in technical writings, have been simplified to the greatest degree possible.
A particular stress has been placed on hidden points, cautionary items, and other areas which will require mastering by students. The detailed explanations, using the very minimum of materials and tools, have not been limited simply to the coloring sequence, but also encompass areas which range from color creation through specific brush technique.
The reader is encouraged to read each section of the explanation with care, and put the techniques to use. Even if faltering along the way, continue on reading to the final page, and then take time to review the process. If persevering, I am certain that confidence in the ability to color perspective drawings will emerge from these efforts.
Beginners are encouraged to browse through Chapter 2, and begin your drills from the "Painting Practice" of Chapter 3. Presented at the end of this volume are checkpoints and actual examples of cautionary items for use in cases when drawings have proved difficult to complete. I have also established Q/A format correction and comment service, to enable drills to be undertaken with maximum energy and confidence.
This book has been compiled with the goal of assisting the reader to succeed. It is envisioned first and foremost as a textbook for the beginner, and to fulfill the role of a perspective dictionary for experts and other professionals.
It is my most earnest desire that the use of this book will serve as a springboard in the creation of perspectives of increasingly high quality and perfection.
This was my purpose in compiling the work, and I sincerely hope that the volume will be of some use in escorting readers in this direction.

Hiroaki Matsubara

Contents

目次

1 第1章 画材と用具の実際 —— 使い易い画材と用具

Chapter 1 Painting Materials and Tools

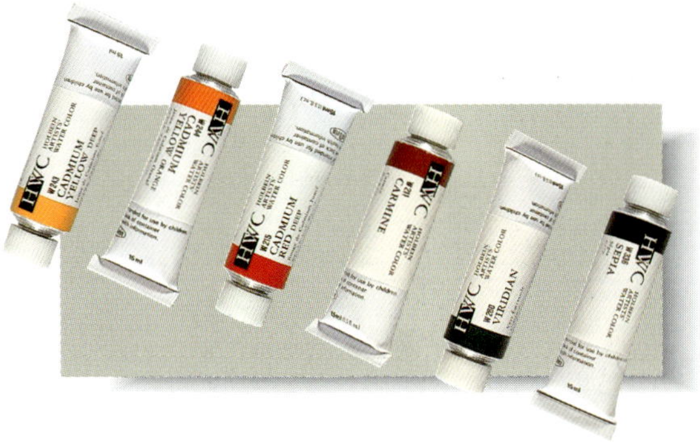

2

第2章
着色のプロセス——いろいろな着色過程の実際

Chapter 2 Painting practice — Different Coloring Process

パース画の着色 Coloring the perspectives

1. 筆塗りパースの不透明着色 Using brushes to light colors perspectives

2. エアーブラシパースの着色 Coloring the perspectives with an airbrush

3. 筆塗り併用エアーブラシパースの着色 Coloring the perspective with combined use of airbrushing and brush painting

3 第3章 表現の実際 — 建物がもっている各部表情のいろいろ

Chapter 3 Painting Practice–Different expressions presented by different elements of buildings

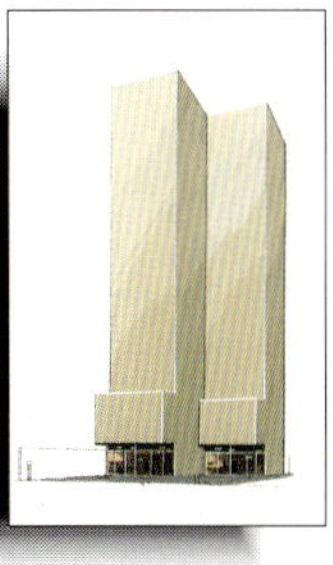

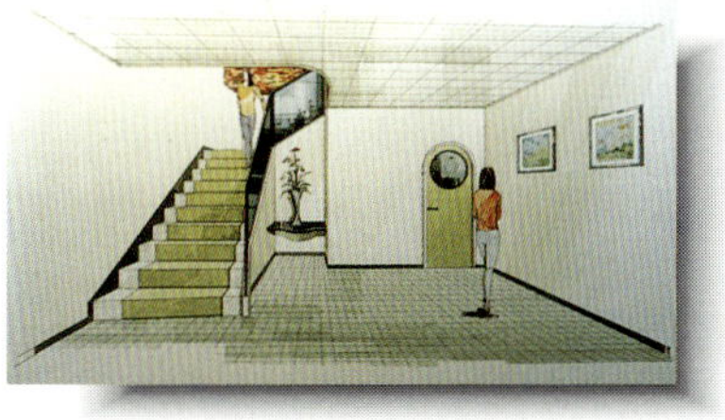

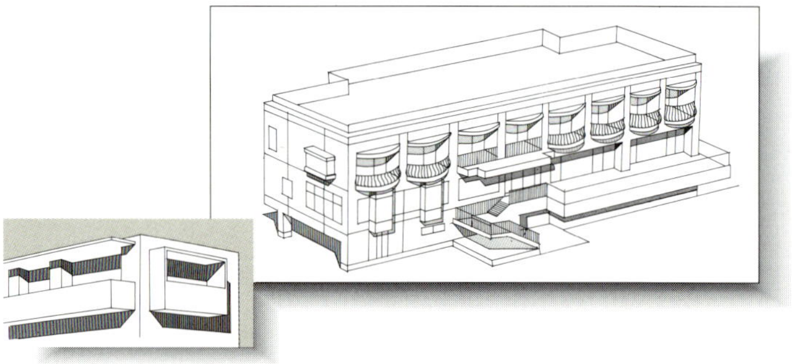

第4章 点景の実際

Chapter 4 How to effectively draw the incidental elements

点景の表現方法 104–128
How to paint the incidental elements

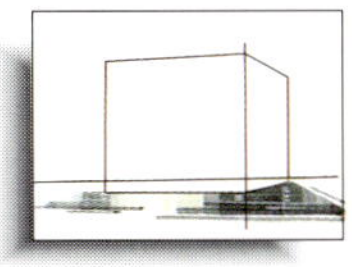

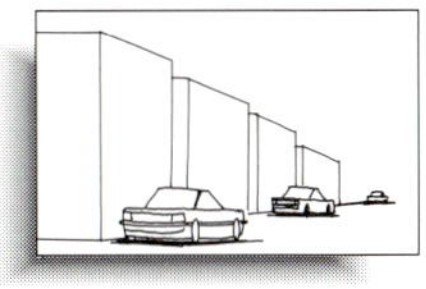

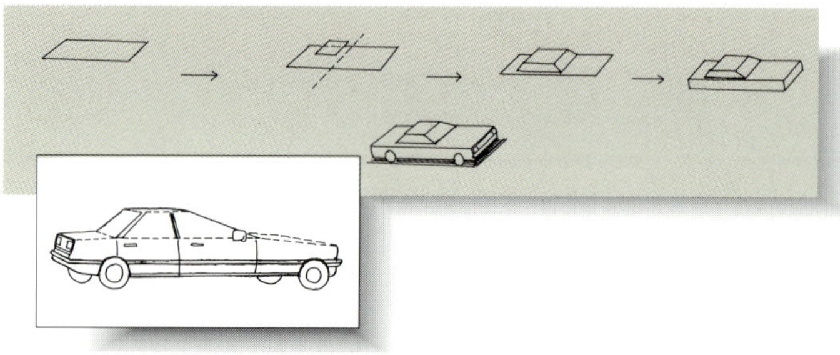

National/Panasonic

第5章
うまく描けなかった場合の処理

Chapter 5 How to touch-up the perspective

うまく描けなかった場合の チェックポイントと注意

Checkpoints and cautions when touching up

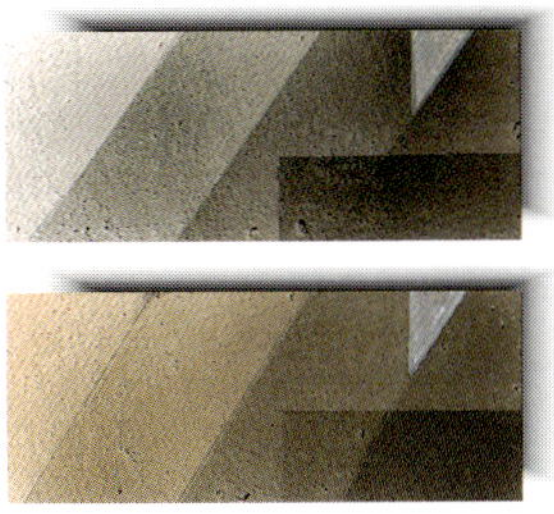

第6章
作品の実際

Chapter 6 Actual works

7 第7章 実技添削 応募規定

Chapter 7 Practical skill and postal tuition course Application procedures

Published by Graphic-sha Publishing Co., Ltd. 1996

ISBN4-7661-0820-5

First Edition 1996
Yanai Building
Graphic-sha Publishing Co., Ltd.
1-9-12 Kudan-Kita, Chiyoda-ku, Tokyo 102 Japan
Phone : 3-3263-4318 Fax : 3-3263-5297

Printed in Japan

第1章

画材と用具の実際

――使い易い画材と用具

Chapter 1

Painting Materials and Tools

1

1

1. 使い易い画材と用具 Painting materials and tools which are easy to use

絵の具に関しては多くのメーカーのものがあり、どのメーカーのものが一番よいかは一概にいえません。一般的にいえば、外国製の絵の具は、発色もよく絵の具の「伸び」もよいようです。そこで、自分に合った使い易いメーカーの絵の具で、しかも比較的安価な絵の具を使うとよいでしょう。
比較的安価な絵の具をすすめる意図は、パレット上で色をつくる場合に、たっぷりとつくっておく方が後で困らないからです。
パース画着色にあたって、最もよく利用される絵の具として、次のような絵の具があります。

A variety of colors offered by many manufacturers are available on the market, and it is quite difficult to make a generalization on which maker's colors are best. In general, the colors made abroad have a reputation for lacking good color development and not spreading as well. Broadly speaking, it is recommended that you use the colors which suit you best; types that are easy for you to use and are relatively inexpensive. The issue of price is important because the colors should be mixed on the palette in ample supply so that they will be quickly available for later use. The following types of colors are widely used in perspectives

2. 基本的な絵の具 Fundamental colors

●ポスターカラー
白…………スノー・ホワイト ―― ❶
黒…………ブラック ―― ❷
●ガッシュ
イエロー・オーカー ―― ❸
●透明水彩絵の具
カドミウムイエロー・レモン ―― ❹
カドミウムイエロー・ディープ ―― ❺
カドミウムイエロー・オレンジ ―― ❻
カドミウムレッド・ディープ ―― ❼
カーマイン ―― ❽
ウルトラマリン・ディープ ―― ❾
コバルトブルー・ティント ―― ❿
プルシャンブルー ―― ⓫
マンガニーズブルー ―― ⓬
ビリジャン ―― ⓭
カドミウムグリーン・ペール ―― ⓮
バーント・アンバー ―― ⓯
セピア ―― ⓰

★本書の説明文では「カドミウム」を省きます。

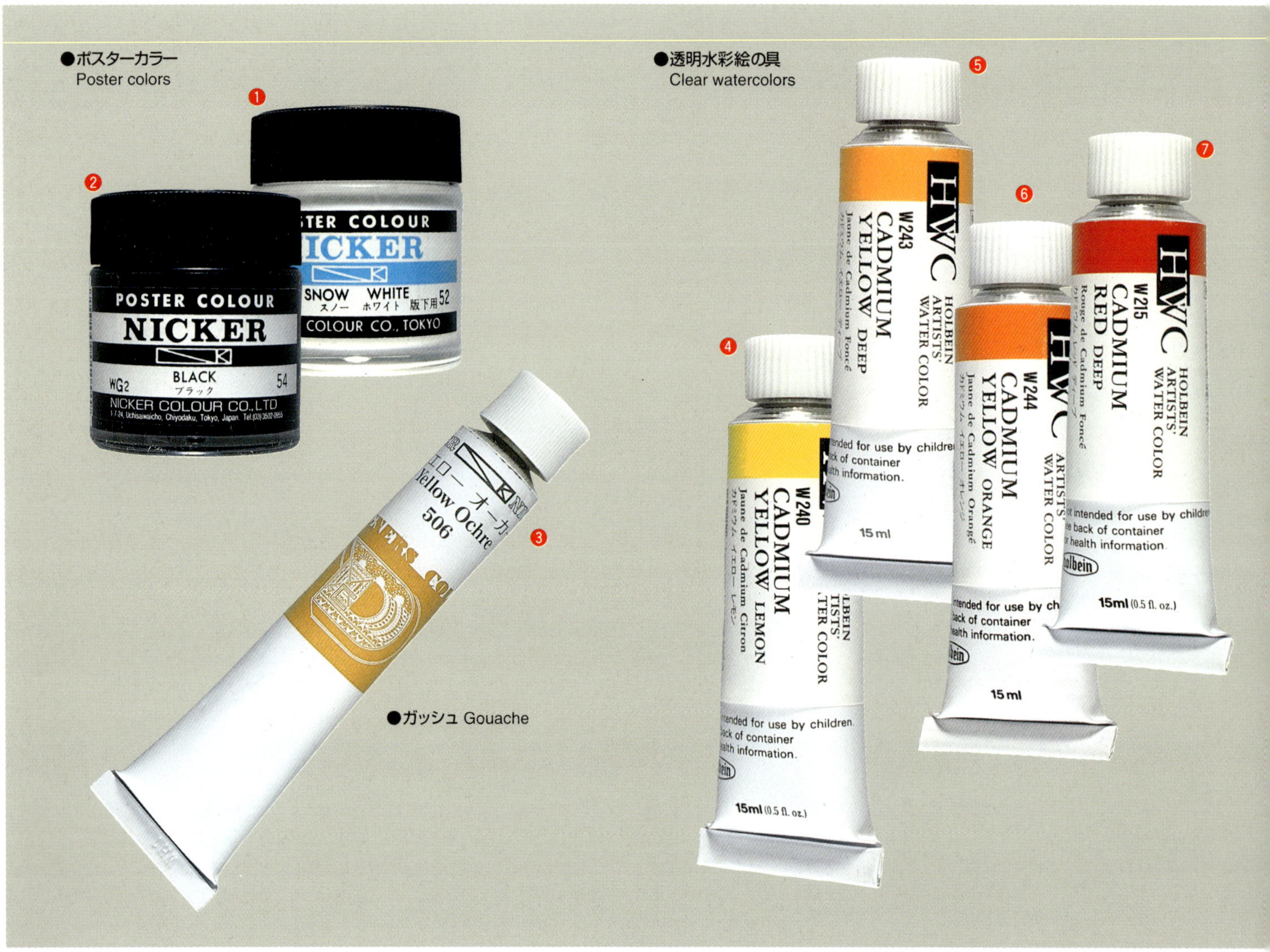

●ポスターカラー Poster colors
●透明水彩絵の具 Clear watercolors
●ガッシュ Gouache

ポスターカラー
Poster colors

不透明水彩絵の具で、比較的厚塗りに向いた絵の具であるので色むらのない着色が可能であると同時に、重ね塗りによって下の色をかくすことが出来ます。

These colors are opaque and are suitable for thicker painting; they are particularly well suited for uniform coloring and can be used to completely cover and hide previous layers of paint.

透明水彩絵の具
Clear watercolors

アラビアゴムが混合された絵の具で、非常に淡い色から濃い色まで着色可能な透明感のある絵の具ですが、色むらが出来易く、一度、紙等に着色されると染まり易く洗い落とすことがむずかしい絵の具です。しかし、重ね塗りによる色の深みや「つや」を出すのには最も適した絵の具の一つでもあります。

Clear watercolors are a transparent type of paint containing a portions of gum Arabic, and can be used to express an extensive range of colors, from light to fairly heavy. The paint tends to mottle on the paper or canvas, however, absorbing quickly through the surface once it is painted on and becoming very difficult to remove. These colors are excellent for producing deep and "luster" colors when they are overlapped.

ガッシュ
Gouache

ポスターカラー等の不透明水彩絵の具と透明水彩絵の具の中間的な絵の具で、淡く着色することも、厚塗りすることもできるという両方の利点を持ち合わせており、初心者には、好ましい絵の具です。

These colors can be thought of as an intermediate between opaque poster colors and transparent watercolors; they have the combined advantages of soft coloring and thick painting, and are preferred by beginners.

●Poster colors:
- White ..... Snow white ―― ❶
- Black ..... Black ―― ❷

●Gouache:
- Yellow ocher ―― ❸

●Clear watercolors:
- Cadmium yellow, lemon ―― ❹
- Cadmium yellow, deep ―― ❺
- Cadmium yellow, orange ―― ❻
- Cadmium red, deep ―― ❼
- Carmine ―― ❽
- Ultra marine, deep ―― ❾
- Cobalt blue, tint ―― ❿
- Prussian blue ―― ⓫
- Manganese blue ―― ⓬
- Viridian ―― ⓭
- Cadmium green, pale ―― ⓮
- Burnt umber ―― ⓯
- Sepia ―― ⓰

★An explanation of "cadmium" colors is not included in this manual.

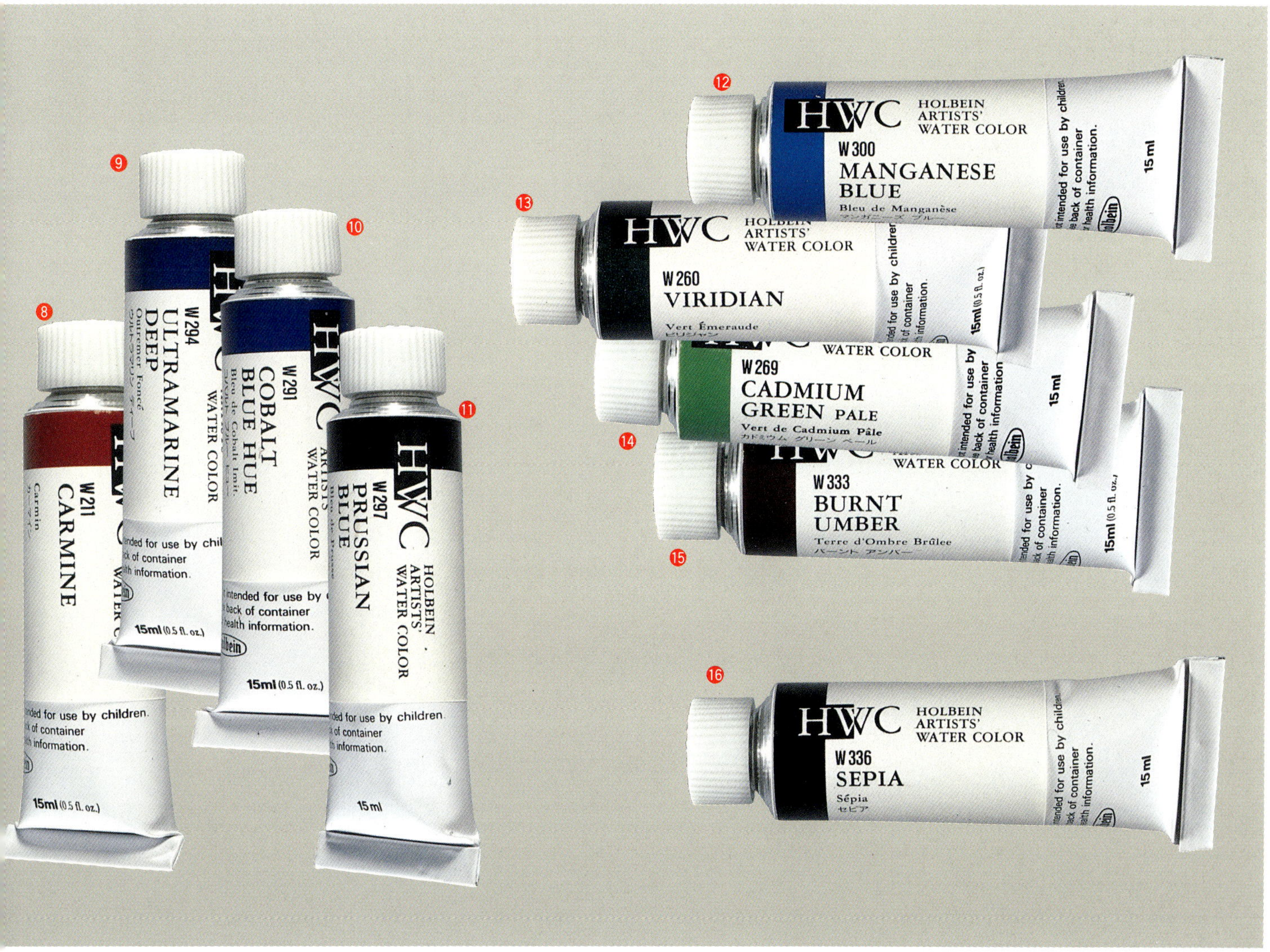

3. 絵の具の性質 Nature of colors

絵の具の混合は減色混合といわれ、混合される色数が多くなればなる程、暗くにごっていきます。従って、絵の具を混ぜ合わせる時、出来るだけ色数を少なくして混合することが、きれいな色づくりのコツでもあります。また、黄等の明るい色は、色むらや顔料の分離が少なく、他方、紫や青等の暗い色は、色むらや顔料の分離がおこり易いので、着色する度に、絵の具をよく混ぜ合わせるように注意し、さらに、着色する色も、たっぷりとつくることが望ましいです。

4. 用具の種類 Types of painting tools

最低限度必要な用具
Most essential tools for drawing

●筆と水入れ及び雑巾
　平筆…２号筆，３号筆各２本と大きな平筆１本 ―― ①
　丸筆…面相筆，極細筆各２本 ―― ②
●鉛筆とシャープペンシル ―― ③
　H，HBの鉛筆とシャープペンシル
●鉄筆…………先のとがったもの ―― ④
●ロットリング ―― ⑤
　1.8mmと２mm各１本
●ボールペンもしくはガラス棒 ―― ⑥
●カッターナイフとペインティングナイフ ―― ⑦
●45cm溝引き定規 ―― ⑧
　プラスチック製，竹製，木製の何れか１本
●刷毛ボウキまたは羽ボウキ ―― ⑨
●デザインパレット(梅皿もあればなおよい) ―― ⑩
　写真のように，多くのくぼみのあるもの
●トレーシングペーパー ―― ⑪
●定規 ―― ⑫⑬⑭
　円形定規，雲形定規，三角定規，あれば楕円形定規
　(作図する場合は，製図板及びT形定規も必要)

●Paintbrush, water container and dustcloth
　Flat paintbrush ....Two No.2 and two No.3 paintbrushes, one big flat paintbrush ―― ①
　Round paintbrush .... Two "Menso" brushes and two ultra-fine brushes ―― ②
●Standard and mechanical pencils ―― ③
　Several H and HB pencils and one mechanical pencil
●Stencil pen .... One with a sharp point ―― ④
●Lottling set ―― ⑤
　One 1.8mm and one 2mm type
●Ball-point pen or glass rod ―― ⑥
●Cutter knife and painting knife ―― ⑦
●A 45mm square ―― ⑧
　A plastic, bamboo, or wooden square
●Brush-type broom or feather brush ―― ⑨
●Design palette (If available a ceramic "Umezara" palette is preferred) ―― ⑩
　A palette with many indentations, as shown in the picture
●Tracing paper ―― ⑪
●Squares ―― ⑫ ⑬ and ⑭
　A circle template, a curved rule, a triangle rule, and if available, an oval rule
　(A design board and T-square are required for drawing figures.)

Color mixtures are sometimes referred to as reduced color mixtures: as more colors are mixed in, the overall color of the mixture tends to darken. Therefore, the trick to producing clean colors is to use as few different colors as possible when blending them. Yellows and other bright colors tend to mottle less and have a lower degree of pigment separation than darker purples and blues. It is necessary, therefore, to be sure that the colors are well mixed, and it is recommended that the mixed colors be produced in sufficient quantities.

エアーブラシ着色に必要な用具
Tools necessary for airbrush coloring

- ●マスキングフィルム ―――― ⑮
- ●エアーボンベ ―――― ⑯
  コンプレッサーがあればよりよい
- ●吹付けピースガン ―――― ⑰
- ●デザインカッターナイフ ―――― ⑱
- ●マスキングテープ ―――― ⑲
- ●金網 ―――― ⑳
- ●歯ブラシ ―――― ㉑
- ●トリパブA液 ―――― ㉒
  (A液は絵の具の定着液で、B液はつや出しや防水用)

- ●Masking film ―――― ⑮
- ●Air cylinder ―――― ⑯
  Air cylinders with compressors are preferred.
- ●Spray piece gun ―――― ⑰
- ●Design cutter knife ―――― ⑱
- ●Masking tape ―――― ⑲
- ●Wire net ―――― ⑳
- ●Toothbrush ―――― ㉑
- ●"Toripabu" A-solution ―――― ㉒
  (The A-solution is a color fixing agent; the B-solution is used for creating luster or water-proofing.)

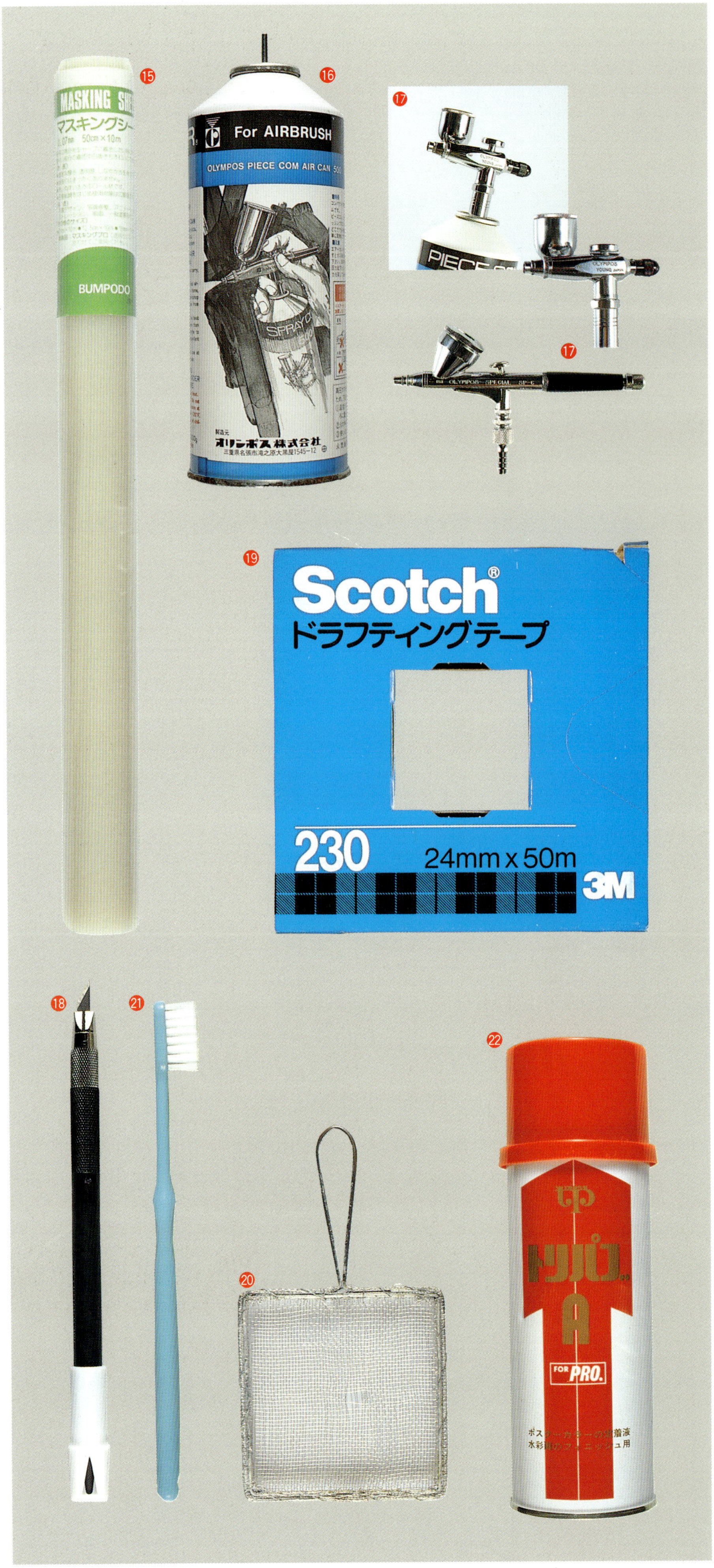

その他、あれば便利なもの
Other materials which are convenient

- ●字消し板
- ●画鋲及びとんがり帽の付いた押しピン
- ●ティッシュ・ペーパー
- ●ドライヤー
- ●スポイト
- ●防じんマスク

- ●Erasing shield
- ●Thumbtacks and pushpins
- ●Tissue paper
- ●Dryer
- ●Pipette
- ●Dust mask

用紙
Papers

- ●キャンソンボード(不透明・透明水彩絵の具用)
- ●クレセントボード(エアーブラシ用)
- ●Canson board
  (For both opaque and clear watercolors)
- ●Crescent board (For airbrush)

第2章

着色のプロセス

──いろいろな着色過程の実際

Chapter 2

Painting Practice

Different coloring process

2

2

パース画の着色

Coloring the perspectives

今日、着色パースの技法として、透明水彩絵の具による着色と、不透明水彩絵の具による着色、さらに、マーカー(マジックペンと同じ)による着色があり、それも筆塗りで仕上げる着色とエアーブラシで仕上げる着色があります。

There are three basic coloring techniques currently used for perspectives (coloring with clear watercolors, with opaque watercolors, and with felt-tipped markers), and two types of finishing methods (finishing with drawing brushes and with airbrushing).

透明水彩絵の具によるパース画(筆塗り)
Perspectives prepared using clear watercolors (with a paintbrush)

透明水彩絵の具は絵の具の「伸び」がよいので、非常に速く着色でき、プレゼンテーション用のパースには時間的無駄がなく、コピーされた下図や、スケッチした下図にも簡単に着色出来ます。

Since clear watercolors tend to "spread" well, the colors can be applied quickly, allowing more time for the preparation of the perspectives for presentation. Reproduced drafts and sketches can be colored easily and quickly.

淡彩外観パース
Exterior perspectives in light colors.

淡彩インテリアパース
Interior perspectives in light colors.

不透明水彩絵の具によるパース画(筆塗り)
Perspectives prepared using light colors (brush painting)

一般に商品パースといわれるもので、実在感を表現するのに最も適しているだけでなく、デザインの変更や設計変更による部分的な手直しも簡単に出来ます。

These perspectives are generally used for commercial purposes; they are the best suited for conveying a sense of realism, and they are ideal for partial touch-ups required after design changes.

透明水彩絵の具での着色を中心にして不透明水彩絵の具を併用したパース画(筆塗り)
Perspectives prepared using mainly clear watercolors combined with opaque watercolors (brush painting)

床面タイルの質感を表現する為に、床面のみ不透明水彩絵の具で、他は全て透明水彩絵の具で着色したパース画
Perspectives prepared using opaque watercolors only to express the texture of the floor tiles, and clear watercolors for the rest.

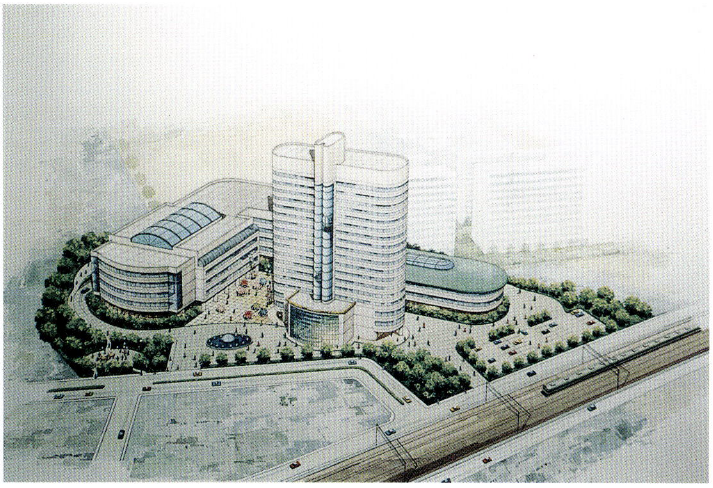

植栽と人物・車の点景のみ不透明水彩絵の具を使い、他は全て透明水彩絵の具で着色したパース画
Perspectives prepared using opaque watercolors only for plants, characters, cars, etc., and clear watercolors forthe rest.

エアーブラシによるパース画
Perspectives prepared applying the airbrushing technique

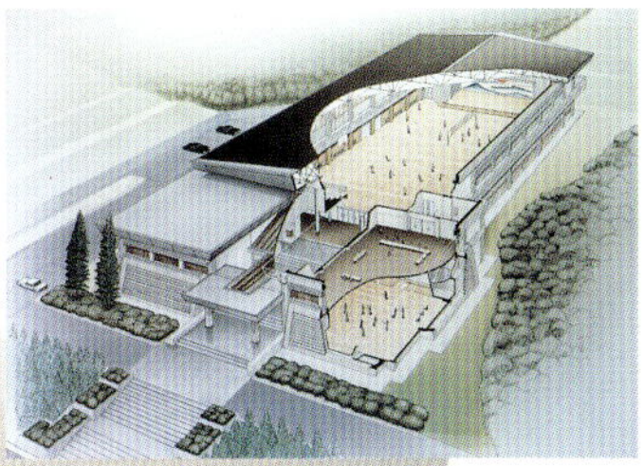

コンプレッサーを用いて、ピースガンといわれる吹付け器具によって、色を吹付けながら着色していくパース画ですが、仕上りが非常にきれいで、現代的なパースとしてマスメディアによく利用されています。ただ、マスキングに時間がかかる他、絵の具の色と吹付けた後の色が違う為に、熟練を要します。また、設計変更による手直しも、描き直しも出来ないという欠点もあります。

These perspectives are prepared using a compressor and special spraying device called a "piece gun." Since a very beautiful finish can be obtained using this method, these types are widely used by the mass media for modern perspectives. There are drawbacks, however: masking takes considerable time, and since the colors tend to differ before and after spraying, special skill is required. Another big disadvantage is that the perspectives can't be touched up or repainted after design changes.

筆塗りとエアーブラシの併用によるパース画
Perspectives prepared by brush painting and airbrushing

山や森を透明水彩絵の具で、あらかた仕上げた上からエアーブラシで再度吹付け着色した後に、強調すべき植栽を重ね描きしたパース画
Perspectives of mountain and forest scenes in which clear watercolors are airbrushed over in the final stages to highlight the plants.

窓ガラスと路面、植栽は透明水彩絵の具で着色し、他は不透明水彩絵の具で着色したパース画
Perspectives prepared using clear watercolors for window panes, street surfaces and plants, and opaque watercolors for the rest.

窓ガラスも建物も、下塗り着色した後、エアーブラシで仕上げたパース画
Perspectives finished applying airbrushing technique after preliminary painting of window panes and buildings.

人物及び噴水等、細かい部分を筆塗り着色したパース画
Perspectives prepared using brush painting for the human subjects, fountains, and other details.

1. 筆塗りパースの不透明着色 Using brushes to light colors perspectives

A. 外観パースの着色過程 Coloring process for exterior perspectives

マンション及び集合住宅の着色過程
Coloring process for a condominium and an apartment house

まず空を着色します。この時、画面の空の部分をあらかじめ水で濡らしておくと着色し易くなります。筆は出来るだけ大きな平筆を使うとよいでしょう。また、窓ガラス面の一部にも見本のように空の色を着色しておきます。

To begin with, paint the sky. If the portion for the sky is dampened in advance, good coloring can be assured. Larger brushes are recommended for this process. Some portions of the windows should be lightly colored with the colors of the sky, as shown in the sample.

窓ガラスの着色に移ります。イエロー・オーカーにバーント・アンバーを少し加えた淡い色から始め、徐々に重ね塗りをくり返し、基準線寄りを暗くします。この時、空の色で着色されているガラス面を一部残すことを忘れてはなりません。

Next, color the window pane. Start with light colors --add a few small dabs of burnt umber to the yellow ocher-- and then repeatedly overlap the colors to express darkness around the reference line. It is important to remember at this stage not to paint over the portions of the window pane where the sky colors are to be painted.

さらに暖色ニュートラル(p.57参照)を加えながら茶黒系の色をつくり、何度も重ね塗りしガラス面の奥行を表現します。

Prepare a series of brownish black hues by adding warm neutral colors (See p.57) and apply them repeatedly to express the depth of the window pane.

イエロー・ディープに白を加えた明るい色で、照明や1階部分の明るい人物のシルエットを描き込みます。その後、サッシの影を描き入れ、サッシを黒っぽい色で描き加えます。アルミサッシや、白っぽいサッシの場合は、白だけか、白に少し黒っぽい色を加えた不透明水彩絵の具で描き加えます。

Silhouette the lighting and human elements on the ground floor using bright colors made by adding white to deep yellow. Recreate the shade of the aluminum sashes by painting the sashes with blackish colors. For off-white aluminum sashes, use only white hues, or use an opaque watercolor with very small amounts of black added to the white.

外壁面の着色に入りますが、正面壁と側面壁の色は、彩度を同じにするだけでなく、明度も2度程度下げた色(p.86の「明度の合わせ方」参照)にしなければなりません。着色は、正面壁から側面壁へと進めますが、絵の具の濃さを化粧品の乳液よりも若干水っぽくして、二、三度重ね塗りして着色します。

Then color the exterior wall. Colors of the same chroma should be used for the front and side walls, and their brightness should be two degrees lower (How to match the brightness: p.86). The brush strokes should start from the front and move towards the side walls; a slightly watery color with a density a bit heavier than milky cosmetic lotion should be overlapped two or three times.

外壁面にみられる色の変化、及び、影の色の変化を3段階の明るさの色で表現します。特に、側面のように壁面の大きな場合は、必ず色の変化を描き入れなければなりません。その着色方法は、下塗りした色に、少しずつ白を加えながら基準線より離れるにつれ、より明るくなるように重ね塗りします。なお、色の変化を描き入れる時、その方向性を一定にします。

Express the color change and shade found in the exterior walls with three stages of color brightness. It is especially important that the color fluctuation in the wider space of side wall is clearly expressed. The trick here is to repeatedly color the area with white so that it becomes brighter farther away from the reference line. When expressing the change in color, the direction in change should be consistent.

屋根や庇、軒裏を着色し、目地を入れたり、ぼやけている部分を暗い色の線描で、はっきりさせます。最後に、白でハイライトの線描をして建物の着色を仕上げます。なお、色みの強い色や、暗い色のハイライトには、白にそれらの色を若干加えた明るい色を使った方が自然です。詳しいことはp.81に述べてあります。

Paint the roof, lean-to roof and eaves. To make the joints clear, describe the darker lines on the faded color portions. Finally, draw in the highlight lines in white to finish the coloring of the building. When expressing the highlights with heavier or darker colors, a natural atmosphere can be expressed by brightening the colors with small amounts of white blended in. For details, see p.81.

点景である植栽や車、人物を描き加え、空に雲を描き加えて仕上りとなります。なお、この見本のパース画は、空と雲をエアーブラシで仕上げています。路面、植栽、車、人物等の点景については第4章で詳しく説明します。

Draw in the cars, plants and people, and finish up the rendering by drawing the sky. The rendering shown here as an example has been finished with an airbrush. The methods used to draw incidental elements such as roads, plants, cars, people, etc., are explained in Chapter 4.

作品例
Samples of works

リビングルームの着色過程
Coloring process for a living room

まず、天井、壁、床の着色から始めます。不透明水彩絵の具による着色なので、絵の具は化粧品の乳液よりも少し水っぽくした濃さで、大きな筆を使って、絵の具のかたまりが画面にのこらないように伸ばしながら着色することが大切です。天井、壁は、イエロー・オーカーに白と黒を加えた色で、床は、イエロー・オレンジに白と若干バーント・アンバーを加えた色であらかじめ全体を着色します。その後、天井、壁、床に色の変化表現を重ね塗りして着色します。

Start by coloring the ceiling, wall and floor. Since opaque watercolors are to be used, the colors should have a slightly moister density than milky cosmetic lotion. The trick is to use a larger paintbrush and spread the colors so that any clog of colors remains on the picture. Paint the ceiling and wall with yellow ocher blended with white and black, and color the entire floor in advance with yellow-orange blended with white and a bit of burnt umber. Then overlap the colors over the ceiling, wall and floor to express the fluctuation of colors.

テーブルや椅子の影から着色し、奥の椅子からテーブル、そして、手前の椅子へと着色すると描き易いでしょう。なお、テーブルの天板には垂直方向に色の変化を描き入れます。

Paint the shade of the table and chairs first. To make the painting easier, it is advisable to draw the chairs in the far back, and then move forward to paint the table. Express the shifts of color on the top surface of the table in a vertical direction.

奥のソファー等から手前のソファーや家具を仕上げていきます。ソファー等布製のものは立体的に描くだけでよいでしょう。

When drawing, start with the sofa in the back and then proceed by drawing the furniture further in the foreground. Three-dimensional drawing is enough for furniture with cloth upholstery such as sofas.

手前の椅子や家具を仕上げます。手前の椅子の背板は、大きな面で表現されているので、明るい色の変化を入れます。

Finish painting the chairs and furniture in the foreground. Since the backs of the chairs in the foreground are expressed in wide forms, use brighter colors for them to express the change of colors.

照明器具を描き上げてから、室内の点景としての観葉植物を描き加えますが、室内がはなやかになるような色調で着色することが望ましいでしょう。

After painting the lighting fixtures, paint in the foliage and similar elements in the room. The use of brighter tones is recommended for these elements to give the interior a gorgeous touch.

最後に、壁面の絵や、置物等の小物を描き込むと仕上ります。

Finally, paint in the pictures on the wall, the ornaments, and other small articles.

作品例
Samples of works

照明等一部にエアーブラシが使われているが、不透明水彩絵の具による筆塗りを基本にしたパース画

Though airbrushing is partially used to depict the lighting and similar areas, perspectives are basically prepared by brush painting using opaque watercolors.

2. エアーブラシパースの着色 Coloring the perspectives with an airbrush

A. 外観パースの着色過程 Coloring process for exterior perspectives

マンションの着色過程
Coloring process for an apartment house

まず、画面全体にマスキングフィルムをかぶせ、空気が入らないように布でこすりながら貼り付けます。マスキングフィルムの足らない部分は、紙をセロテープで貼り付けて被います。その後、デザインカッターで、下図の全てに切り込みを入れます。

To begin with, place a sheet of masking film over the entire picture. Rub the surface firmly with a cloth to prevent air bubbles from becoming trapped inside. Cover areas that are not to be covered by the film with paper or cellophane adhesive tape. Perform all the necessary cutting over the entire surface of the rough sketch with a cutter knife.

最も暗い屋根から、マスキングフィルムを外し、ニュートラル・ブラック(p.57参照)を吹き付けます。この時、色の濃淡が、はっきり見えるように吹き付けることが大切です。

Remove the masking film from the roof portion, the darkest portion in the picture, and spray on a coat of neutral black (see p.57). When spraying the surface, it is important to make sure that the color of the shade is clearly expressed.

次に側面壁の影のマスキングフィルムを取り外し、側面壁の暗い色をつくり、吹き付けます。この時も、必ず、色の濃淡がはっきり見えるように吹き付けることが大切です。この建物の場合、ニュートラル・ブラックにイエロー・オーカーを混ぜ合わせた暗い色で吹き付けます。

Next, remove the masking film from the shade portion of the side wall, mix a darker color for the side wall, and spray it on. It is also important that the color of the shade is clearly expressed during this step. When spraying this building, use a darker color made by blending the neutral black with yellow ocher.

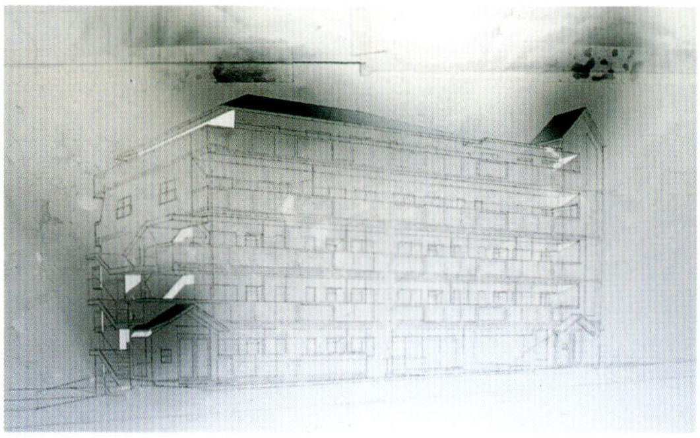

側面壁の影を吹き付けた後、階段の裏も吹き付け、正面壁の影のマスキングフィルムを取り外します。

After spraying the shaded area of the front exterior wall, remove the masking film covering the eaves of the building.

正面壁の影を吹き付けた後、軒裏のマスキングフィルムを取り外し、側面壁の影と同じ色を吹き付けます。なお、色の指定があれば、その色にしなければならないので、後廻しにします。

After spraying them with the same color used for the shade of the side exterior wall. The exterior wall should be colored at some point after the appropriate coloring is designated.

軒裏の吹き付けが終ると側面壁のマスキングフィルムを取り外します。見本の建物の外壁色は、影と同様に、ニュートラル・ブラックにイエロー・オーカーを混ぜた色です。

After spraying the eaves, remove the masking film covering the exterior side wall.For sample perspectives, the color used for the exterior wall is a blend of neutral black and yellow ocher, similar to the color used for the shade.

側面壁は、最も広い面積をもっているので、濃淡表現を強くしなければなりません。側面壁の吹き付け後、正面壁のマスキングフィルムを取り外します。

Since the side wall takes up the widest area in the painting, it is important to stress the contrast of the shade. After spraying the side exterior wall, remove the masking tape covering the front exterior wall.

側面壁と同じ色で、正面壁の基準線寄りに集中して吹き付けます。特に、正面壁の吹き付けで注意する点は、周りの色が暗い為、白く明るく吹き付けたように見えても、全体のマスキングフィルムを取り外すと、かなりの色が吹き付けられている点です。従って、基準線より離れている部分は、白く明るく吹き付けます。この写真の吹き付け状態で下の写真の色の状態になるので、よく比較して見て下さい。特に、白っぽく見えている部分が下の写真の色まで暗くなることを頭に入れなければなりません。

Spray the same color used for the side exterior wall over the front exterior wall, concentrating the spray around its reference line. Be very careful to avoid spraying too much over the front exterior wall. Even when efforts are made to spray white and brighter colors, fairly large amounts of color tend to be sprayed on because the surrounding color is dark. A good way to avoid this is to spray the areas at a distance from the reference line with white or bright colors. Keep in mind that the gradations of spray shown in this photo are developed into the color conditions shown in the photo immediately below it. So, compare them carefully for your study. Be sure to remember that the portion which looks white darkens to the level shown in the lower photo.

建物の外壁が仕上ると、もう一度、マスキングフィルムを貼り付けて、建物の輪郭と路面にデザインカッターで切り込みを入れます。その後、窓ガラス面、及び窓ガラス面の濃淡の切り込みも入れます。

After painting the exterior of the building, adhere the masking tape again and cut in the outline of the building and the road with the design cutter. Cut both the shaded and unshaded portions of the window panes.

まず、路面の暗い部分から、マスキングフィルムを取り外して、吹き付け、明るい色の部分へと移ります。路面の吹き付けが仕上ると窓ガラスの吹き付けに移ります。窓ガラス面に切り込まれた濃淡表現の暗い部分から順次明るい部分へと、外壁面の吹き付けと同様に、マスキングフィルムを取り外しながら吹き付けます。詳しくは、「窓ガラスの描き方」(p.56参照)で述べてあります。最後に、空の部分のマスキングフィルムを取り外し、マンガニーズブルーで吹き付けます。

Begin by removing the masking film from the bright portion of the road and spraying it, and then move on to the darker portion. After finishing the road spray, move onto the portions of the window panes to be sprayed. Apply the colors in the same manner used for the exterior wall: begin by removing the masking film and spraying the darker portions in the shade, and then repeat the process for the progressively lighter portions. For details of this step, refer to "How to color windows"(p.56). Finally, remove the masking film covering the sky portion and spray on a coat of manganese blue.

窓ガラス面や、ベランダのガラス面のサッシの影を、寒色ニュートラル(p.57参照)で、少し太めに描き加えます。

Paint the window sashes and the shade of the sashes of the window panes at the verandah with a cold neutral color(see p.57) so that the lines becomes slightly thicker.

外壁面のタイル目地、屋根のシングル表現を極細筆で仕上げ、サッシやガラス枠を描き込み、窓ガラス面の周りに壁の厚みやハイライトを描き入れて建物の仕上りとなります。

Finish the tile joints in the exterior wall and single expression of the roof using an ultra fine paintbrush, and paint the sash and window pane frames. Next, complete the rendering of the building by drawing in the thickness of the wall and highlighting around the window panes.

点景である植栽、車、人物を筆塗りで着色すると仕上ります。エアーブラシで点景を着色する場合は、建物と同様に進めればよいでしょう。ただ筆塗りの方が速く仕上ります。

Finish up the perspective by coloring the plants, cars, people, etc. When using an airbrush to color the items, follow the same steps as those applied to painting the building. Brush painting can achieve a quicker finish.

作品例
Samples of works

B. 室内パースの着色過程 Coloring process for interior perspectives

リビングルームの着色過程
Coloring process for a living room

㈱リクルート月刊誌「ハウジング」より
Source: "Housing" published by Recruit

まず、マスキングする前に家具の立体感の下塗りを透明水彩絵の具でしておくと速く仕上りますが、筆塗りが苦手な人は、その部分の吹き付け時に、マスキングフィルムを暗い部分から取り外しながら吹き付けます。簡単な下塗りの後、マスキングフィルムを貼り付け、デザインカッターで、下図に切り込みを入れます。
The rendering can be finished more quickly by painting in a three-dimensional draft of the furniture in clear watercolors before masking. Artists less skilled at brush painting can achieve more successful results by removing the masking film from the darker portions and spraying them. After finishing up with the simple preliminary painting, adhere the masking film and cut it with a design cutter as shown in the drawing below.

黒っぽい家具（ステレオ、テレビ等）や２階の窓ガラスの暗い部分からマスキングフィルムを取り外し、ニュートラル・ブラックを吹き付け、色味の違った植木鉢等は吹き付け着色した後、再度、取り外したフィルムを被いかぶせます。また、ソファーは、下塗り着色がされているので一度にフィルムを取り外し、濃く吹き付けたりして立体表現をし、その後で、床のジュータンの吹き付けをします。
Remove the masking film from the darker portions of the furniture (stereos, TVs, etc.) and window panes on the first floor, and spray on a coat of neutral black. Reapply the masking film over items that are differently tinted such as plant pots, etc., after their coloring has been finished. Since the preliminary coloring of the sofa has been already finished, completely remove the masking film and spray generously over it to express the three dimensions. Next, spray the carpet on the floor.

２階の窓ガラスやステレオ、テレビ等の黒っぽい家具の吹き付けが終ったら、それぞれ取り外したフィルムを再度貼り付け、茶黒系の本棚や飾り棚のガラス面や、セピア系のサッシを吹き付けます。それが終ったら、その茶黒系の部分にも、再度、取り外したフィルムを貼り付け、木製の家具の吹き付けに移ります。最も暗い影から明るい影へと順々に吹き付けますが、テーブルのように暗い家具から離れている場合は、同時にフィルムを取り外してもかまいません。茶黒系の色は、バーント・アンバーに暖色ニュートラル（p.57参照）を加えてつくります。
After the window panes on the first floor and the dark-colored furniture have been finished, cover them again with the masking film and spray over the glass panes of the bookcase and dressing rack with a brownish black, and spray the sashes surrounding them with a sepia color. After completing this step, cover the brownish-black portions with the masking film and spray over the wooden furniture. In this step, the spray should be applied at first to the darker portions, and then should move progressively to the brighter portions. The masking film can be removed throughout this step. The brownish-black color is made by adding a warm neutral color (see p.57) to the burnt umber.

家具の暗い部分の吹き付けが終ったら１階リビングルームのガラス面のフィルムを取り外し、上部に空の色を、下部に芝生の色を淡く吹き付けます。空の色は、マンガニーズブルーで、芝生の色は、グリーン・ペールがよいでしょう。

After spraying over the darker-colored furniture, remove the masking film covering the window panes in the living room on the ground floor. Spray the upper portions with the color of the sky and lower portions with the color of the lawn. Manganese blue is recommended for sky colors, and pale greens for the lawn.

１階のガラス面の吹き付けが終ると、再度、その面のフィルムを貼り付け、木製家具の明るい部分や、壁面の幅木、テーブルの天場、カーテン等、同系色のものの吹き付け着色をします。この場合、カーテンは、少し色味が異なるので、他の木製の部分を三角定規等、少し重みのある物で被うとよいでしょう。木製家具等の明るい部分の色は、イエロー・オレンジにバーント・アンバーを混ぜ合わせた色でつくります。

After finishing up the glass surface on the ground floor, reapply the masking film over the same portions so that similar colors can be sprayed over the brighter portions of the furniture, the baseboard of the wall, the tabletop, the curtains, etc. Since the tone of curtain color differs slightly, it is advisable to cover the wooden portion with a slightly weighted triangle. The colors for the brighter portions of the wooden furniture should be made by blending yellow-orange with the burnt umber.

カーテンの吹き付け後、再度、フィルムを貼り付け、床のフローリングの映り込みの暗い部分や、奥の家具(システムキッチン)を吹き付けます。

After spraying over the curtain, reapply the masking film over the curtain so that the darker shades of the flooring and the furniture (system kitchen) in the back can be sprayed.

さらに、床のフローリングに映り込む、壁の明るい部分のフィルムを取り外して吹き付け、テーブルの吹き付けに移ります。この時、左手の家具や、２階の窓ガラス、さらに、テーブルの木製の部分等、紙や、マスキングテープで被ってもかまいません。特に、取り外したフィルムをなくしたり、細かくて貼り付けにくい場合は、紙やマスキングテープを利用すると速くマスキングが出来ます。

Remove the masking film covering the brightly-colored portion of wall reflected on the surface of the flooring, and continue spraying, moving towards the table. You can cover the furniture on the LH side, the window panes on the first floor, and the wooden portion of the table with paper or masking film in this step. If you lose any of the previously removed masking film, or if the film is too narrow to stick, the use of paper or new masking film will help to finish the masking process more quickly.

次に壁面の吹き付けに入りますが、今までに吹き付け着色した部分を紙やマスキングテープで、全て被います。壁面の吹き付けは、天井面の吹き付け後に、側壁から始めます。特に壁面は、面積が大きいので、色の濃淡が強く感じられる程度まで、正面壁との境目に集中して吹き付けます。この時、正面壁の吹き付け時に暗い色が重なり、さらに暗くなることを考え、暗くなり過ぎないように注意しましょう。ただし、側面壁の吹き付け後、再度、マスキングする場合は、気にしなくてもよいでしょう。

Remove the masking film covering the brightly-colored portion of wall reflected on the surface of the flooring, and continue spraying, moving towards the table. You can cover the furniture on the LH side, the window panes on the first floor, and the wooden portion of the table with paper or masking film in this step. If you lose any of the previously removed masking film, or if the film is too narrow to stick, the use of paper or new masking film will help to finish the masking process more quickly.

側面壁が終ると、正面壁のフィルムを取り外し、側面壁と同じ色で淡く吹き付けます。外観パースの場合と同様に、全体のマスキングフィルムを取り外した時に、暗くなり過ぎることが多いので、明る過ぎると思われる程度で吹き付けを止めます。

After the side wall has been finished, remove the masking film covering the front wall portion and lightly spray the area with a coat of the same color used for the side wall. When removing the final portions of masking film from exterior renderings, artists are often disappointed to discover the excessive darkness of the perspective. So, spray a little brighter.

最後に、全てのマスキングしたものを取り外し、吹き忘れた部分や、筆塗り仕上げの方が簡単な細かい部分の着色をします。同時に、暗い色の線で形を整えたり、ハイライトを入れます。

Finally, remove all the masking film and touch-up or color the areas where the spraying missed or the detailed areas which can be easily finished by brush painting. At the same time, adjust the rendering by adding some darker lines or highlighting.

点景としての植栽や、細かい小物を描き加え、さらに、ガラス越しの庭の植栽を淡く描き入れると、見本のように仕上ります。

Finally, remove all the masking film and touch-up or color the areas where the spraying missed or the detailed areas which can be easily finished by brush painting. At the same time, adjust the rendering by adding some darker lines or highlighting.

3. 筆塗り併用エアーブラシパースの着色 Coloring the perspective with combined use of airbrushing and brush painting

A. 下塗りエアーブラシパースでのテナントビルの着色過程
Preliminary airbrushing in the coloring process for a perspective of a tenant building

空、ガラス面、ハーフミラーの着色
Coloring process for skies, glass surfaces, and half-mirror textures

画面の空の部分をあらかじめ水で湿らせておき、プルシャンブルーとビリジャンの混合色に白を加えた空の色を、比較的大きな平筆で、絵の具を伸ばしながら下の方はぼかすようにして下塗りをします。なお、エアーブラシのみで着色する場合は下塗りはいりません。

Moisten the sky portion in the picture in advance and spread a mixture of white, Prussian blue and viridian across the surface. Use a relatively large flat brush and start the strokes from the lower area so that the preliminary painting color can be faded. The only way to skip the preliminary painting in the coloring process is to use an airbrush.

1階ロビーのガラス面は、ハーフミラーと御影石の色調に合わせて寒色系で表現します。描き方は後に「店舗のガラス面の着色手順」(p.71参照) で述べます。また、外壁面にはみ出したガラスの色は、平筆を使って水で洗い落しておくとよいでしょう。なお、エアーブラシで着色する場合は、ガラス面全体をマスキングして、最も暗くする部分から順次明るい部分へと取り外しながら吹き付けます。

Cold colors should be used to express the glass of the lobby on the ground floor so that its colors match a "half-mirror" and granite color tone. This coloring process is explained in "Coloring process for windows of a showroom" (see p.71). The color extending from the exterior wall should be removed with a flat brush and water. Cover the entire rendering of the surface of the glass with the masking film before coloring with the airbrush. Begin by peeling the masking film away from the darkest portions and spraying them, and proceed in stages to the progressively lighter portions.

ハーフミラーの質感を強調する為に、白でガラス面全体を下塗りしますが、この白は、あまり濃くならないように注意します。エアーブラシパースの場合は、用紙が白色なので、その紙の白を利用するので下塗りはいりません。

In order to stress the "half mirror" texture, apply a preliminary coat of white over the entire surface of the glass area. Take care to prevent the white from becoming too heavy in these preliminary painting stages. If you are using an airbrush, it is not necessary to apply the white color onto the paper, since the paper used in this process is white to begin with.

マスキングフィルムをかぶせ、足らない部分は紙をセロテープで留めます。その後、カーテンウォールの部分を切り取り、マンガニーズブルー等の空の色を見本のように右上部分だけに吹き付けます。

Use the masking film to cover the surface wherever possible, and use cellophane adhesive tape to cover areas where the film can't be used. After adhering the masking film, cut the portion of film covering the curtain wall and spray on manganese blue and other colors to express the sky. Make sure to only spray over the upper RH side, as shown in the sample.

カーテンウォールの下の部分をガラスの色で吹き付けますが、下地に着色された白色の部分がなくならないように注意しなければなりません。見本では、ビリジャンとプルシャンブルーの混合色で緑みの強い色を基調にして、暗い部分には、寒色ニュートラルを加えた色で吹き付けています。

Spray a color similar to that used to express the glass over the lower portion of the curtained wall, but take care during this process to prevent the white-colored portion on the preliminary painting from disappearing. A blend of viridian and Prussian blue is used to produce the dark green color shown in that portion in the sample, and a cold neutral color is used for the darker portion.

マスキングフィルムをはがすと、このようになります。

This shows the condition when the masking film is peeled off.

さらに、再度マスキングフィルムでカーテンウォールの部分を被い、ガラス面に映り込む建物の輪郭をデザインカッターで切り込み、最も暗い部分から明るい部分へと、順次、フィルムを取り外しながら吹き付けていきます。この時、あらかじめ別のコピーした下図に映り込む建物の形を描いておき、それを見ながら、最も暗くする部分から切り抜きながら吹き付けるとよいでしょう。

Cover the curtained wall area with the masking film again, and cut the outline of building reflected on the glass panes using a design cutter so that area can be sprayed from the darkest portions to the brighter portions by peeling off the film in sequence. Sketch the configuration of the building on a separate sheet of draft paper before beginning the process, and refer to the sheet to determine the darkness that needs to be described in the respective portions, and the required sequence of spraying.

映り込んだ建物の窓ガラスを平筆で描き加え、照明を描き込みます。この時、映り込んだ建物のガラス面を平筆で描き込むので、その絵の具の水ぼてがガラス面に生じないように、カーテンウォール面から外壁へと筆を運びます。エアーブラシで表現する場合は、前の段階で、その窓ガラス面も切り込み、最も暗い部分から順次吹き付ければ失敗せずに仕上ります。さらに、白の入った明るい色で、照明を描き加えます。

Paint over the window panes of the building that have reflections using a flat paintbrush, and then draw the lighting inside the building. Since the glass reflecting the landscape is painted with a flat brush and droplets of watery color are likely to fall on these portions, the stroke of the flat brush should move from the curtain wall to the exterior wall. When using an airbrush, cut the window pane portion in advance and start spraying from the darkest portion to the brighter portion to obtain a satisfactory finish. The lighting should be painted using a bright color with white blended in.

サッシの影を入れ、不透明水彩絵の具でサッシを描き入れます。この見本では、黒っぽいサッシとしてセピアに白を加えた色で着色しています。

Paint the shading of the sashes, and then paint the sashes with opaque watercolors. The blackish sash in the sample shown here is painted in sepia with a small amount of white added.

イエロー・オーカーに白と黒を加えてつくったグレー系の色で外壁の下塗りをします。この下塗りの絵の具は、あまり濃くしない方がよいでしょう。エアーブラシの場合は、下塗りしなくてもよいでしょう。下塗りの絵の具が濃い場合、マスキングフィルムを取り外す時に絵の具がはがれることがあります。

Apply a preliminary coat of grayish colors produced by adding small portions of white and black to yellow ocher on the exterior wall. If this preliminary coat is applied to heavily, the coloring has a tendency to come off when the masking film is peeled off. If an airbrush is used, the coat is not necessary.

下塗り後、マスキングし、まず、正面から側面へと下塗りした時の絵の具で色むらがなくなるように吹き付け、その後で、明るくする部分には白を、より暗くする部分には黒とイエロー・オーカーを加えた暗い色を吹き付けます。この時、正面を吹き付けた後、側面を取り外す前に、抜き取った正面のフィルムを元の位置にかぶせ直すと、マスキングの回数が少なくて済みます。

After the preliminary coloring has been applied, mask the perspective. Next, spray the same colors used in the preliminary painting uniformly from the front to the side exterior walls in order to avoid mottling. Spray white over the bright portions, and cover the darker potions with a darker blend of yellow ocher and black. Masking does not have to be carried out as often if the removed masking film is used again to cover the front exterior wall before removing the masking film from the side wall portion after the front exterior wall has been completely sprayed.

外壁面を吹き付けた後、材質感を表現する為に、金網を使って粗めの「ザラ目ツブ」を壁面に落として石の表現をします。
After the spraying of the exterior wall has been completed, drop coarse sand through a wire screen over the exterior wall to express the stone texture.

●金網ブラシの使い方 How to use the wire screen and brush

金網に絵の具をつけて、歯ブラシでこすり落とします。
Put the colors on the wire screen and scrub them with a toothbrush so that they drop onto the painting.

建物の影を着色し、御影石の目地を描き込みます。
Color the shaded portions of the building and describe the joints on the granite.

建物全体をマスキングし、空の部分を切り抜き、空の色を吹き付けて色むらをなくした後、白で雲を吹き付けます。
Cover the entire building with masking film, cut away the sky portion, and spray the sky color over it in a uniform manner to avoid mottling. Then spray white over the clouds.

点景を路面→街路樹→車→人物の順に描き入れて仕上げます。
Finish up the rendering by first painting the road, then the roadside trees, the cars, and finally the people.

B. 住宅の着色過程 Coloring process for a residential house

窓ガラス、照明、瓦の着色
Coloring process for glass windows, lighting fixtures, and roof tiles

空の画面をあらかじめたっぷりと水で湿らせた後に、空色を伸ばしながら着色し、その色が乾いたら窓ガラスの着色に入ります。窓ガラスの一部に空色を着色し、イエロー・オーカーにバーント・アンバーを加えた色から着色し始め、暗く着色するに従って、暖色ニュートラルを加えます。窓ガラスの下地着色が終ると、白を加えた明るい色で照明や室内の家具のハイライトを描き入れ、サッシの影を少し太めに描き込み、サッシを最後に描き入れます。なお、外壁面にはみ出した色は水で洗い流すとよいでしょう。

After applying ample moisture to the sky portion of the painting, color the sky by spreading the colors. Once the sky colors have dried, color the window panes. Spread sky colors over some portions of the panes. Begin spreading a mixture of burnt umber with yellow ocher, and then add warm neutral colors as you progress to the darker portions. After finishing the preliminary coloring of window panes, highlight the lighting and interior furniture in bright colors with white blended in, paint the shaded parts of the sashes in generous strokes, and finally paint the sashes themselves. If there is any excessive color out of the exterior wall, it should be removed with water.

イエロー・オーカーに白とセピアを加えた色で外壁面の下塗りをします。このパース画では、下塗り後にエアーブラシ着色をするので、正面壁と側面壁の明度差は無視してもかまいません。つまり、明度差が弱くても、強すぎても、エアーブラシ着色時に調節出来るからです。筆塗りの場合は明度差を守らなければなりません。

The preliminary coloring of the exterior wall should be done with a blend of yellow ocher with white and sepia. Since airbrushing is employed after preliminary coloring in this perspective, the difference in brightness between the front exterior wall and side exterior wall can be ignored --weak differences and strong differences can be easily adjusted with the airbrush. If brush painting is employed, the correct difference in brightness should be expressed during the preliminary coloring.

エアーブラシを使って、正面と側面との境界部分の明度差が２度程度になるように、同系色を吹き付けます。見本の影は手塗り着色されていますが、その場合、基準線より離れている部分は明るくなるように濃淡表現をしておきます。また、この時点で、戸袋等の外壁面は全て仕上げておきます。

Spray a color of a similar system over the boundary between the front and side exterior walls using the airbrush so that a difference in brightness of two degrees can be achieved around the boundary. In the sample, the shade is manually colored. In this case, the portion set apart from the reference line is expressed by the shade so that it can be brightly rendered. The entire surface of the exterior wall, including the doorcase, should be finished during this process.

イエロー・オーカーに白と黒を加えて暗いグレーをつくり、屋根瓦の下塗りをします。

Apply the underpainting of the roof tiles with a dark gray mixture of white and black added to yellow ocher.

エアーブラシを使って濃淡を表現し、白っぽく光っている部分は白だけで吹き付けます。

Use an airbrush to express the shade and take care to spray only white over the shiny white portions.

瓦を仕上げます。瓦の描き方は「点景の表現方法」で説明しますが、暗い色と明るい色とで瓦の流れを間隔を開けて、交互に描き入れ、最後にのせ瓦や、瓦の厚みを描き加えます。

Finish the roof tiles. Though the methods used to draw roof tiles will be explained in detail in the chapter entitled " How to paint the incidental elements," paint the roof tiles using alternating sections of dark and bright colors spaced at a certain interval, and finally draw the roof tiles and the thickness of these portions.

建物の基礎部分の着色をしますが、屋根瓦の色に白を加えてつくると簡単で速く描けます。パース着色の速さは、いかに色を速くつくるかによって決まります。従って、同系色は同時に着色するようにします。

Color the foundation of the building. If white is added to the color for the roof tiles, simple and quick brushstrokes can be applied. How quickly the color is laid in the perspective depends on how quickly the color is produced. Therefore, try to apply colors of similar systems at the same time.

基礎部分に着色した色を少し暗くして、外構の着色をします。石や土の表現は金網ブラシを使って「ザラ目」をつけ、目地も入れます。

Lay darker colors on the building foundation before laying the color on the landscape. Scrub coarse sand through the wire mesh with the toothbrush to express the stone and earth, and paint in the joints.

建物が仕上ると空の部分を再度マスキングし、空の色むらがなくなるように、上の方は青みが強くなるように、他方、下の地面に近い部分は白っぽくなるように吹き付けます。空の吹き付けが済むと雲を白だけで吹き付け着色します。

After coloring the building, mask over the sky portion again so that a bluish color can be uniformly sprayed over the upper portion, and so white can be sprayed over the portions closer to the ground. After spraying over the sky, spray on the clouds using only white.

植栽や車を描き加えてからフェンス等を描き、路面を仕上げます。ただ、住宅の路面は、テナントビル等の路面と違って垂直方向の濃淡表現をしないで、見本のような曲線表現をするとやわらかな感じになって好ましいでしょう。

Draw the fence after finishing the coloring of the plants and cars to finish the road. If the surface of the road in the residential area is expressed by the curved lines, as shown in the example, and not by the shading in the vertical direction, i.e., not by the method employed to express the surface of the road in the perspective of the tenant building, an excellent soft feeling can be conveyed,

作品例
Samples of works

下塗りエアーブラシによる作品

Example of works with airbrushed underpainting.

筆塗りだけによる作品

Example of works prepared with brush painting only.

C. 山や森のある建物の着色過程 Coloring process for a building with mountains and a forest in the background

小さな窓ガラス、外構、石畳、遠景の着色
Coloring process for small glass windows, landscapes, stone pavements, and distant sceneries

「ルックＪＴＢヨーロッパ」よりリンダーボーブ城
Linderhope Castle from "Look JTB Europa"

窓ガラスの着色から始めますが、窓ガラス面が小さいので、大まかな濃淡表現で仕上げます。その後、建物や外構面を仕上げます。ただ、このパースのように建物や外構面が全体的に小さくて細かい場合は、壁面等の色の変化を省いてもかまいません。

Start by coloring the window panes. Since windows take up quite a small area, a rough shading technique is used for finishing them. Next, finish the coloring of the building and landscape. In cases where all of the building and landscape is rendered in fine detail, as shown in this example, it is not necessary to express the change in color on the exterior wall.

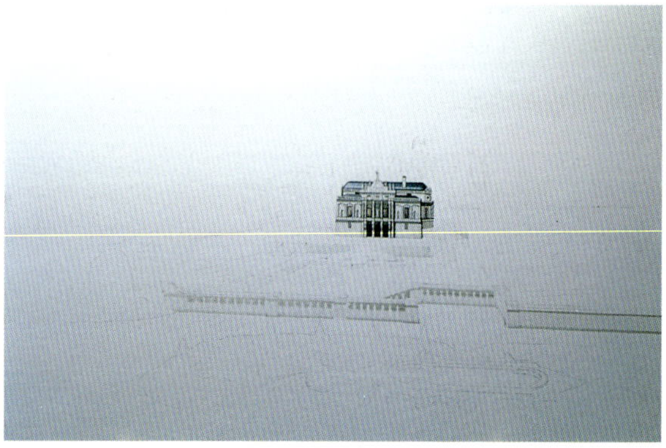

広場の石畳や池等の着色に入りますが、着色面が建物と違って大きくて単純な面なので、必ず、濃淡表現をしなければなりません。それには手前の方を暗く表現するようにします。見本ではエアーブラシを使って濃淡表現をしていますが、手前の方を暗く表現することで建物の遠近感がよく表現出来ます。

Then color the stone pavement and pond in the plaza. Since the area that needs to be colored here is large and simple, in contrast to the portions of the building, never fail to express the shade. To successfully achieve this expression, color the foreground dark. In this way, the distance of building can be clearly expressed.

遠くに見える山は青みのある透明水彩絵の具で簡単に描き上げ、建物の後にある芝生の庭は、不透明水彩絵の具で明るく描きます。これらの山や庭は、面積が大きいので大まかな色の濃淡表現が必要です。見本はエアーブラシを使って着色しています。

Paint the mountains in the distance simply in bluish clear watercolors, and paint the lawn-covered garden behind the building in bright colors using opaque watercolors. Since the mountains and garden occupy a large portion of the perspective, it is important to use simple coloring in expressing the shade. The sample shown here is colored with an airbrush.

遠くの山は、カエデの葉の形のかたまりで下塗りし、手前の森は杉の木の形で下塗りしておきます。前面にある花壇は下図通りにベタ塗りします。特に、前面の花壇に関しては、芝生は明るめの色で、密植されている低木は暗めの色で、中木等は低木よりも明るめの色で着色します。

The underpainting of the mountains in the distance should convey the maple leaves as lumps of shapes, and the shapes of the cedar trees should be emphasized in rendering the forest in the foreground. Paint all of the flower bed in the foreground as shown below. Especially bright colors should be used for the lawn, just as in the flower bed in the foreground. A dark color should be used for the densely planted shrubs, and a slightly brighter color should be used for the moderately tall trees.

遠くの山は、先のすり減った丸筆の先を使って、下塗りされたカエデの葉の形が自然な色の流れになるように、小さな木の葉を描き加えながらぼかします。森は下塗りの色より暗めの色で木の形を整えていきます。また、前面の花壇も同様に着色していきます。

Apply stump-like strokes using a paintbrush with a worn tip for the underpainting of the maple leaves in the distant mountains, and paint in the leaves of the small trees. By doing this, the shapes of the maple leaves can be graded into the surroundings in a natural flow of colors. Paint the trees in the forest in darker colors than the underpainting, and color the flower bed in the foreground in the same manner.

さらに白を多く混合した明るいグリーン系の色で、森の木を細かく仕上げ、よりリアルになるように着色します。この時、後ろの山のつらなりが、自然な色の流れになるように、木の形をぼかしていきます。最後に、花や人物、噴水等の点景を描き加えて仕上げます。

To create a more realistic expression, paint the details of the trees in the forest in bright greens with generous amounts of white mixed in. Shade over the shapes of the trees in the mountain range in the distance during this process to achieve a natural flow of color. Finally draw the flowers, people, fountain in the pond, and similar items.

作品例
Samples of works

D. 湖や池に映り込みのある建物の着色過程
Coloring process for a building perspective reflected on the surface of a lake or pond

建物や背景、映り込みの着色
Coloring process for reflections on buildings and landscapes

井上宗和著「ヨーロッパ古城物語」よりアニフの城
Anif Castle from "The Story of Ancient European Castles" (written by Munekazu Inoue)

空を着色した後で、湖を空よりも濃いめに着色し、建物のガラス面の着色に移ります。この建物の窓ガラス面は小さいので、大まかな濃淡表現だけで仕上げます。見本はエアーブラシを使って空と湖を着色していますが、筆塗りで着色する場合は、山や森に空の色がはみ出してもかまいません。同様の事は、湖の色についても言えます。

After coloring the sky, lay a heavier color on the lake, and then begin coloring the glass panes of the building. Since the window panes take up only a small part of this building, the shaded areas can be somewhat rough. In the sample, an airbrush is used to color sky and lake. If brush painting is used, however, the color of the mountain and forest can be overlapped with the color of the sky, and even the lake.

建物を着色する場合、映り込みの建物も同時に着色し、映り込みの建物には、白を部分的に吹き付けてぼかしておきます。筆を使う場合は、白を薄くして平筆で、素速く重ね塗りをすれば同様の効果が現れます。また、筆による着色では、映り込んだ建物の正面壁と側面壁の明度差は少し弱くして、全体的にぼやけた感じになるように着色します。建物が仕上がったら、森と映り込んだ森の着色に入り、建物同様に、映り込んだ森は少し明るめに着色し、明るいハイライトの色も暗い部分も、あまりコントラストが強くならないように表現します。

Reflection of the building on the lake should be rendered when the building itself is colored. Shade off the reflection of the building, partially spraying it with white. When brush painting is used, the same effect can be achieved by a quick overlap of coloring using a flat brush soaked with a thinner white. Try not to stress the difference in brightness between the reflection of the front exterior wall and that of the side exterior wall with the brush; draw the entire reflection dimly. After coloring the building, color the forest and its reflection on the lake. The reflected forest should be painted brighter, just as the building had been. Avoid excessively strong contrast between the highlighted portions and dark portions.

遠くの山は青みのある色で、近くの森は緑みの強い色で着色し、映り込みの山や森は、あまり明暗のコントラストは避け、少々ぼかし気味に着色すると見本のような感じになります。この後、湖に浮いている水草や、水面に反射される光を描き加え、手前にある植栽を描き込むと仕上ります。

Color the mountains in the distance with a bluish pigment, and use a heavy greenish color for the forest surrounding the building. Avoid excessively strong contrast in brightness between the reflection of the mountain and that of the forest; coloring a bit dimly will produce the atmosphere seen in the sample. Then draw the waterweeds floating on the lake and the light reflected across its surface. Finally, finish up the rendering by painting in the plants in the foreground.

E. 河と森越しに見える遠景の建物の着色過程
Coloring process for a building in the distance beyond a river and forest

小さな建物、距離感を出す着色
Coloring process for small buildings from a distant view

「ルックＪＴＢヨーロッパ」より
From "Look JTB Europe"

空の下塗り後、建物の窓ガラスの着色をします。窓ガラス面が小さいので、大まかな濃淡表現で着色します。

After underpainting the sky, color the window panes of the building. Since the windows take up only a small area, rough shading is enough.

建物が小さくて細かいので丸筆で着色し、屋根以外は外壁面の色の変化も省いてよいでしょう。

Since the building is small and fine, use the round brush to paint it. The changes in color of the exterior wall can be left out, but not the changes in the color of the roof.

植栽の部分を除いて、外構面や石畳を描き上げ、建物からの距離感を強調する為に、木の影を暗く着色します。

Draw the landscape and stone pavement, but leave the area with the plants for later. Use a darker color for the shade of the tree to stress the distance of the building.

不透明水彩絵の具で植込みや森、並木等の植栽を出来るだけ細かく描き込みます。

Use as much detail as possible in rendering the thick block of shrubs, forest, roadside trees, and other plants.

河の下塗りを明るめのブルー系の色で着色した後、エアーブラシを使ってコバルトブルー等の暗い色で吹き付けます。光った水面や、映り込みの明るい部分は、より明るい色で吹き付けます。その後に、船を描き入れ、細い丸筆を使って波の表現を細かく描き込みます。空の雲は、河の吹き付けと同時に白で吹き付けると速く仕上ります。

After laying the underpaint on the river in a bright bluish color, spray on a darker cobalt blue with an airbrush. Spray brighter colors on the shiny portions of the river surface, and make the reflections bright. After that, paint the ship, expressing the wave in as much detail as possible using the round brush. To save time, spray the clouds in the sky with white while the river is being colored.

作品例
Samples of works

海の表現着色を河の着色と同様の方法で描き上げたパース画。

Perspective in which the same method is used to color the sea and the river.

ゴルフ場の芝生表現を河と同様に、明るい芝色で下塗りし、その上にエアーブラシを使って、少し暗めの色で濃淡をつけたパース画。

Perspective in which a bright layer of underpainting is laid on the lawn using the same method applied to the of coloring golf courses, and in which the shade is finished in darker colors by airbrush.

F. 鳥瞰的な日本の城の着色過程 Coloring process of bird's-eye view of a Japanese castle

芝生、石積みの着色
Coloring process for lawns and stonewalls

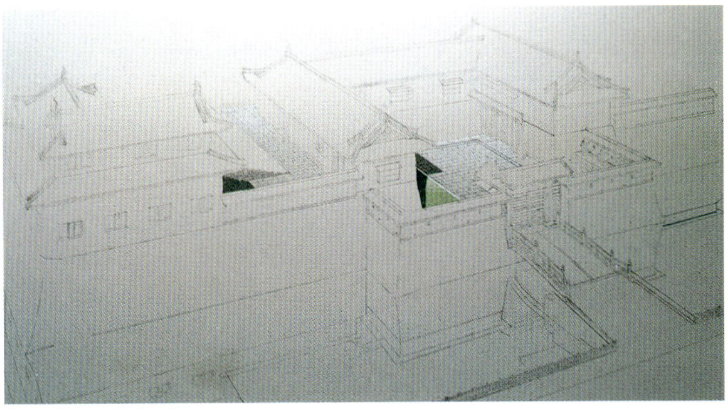

城内の庭、芝生を描きます。鳥瞰パースの着色は、建物を着色する前に、敷地内の外構を描き上げておかなければなりません。

Draw the garden and lawn inside the precinct of the castle. When coloring a bird's-eye view perspective, it is necessary to finish the coloring of the exterior landscape inside the precinct before starting the coloring of the building.

城内の庭と石積みの色が同じなので、石積みの着色から始めます。石積みは質感を表現する為に色むらを出しておきます。映り込みの石積みは、大きな池や河と違って、比較的小さな池である上、見下げの表現である為、全体的に暗めに下塗りします。このことは外観パースと鳥瞰パースの大きな違いです。

Since the colors used for the garden inside the precinct and the stone wall are the same, start coloring from the stone wall. To express the texture of the stone wall, try to deliberately mottle the colors. Since the reflection of the stone wall on the moat is relatively small compared to the reflection on the pond and river, and since it is expressed as seen from above high up in the air, this portion should generally be painted in dark colors. This is the point where exterior perspectives differs strikingly from bird's-eye view perspectives.

石積みの目地を描き入れ、映り込みの石積みの目地は部分的に描き込み、薄くした白で重ね塗りしてぼかしておきます。

Draw the joints on the stone wall. The joints in the reflection should be partially overlapped with a lighter white color to produce the shading off in that area.

池に空の色を下塗りします。筆塗り仕上げの場合は、出来るだけきれいに着色し、次段階の色の変化表現も生乾きのうちに済ませておきます。

Spread the sky color over the lake in a layer of underpainting. If you are using a brush, try to make the color as beautiful as possible, and finish spreading the subsequent layers of color while the underpaint is half dried.

池の空色をエアーブラシで吹き付け、色むらをなくすと同時に、色の濃淡を表現します。つまり遠くの方は、白っぽく表現します。また、城壁面も着色しておきます。

Spray the sky color over the lake to eliminate any mottling and express the color of the shade. That is to say, express the portion in the distance with a more whitish color.

城壁面の影を着色します。ただし、映り込みの影については、正面も側面も暗めに着色します。

Then, color the castle's exterior stone wall and its shaded portions. Somewhat darker colors should be spread over the shaded portions on both the front and side walls.

映り込みも含めて、城壁面を仕上げます。

Finish the stone wall and its shaded portions.

城門を全て仕上げますが、同時に、池に映り込む城門も、少し暗めに描き進めます。また、同系色である窓の格子も描き上げておきます。

Finish the castle gate. Somewhat darker colors should be spread over the castle gate reflected on the lake. The color used for the window grilles should be similar to that of the castle gate.

屋根の下塗りをします。鳥瞰パースなので、外観パースとは違って明るめに着色します。

Spread a layer of underpainting over the roof areas. Since this is a bird's-eye view perspective, the colors should be brighter than those used in regular perspectives.

エアーブラシを使って屋根の面々の明暗をはっきりさせると同時に、同じ面での色の濃淡を表現します。筆塗りの場合は、前の段階で、面々の明暗を表現しておいた上に、重ね塗りで、同じ面での色の濃淡を表現します。

Paint the shade of each side of the roof clearly using an airbrush, expressing the shade evenly on the same planes. When using a brush, clearly express the shade of each roof plane by overlapping the colors over the shaded portions that had been painted beforehand.

屋根の瓦を描き上げますが、乗せ瓦の下場の線は、特に、暗くしてメリハリをつけます。

Draw the roof tiles. Use a dark color to render the line of the eaves of the tiled roof dark to make it clearer.

城全体を仕上げてから、前面の道路や橋も描き加え、池に映る影も描き入れます。また、背後の植栽も、遠くの木は淡くぼかし、近い所は少し濃いめに表現し、城内の木も仕上げておきます。

After finishing all of the castle, draw the road and bridge in front of the castle and the shade reflected on the moat. Paint the plants in the distance in fairly dim tones, and make those in the foreground darker. Finish the trees inside the precinct of the castle at this stage.

池以外をマスキングして、白で、映り込んだ城を部分的に吹き付けてぼかし、同時に、映り込む雲を吹き付けます。

Mask everything except the moat. Spray partially over the shaded portion of the castle reflected on the moat until the color starts to appear faded, and also spray the colors over the clouds reflected on the moat.

細い丸筆を使って、水面に小さな波を描き、特に、映り込んだ城の輪郭の所は、多くの白っぽい波でぼかしておきます。その後に水草を描き加え、水面と石積みの境を暗い色で区切りをつけて仕上げます。外観パースの場合は、この区切りはいりません。

Paint ripples on the moat using a fine round paintbrush. Shade off the outline of the castle reflected on the moat with whitish ripples. Then paint the waterweeds. Make the boundary between the surface of the water and the stone wall clear by using a darker color. If this was a regular perspective preparation, it would not be necessary to express this boundary.

点景を描き入れて仕上がりです。

Finish the perspective by adding the smaller incidental elements.

4. 淡彩パースの着色 Preparation of light coloring

A. 外観パースの着色過程 Coloring process for exterior regular perspectives

側面壁と正面壁の違いを出す着色
Coloring process for highlighting the difference between front and side exterior walls

イエロー・オーカーに暖色ニュートラルを加えた、水っぽい色で外壁面を着色します。窓ガラスは後から暗い色で着色するので無視すると着色し易いでしょう。それが乾いたら、側面壁だけを同じ絵の具で重ね塗りします。

Cover the exterior wall with a watery mixture of warm neutral colors and yellow-ocher. The window panes should be left unpainted at this stage, since they will later be painted over in a darker color. When the color on the exterior wall is dried, only overlap the same color over the exterior wall.

さらに、外壁面の色の変化を表現する為に、同じ絵の具で重ね塗りをして、基準線寄りを暗くしていきます。この時、側面壁の絵の具を少し濃くして着色した方が、正面壁との明度差が出易いでしょう。また、正面壁と側面壁の色の変化にみられる方向性を一定にします。

To express the change in colors on the exterior wall, overlap the same color on the wall until the area closer to the reference line darkens a bit. If thicker coloring is used over the side exterior wall, the difference in brightness between the side and front exterior walls can be more clearly expressed. When drawing the change in color, make the direction of change consistent.

次に窓ガラスの着色に入りますが、淡彩パースなので外壁面に色がはみ出ないように着色しなければなりません。もし、はみ出した場合、乾いてから、平筆の先で洗い落として下さい。なお、水ぼてによるシミが出来易いので、暗く着色する部分に筆を運び、余分な絵の具は、筆で吸い取るようにします。暗い部分にシミが出来ても、後で暗く着色すると目立たなくなります。

Next, color the window panes. Take care to prevent the lighter colors from spreading out of the exterior wall area. If these colors do spread out of this area, they should be washed away using a water and a flat brush after the color has been set. It also should be noted that smearing easily occurs if too much water is used in painting the lighter areas. It is therefore recommended to soak up any smearing over the dark areas with a wet paintbrush. If smearing remains on the dark area, however, it can be hidden by additional coloring in the finish stage.

窓の腰壁の着色をして、窓ガラス面を仕上げますが、腰壁は、窓ガラスと同色なので、筆をガラス面に向けて着色すれば、余分な絵の具によるシミがガラス面に逃げる為、きれいに着色出来ます。

Color the wainscots of the windows to finish the window panes. Since the same color is used for the wainscots and the panes themselves, move the brush towards the panes when coloring them. Any smearing caused by excessive coloring will escape into the window panes in this process, so the final coloring will be clear.

路面の着色は、不透明水彩絵の具で描かれたパースと同様にして下さい。ただ、紙が白色なので、少し、淡めの色で着色し始めるとよいでしょう。描き方は、p.104「路面の描き方」に詳しく説明してあります。

When coloring the road surface, follow the techniques used to prepare for rendering in opaque watercolors. Since the paper is white, however, it's better to start by using lighter colors. A good way to paint this portion is described in "How to paint the road surface," on p.104.

車等の点景の着色に入りますが、透明水彩絵の具による淡彩仕上げですので、暗い色をつくる場合は、暖色ニュートラルや寒色ニュートラルを加えてつくって下さい。なお、着色は重ね塗りで暗くするようにします。

Next, color the cars and other incidental elements. Since this light coloring is finished using clear watercolors, add warm neutral or cold neutral colors to produce the darker colors, and overlap them to express the dark portions.

木や人物、雲を描き入れると仕上がりますが、暗い色は、ニュートラル色を加えた色で重ね塗りする点は、前段階と同じです。

Finish the rendering by adding trees, people, clouds, and other incidental elements. Use the same method employed in the previous step to color the dark portions; i.e. by overlapping blends of neutral colors.

植栽、建具、カーテン、ジュータンの着色
Coloring process for plants, home fixtures, curtains, and rugs

透明水彩絵の具を使って、窓ガラス面を着色しますが、空の色から着色し、外の植栽は重ね塗りで仕上げます。その後、壁面の着色に移りますが、下図から色がはみ出しても気にしなくてよいでしょう。

When coloring the window panes using clear watercolors, start by coloring the sky, and paint the plantation outside of the room by overlapping the colors. Move on to the coloring of the surface of the wall. Even if the underpaint color comes out, never mind.

建具や木製枠は必ず重ね塗りで暗くすると同時に、暖色ニュートラルで暗い色をつくって下さい。カーテンの着色も、淡い色から着色し、重ね塗りで立体感を出して下さい。

Render the furniture and wooden frames by overlapping the colors, adding warm neutral tones to the darker colors. When coloring the curtain, begin by using the lighter colors and then gradually overlap them to express the depth.

次に床のジュータンの着色に入りますが、これも淡い色から着色し始め、暗い影等は、暖色ニュートラルを加えた濃い色で重ね塗りして着色します。なお、暗い色が下図からはみ出した場合、乾いてから、平筆に水をつけてきれいに洗い出しておきます。また、出来るだけ、広い面から塗り始めて、細かい部分は、細い丸筆で塗り上げるとよいでしょう。

Then color the carpet on the floor, again beginning with the lighter colors. To express the dark shade, overlap the dark colors produced by adding the warm neutral colors. If the dark underpainting cannot be hidden by the later overlapping, these portions should be washed away using a round watery brush after the underpainting has completely dried. When applying the color, it is generally better to start with the larger area, and then to move on to the details using a fine flat paintbrush.

椅子の着色では、手前程、暗い色になるように着色しますが、布製の場合、色むらがあっても気にしなくてよいでしょう。

When coloring the chairs, spread the darker colors over the chairs in the foreground. Do not be overly concerned if the colors on the cloth-covered chairs mottle slightly.

椅子の模様を描き込み、立体感を付けます。これらの着色も、重ね塗りで進めると容易に出来ます。また、テーブルの天板も、寒色系の淡い色で、部分塗りや重ね塗りで表現着色しましょう。

Paint in the designs of chairs to express their depth. Another way to get good results in this step is to apply the color overlapping technique. The top plate of the table can be rendered in cold light colors, employing both partial coloring and overlapping.

カウンターの着色も、方向性を決めた上で、重ね塗りで暗くしていくと、色の変化表現も出来て、きれいに着色出来ます。また、椅子の白い部分の立体感も、重ね塗りで表現します。なお、点景の着色の前に、木枠やカウンター、テーブル、椅子等のハイライトを入れ、ぼやけている部分は、暗い色ではっきりさせておきます。

When coloring the counter, decide the direction of coloring beforehand and darken the surface of the counter by overlapping the colors. This technique enables you to express the changes in color beautifully. The depth of the chairs can also be expressed by overlapping the colors on the white portions of the chairs. Before coloring the incidental elements, improve the expression of the darkness by adding highlights to the wooden frames, counters, tables and chairs, and spreading darker colors over the areas which look dim.

点景を着色して仕上げますが、やはり立体感を表現するには暖色には暖色ニュートラルで、寒色には寒色ニュートラルで暗い色をつくり、重ね塗りで表現して下さい。植栽等で、暗い部分に明るい葉を描き加える場合は、白を加えた不透明色で着色するときれいに仕上がります。

Finish up the rendering by adding the incidental elements. To express the three dimensions of the incidental elements, overlap warm neutral colors for the expression of warmth and cold neutral colors for coldness. When painting the bright leaves of the plants against the dark background, use opaque colors blended with white to give them a clear finish.

第3章

表現の実際

——建物がもっている各部表情のいろいろ

Chapter 3

Painting Practice

Different expressions presented by different elements of buildings

建物の表現方法

How to render the buildings

パース画の着色手順は、その着色方法によって異なります。筆塗りパースで、不透明水彩絵の具を中心に着色する場合は次の手順で進めばよいでしょう。

The coloring sequences used in rendering vary with the painting method. The following coloring sequence is recommended for brush painting perspectives using mainly opaque watercolors.

- ●第1段階…窓ガラス面の着色
- ●第2段階…正面壁の着色
- ●第3段階…側面壁の着色
- ●第4段階…正面壁の影の着色
- ●第5段階…側面壁の影の着色
- ●第6段階…ハイライトと最暗部の着色

1st step: Coloring of the window panes
2nd step: Coloring of the front exterior wall
3rd step: Coloring of the side exterior wall
4th step: Coloring of the shade on the front exterior wall
5th step: Coloring of the shade on the side exterior wall
6th step: Coloring of the highlights and darkest portions

着色のコツは、大きな面から小さな面へ、また、淡い色から暗い色へと描き進み、絵の具は、あまり濃くせずに2度塗り、3度塗りといった重ね塗りをくり返します。さらに、建物の奥のものから手前の方へ(例えば、窓ガラスから外壁へ、さらに門扉等の外構へ)着色します。奥のものから着色するのは、はみ出した色を次の手前のものを着色する時に、塗りかくすことが出来るからです。
透明水彩絵の具を中心に着色する淡彩パースでは次の原則を守ればきれいに着色出来ます。
原則1……白っぽい建物や壁面等、淡い色や白っぽい色の多いパースには、まず、水っぽくて淡い色から着色し始め、高彩度の部分や暗い部分の着色は後廻しにします。
原則2……同色の暗い色は、重ね塗りすることで暗くします。従って、やや暗い部分は同じ色で、より暗い部分は、さらに絵の具を濃くして重ね塗りしながら暗くします。
エアーブラシを中心に吹き付け着色する場合では、同系色の部分は一度にマスキングし、最も暗い色の部分から取り外して順次明るい部分へと吹き付けると同時に、吹き付けた色の濃淡をはっきりさせます。また、小さな部分や、細かい部分、形が複雑なものは、筆塗りで着色する方が速くきれいに着色出来ます。

The trick to successful coloring is to begin in the largest areas and proceed in sequence to the smaller areas, using lighter colors followed by darker ones. Avoid applying any of the thick colors in the beginning stages. Repeat the coloring two or three times, overlapping the layers. Begin from furthest areas of the building and work your way towards the foreground (e.g., from the window panes to the exterior wall, and then to the exterior landscape like gate). The advantage of this technique is that the colors painted in advance and expanded to the adjacent area can be hidden by the subsequent coloring.
By sticking to the following principles, you can achieve beautiful results with light color perspectives in clear watercolors.
Principle No. 1: When preparing perspectives of whitish buildings or exterior walls with many whites and light colors, start by applying the watery light colors, and then proceed on to the coloring of the heavier shaded portions and dark areas.
Principle No. 2: If colors of a similar system are overlapped, they naturally tend to darken. Use this to your advantage by overlapping similar colors and thicker colors on the relatively dark portions to obtain the proper effect.
When using mainly an airbrush, completely mask over areas that should be painted in similar colors, and remove and paint over the darkest portions first, moving on to the progressively lighter portions. At the same time, express the shade of the sprayed colors distinctly. You can finish renderings of smaller and more detailed or complicated areas more quickly if you use a brush.

1. 窓ガラスの描き方 How to color windows

絵の具は透明水彩絵の具でも、不透明水彩絵の具でもよいですが、窓ガラスは一般的に透明ガラスが多いので、透明水彩絵の具による着色はガラスの透明感を強調するのに適しているでしょう。
また、ガラスには、無色透明のガラスの他、ブロンズペン、グレーペン、ブルーペン等、色のついたものもあり、それぞれの色づかいは異なります。また、建物全体から見た場合、それらのガラスの色は、その建物全体の色調に影響されて、人間の目には色の錯覚がおきて、暖色系の建物のガラスは、概して、茶黒系の暖色に見え、寒色系の建物では青黒系の寒色に見えます。

Either clear or opaque watercolors will do for windows. Watercolors are generally the most suitable for conveying the clearness of the glass.
Windows of course are not made only from clear, colorless glass, and can be colored bronze, or gray, or blue. The colors might be influenced by the color tone of the painted building, which can trick the human eye. Windows of warm system colors are usually seen as brownish black system colors. Windows in buildings drawn in cold color systems can be perceived as cold bluish blacks.

暖色系ガラスの着色
Coloring of windows with warm color

寒色系ガラスの着色
Coloring of windowswith cold colors

A.窓ガラスの色づくり How to produce colors for window panes

ニュートラル色
Neutral colors

チューブから直接取り出した色は、彩度が高くケバケバしい色になります。そこで、純色（チューブに入っている色）に、他の色（例えば、バーント・アンバー等）を若干混ぜ合わせることによって、彩度をおさえた落ち着いた色をつくる必要があります。
このように、彩度をおさえて落ち着いた色にすることを、ニュートラル化といいます。市販されている絵の具のなかには、ニュートラル化した色も多く、ニュートラル化させる絵の具もありますが、2，3の透明度の高い色を混合すると、比較的簡単に、どの色をもニュートラル化させ、しかも、にごりのない色をつくることが出来ます。
ここで取り挙げるニュートラル色は、現代構造研究所のニュートラル色に若干の修正を加えた色で、最も合理的なニュートラル色の一例であると思われますので、その説明と利用方法を述べます。

Colors tend to be quite high in chroma and noisy when they are freshly squeezed out of their tubes. It is very important to calm these colors; to tone them down and reduce their chroma by blending them with small amounts of other colors（such as burnt umber）.
This process of producing the calm colors with reduced chroma is called neutralizing. Although many of the colors on sale commercially have already been neutralized, those which have not been can be easily neutralized by adding a couple of high clearness to produce clear colors.
The neutralized colors introduced are slight adjustments of colors produced at the Modern Structure Research Institute. Since they seem to be good samples of the most appropriate neutral colors, let me explain a little more about them and how to use them.

■ニュートラル色の調合の仕方 How to blend the neutral colors

まず、ニュートラル色の一覧表に示されている調合比に合わせて、梅皿内に、帯状に各々の絵の具をしぼり出して、その帯状の長さの比較で比率を合わせ、箸でよく混ぜ合わせると正しく調合出来ます。調合する際には、水を加えないで調合し、試し塗りする時には筆に水を含ませた上で調合した絵の具を白い紙に塗って、見本の色と比較します。その比較で、足らないと思われる色を加えたりしながら調合していきます。
このニュートラル色は、何度も、直接筆で溶かしながら混合する色ですから、梅皿等にたくさん調合しておくと便利です。

To begin with, squeeze the colors out of the tubes onto the palette in strips according to the mixing ratios specified in the schedule of neutral colors. Blending the colors well by adjusting the ratios according to the relative lengths of the color strips will bring out the appropriate mixtures. Do not add water when mixing the colors. When applying the trial coloring, add water to the paintbrush, lay the trial colors on a white paper, and compare them with the sample colors. If some of the colors appear to be short in the mixture, gradually mix in more of the short colors until the appropriate color blend is obtained.
Since the mixture of these neutral colors is repeated many times by melting them directly with water and a brush, it will be much more convenient for you if you prepare sufficient amounts on the palette in advance.

ニュートラル・ブラック（黒） Neutral black

調合比●ビリジャン（2）：カーマイン（1.5）
Mixing ratio ● 2 viridian : 1.5 Carmine

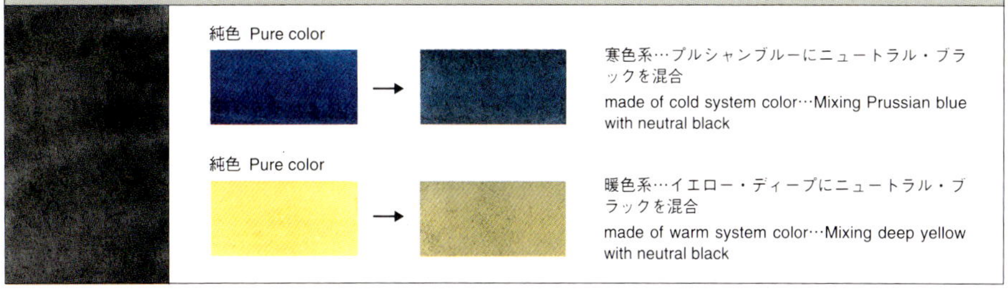

暖色ニュートラル（茶系の黒） Warm neutral color（Black of brown system）

調合比●ニュートラル・ブラック（4）：カーマイン（1）：バーント・アンバー（4）：コバルトブルー・ティント（0.5）
Mixing ratio ● 4 parts neutral black : 1 Carmine : 4 burnt umber: 0.5 cobalt blue tint

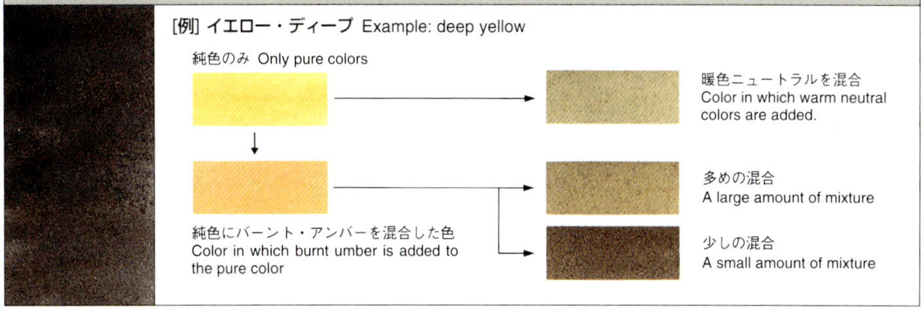

寒色ニュートラル（青系の黒） Cold neutral color（Black of blue system）

調合比●暖色ニュートラル（3）：ニュートラル・ブルー（2.5）
Mixing ratio● 3 warm neutral : 2.5 neutral blue

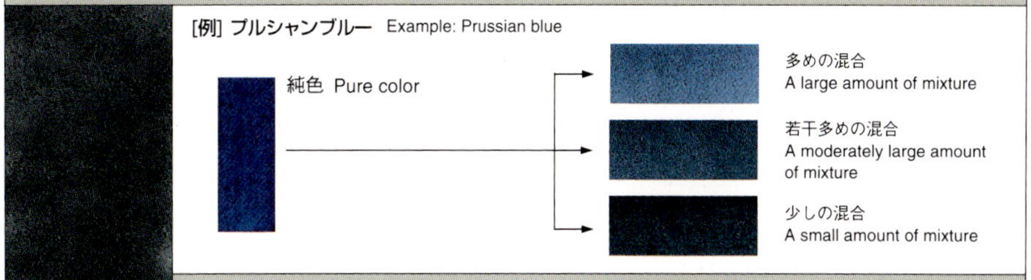

ニュートラル・ブルーの調合比は…コバルトブルー・ティント（3）：ニュートラル・ブラック（2）：プルシャンブルー（5）
Mixing ratio of neutral black is…Cobalt blue tint（3）: neutral black（2）: Prussian blue（5）

●ニュートラル色の一覧表
Schedule of neutral colors

絵の具と水加減
Ratio of colors and water

イメージパースやインテリアパースに多く見られる技法に、淡彩仕上げによる方法があります。
この淡彩仕上げによる技法は、ハイライト等にポスターカラー等の不透明水彩絵の具を一部に使用する以外、ほとんどが透明水彩絵の具で着色します。従って、水の混入加減によって、淡い白っぽい色から暗い色まで、透明水彩絵の具のみでつくることになります。

A lighter coloring technique is sometimes used for finishing images and interiors.
Watercolors are mostly used in this lighter coloring finish technique, but poster colors and other opaque watercolors are used to express highlighted areas. Therefore, light whitish colors can be darkened somewhat using only clear watercolors by adjusting the amount of water added to them.

■ 絵の具の濃さ加減 Depth of colors

絵の具を水でうすめると、その水の量によって、ほとんど色みのない淡い色から、絵の具によっては高彩度で暗い色まで、無限の色が出来ます。そこで、無限の色の濃さから下に示したような代表的な濃さをもつ色を目安にして、7段階の濃さの色をつくり出すことが出来れば、淡彩画としての表現には十分です。この濃さ加減は、あくまで感覚的な目安の濃淡加減ですから厳密に考える必要はありませんが、何度も練習しておく方がよいでしょう。

By diluting the colors with water, a near infinite number of colors of various depths can be obtained; from almost colorless light colors to high chroma dark colors. If seven degrees of colors with the representative depths shown below can be used to produce such an unending variety of colors, then of course there is nothing preventing you from painting the rendering in lighter colors. Since the depth tends to vary with the sensitivity of the artist, it is not necessary to think about this too seriously. It is better to practice the production of the colors.

【絵の具と水加減による濃淡参考図】 Reference chart of depth of colors by type of color and amount of water added

(例) バーント・アンバー 〈Example〉Burnt umber

❶ほとんど水だけの状態の色で、絵の具に水を加えるというよりも、水に微量の絵の具を加えるといった感じでつくるとよいでしょう。そうすれば、水に、ほんのりと色みが感じられる程度になります。(壁面着色に効果的)
Color❶: This color is almost the color of water. The appropriate color can be produced by adding slight amounts of color to the water; not by adding water to the color. Slight amounts of color can be seen mingled in the water. (Effective if used for exterior walls)

❷❶より純色を多めに、色みがはっきりするまで純色を加えます。❶と違って、絵の具に水をたっぷり加えた感じでつくります。(壁面着色に効果的・ガラス面着色の第1段階の濃さ)
Color❷: This color is produced by adding more pure color than used for color q to water until the color is clearly identifiable. Unlike color q, this color is produced by adding ample water to the color. (1st degree of color depth; effective if used for exterior walls)

❸❷よりも少し色みが強く感じられる程度まで純色を加えます。まだ水っぽい状態の色です。(ガラス面着色の第2段階の濃さ)
Color❸: This color is produced by adding pure color to the water so that more color is identifiable, but it is still watery. (2nd degree of color depth; suitable for coloring windows)

❹若干、不透明感が感じられる程度まで純色を多くしてつくります。一般的な水彩画に見られる絵の具の濃さに近いですが、かなり色みが強く感じられます。(ガラス面着色の第3段階の濃さ)
Color❹: This color is produced by adding ample amounts of pure color until an opaque sense of color can be seen. The depth is closer to that seen in ordinary watercolors, but the color appears a bit heavier. (3rd degree of color depth; suitable for coloring windows)

❺純色に水を加える時に、絵の具が少し濃く感じられ、しかも、不透明感がある程度まで水を加えます。(ガラス面着色の第4段階の濃さ)
Color❺: This color looks heavier when water is added to the pure color, but an opaque feeling still remains. (4th degree of color depth; suitable for coloring windows)

❻パレット上で絵の具と水を混ぜ合わせる時、少し絵の具に粘り気が感じられる程度まで絵の具を多くします。かなり暗い色になります。(ガラス面着色の第5段階の濃さ)
Color❻: When mixing the color with water on the palette, continue to add more color until it begins to appear sticky. This color can get fairly dark. (5th degree of color depth; suitable for coloring windows)

❼若干、こってりした感じのある濃さの色であり、純色に少量の水を加えてつくります。(ガラス面着色の第6段階以降の濃さ)
Color❼: This color looks rich in depth,and is produced by adding a slight amounts of water to pure colors. (6th degree of color depth; suitable for coloring windows)

B.テナントビルの表現着色 Coloring of tenant building

暖色系の窓ガラスの着色手順
Coloring sequence for window with a feeling of warm color

●正方形に近い建物
Nearly square-shaped building

●縦長の建物
Tall building

●横長の建物
Large and flat building

第1段階 Step 1

ビリジャンに白を加えた空の色を水でうすめて図の部分に着色し、それが乾いたら、イエロー・ディープにバーント・アンバーを少し加えた色を淡くして、窓ガラス全体を着色します。絵の具の濃さについては、p.58「絵の具の濃さ加減」を参照して下さい。

Mix a sky color by adding white to viridian and diluting with water, and spread over the area indicated by the black circle. After the color is dried, apply a layer of light colors produced by adding slightly burnt umber to deep yellow over the entire window area. For more details on the depth of colors, refer to the "Depth of colors" section on p.58.

第2段階 Step 2

さらにバーント・アンバーを加えた少し濃い色で、視点（基準線）から離れている部分を一部残して重ね塗りします。

Lay a heavier color produced by mixing in small amounts of burnt umber; cover the entire area except for the section which is apart from the visual point （reference line）

第3段階 Step 3

第2段階の色に暖色ニュートラルを少々加えた色で、全体的な窓ガラスの濃淡着色をします。

Cover the entire window pane area with a color produced by adding small amounts of warm neutral colors to the color produced in step 2.

第4段階 Step 4

さらに第3段階の色に暖色ニュートラルを多めに加えた色で他の建物のシルエットを描き込みます。絵の具の濃さは見本に合わせて下さい。

Paint the silhouette of the building using a color produced by adding fairly large amounts of warm neutral colors to the color produced in step 3. Select the depth of the colors according to the sample.

第5段階 Step 5

窓ガラス越しに見える奥の壁面を、第 4 段階の色にさらに暖色ニュートラルを加えた色で、下の階から着色し、上の階へ描き進む度に水を加えて、絵の具を淡くして着色します。同時に、階高が高くなるに従って奥の壁の幅も細く着色します。

Spread a color produced by adding warm neutrals colors to the color produced in step 4 over the exterior wall in the back as seen through the window. In this step, start painting from the lower floor and add water to the colors as you progress to the upper floors so that they lighten somewhat. Also narrow the width of the wall in the back as the painting progresses upwards.

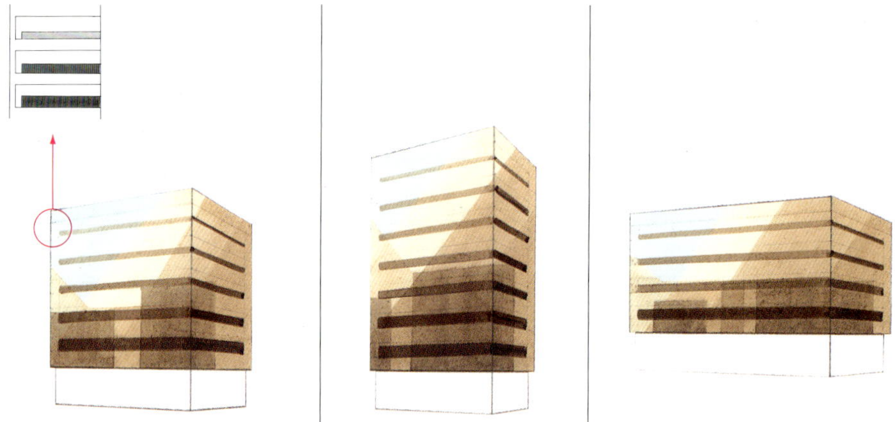

第6段階 Step 6

窓ガラス越しに見える室内の影を描き加えますが、色は第 5 段階と同じで、階高が高くなるに従って、水で淡くすることも大切です。

Draw the shaded interior sections which can be seen through the window. Use the same color used for step 5. It is important here, also, to lighten the colors by adding water as the painting progresses further upwards.

第7段階 Step 7

室内の柱やロッカー等のシルエットを描き入れますが、第 6 段階と同様に、階高が高くなる度に水で絵の具を淡くし、細く描き加えていきます。色は第 6 段階の色に暖色ニュートラルをさらに加えます。

Draw the columns inside the room and a silhouette of the lockers. Use lighter and finer colors for the upper floors, as in step 6. Mix the color used for this step by adding more warm neutral colors to the color used in step 6.

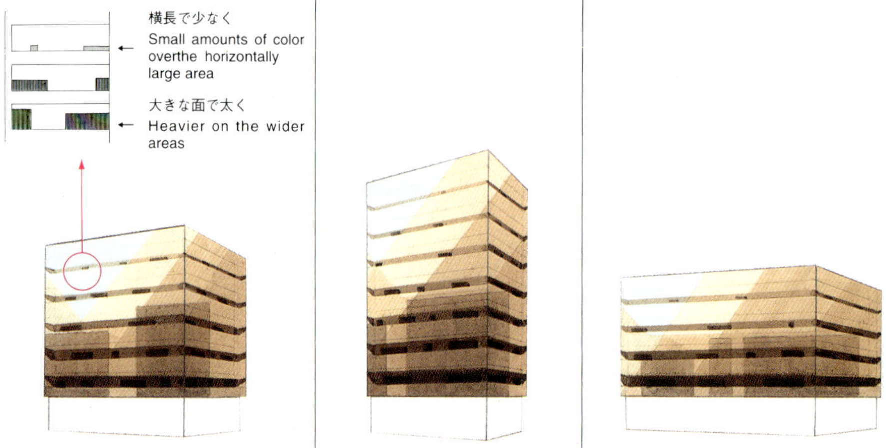

第8段階 Step 8

室内の人物をシルエットで描き込みますが、色は第 7 段階の色に暖色ニュートラルをさらに加えて濃くした色から始め、階高が高くなるにつれ、人物の背高を低め、同時に、淡く着色します。

Silhouette the people in the room. The colors used here should be made heavier by adding more warm neutral colors to the color used in step 7. Again, this color should lightened as the drawing moves to the higher floors. Make the people on the upper floors shorter, and render them in lighter colors.

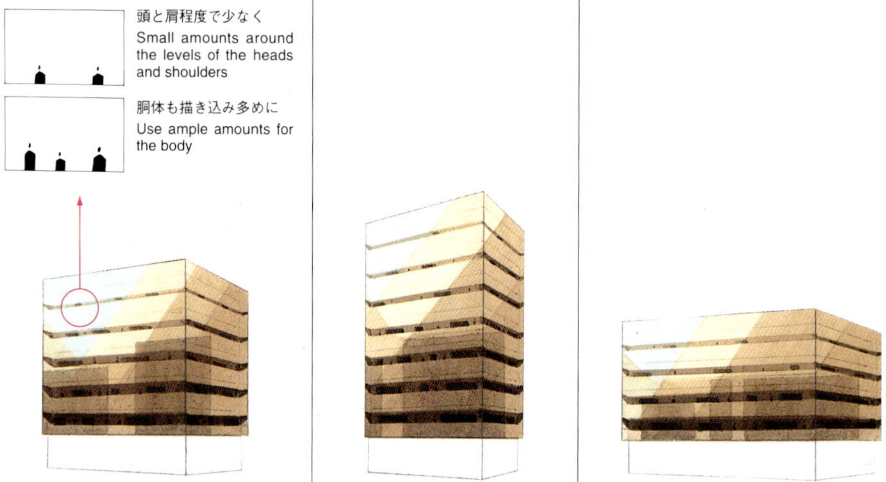

第9段階 Step 9

窓ガラスの全体的な着色が済んだら、色の濃淡コントラストが強い部分に、淡い色を棒グラフ状に描き足して、極端なコントラストを弱めます。

After the comprehensive coloring over the window pane is completed, alleviate any extremely sharp color contrast by applying additional layers of lighter colors in bar-graph-like layers of shape.

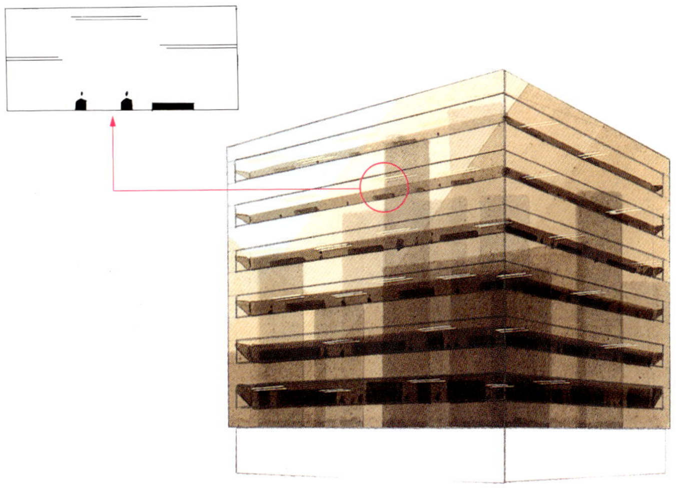

第10段階 Step 10

イエロー・ディープに白を加えた明るい色で照明を描き入れます。一本線でもよいのですが、二本線で焦点に合わせて描きます。

Paint the lighting using a bright color produced by adding white to deep yellow. A single line is enough, but it is preferable to have two lines that vanish to the focal point.

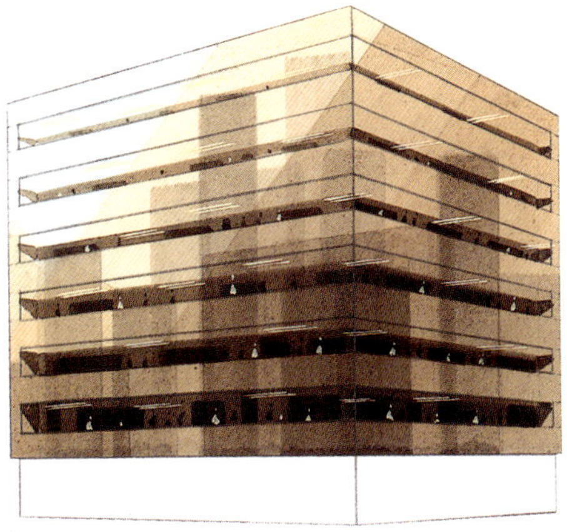

第11段階 Step 11

照明を描いた同じ色に、水を少し加えた色で、明るい人物のシルエットを描き入れます。

Paint in brighter silhouettes of the people. Use the same color used for the lighting with a slight amount of water added.

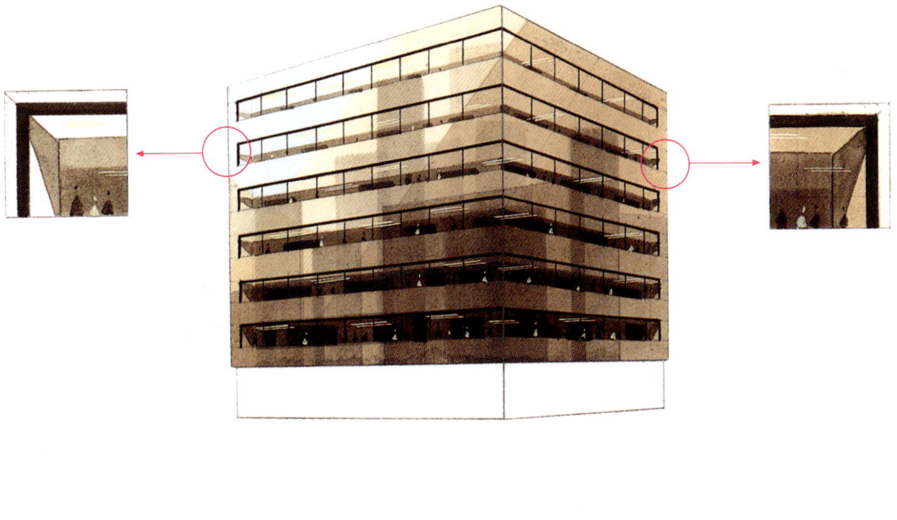

最終段階 Final step

第8段階で使った程度の濃い色で、ガラス面に現れる影を見本のように太く描き加えます。特に、基準線に対して正面と側面では描き込み方が異なるので注意して下さい。

Paint the shade reflected on the window more heavily, as shown in the sample. Use the same degree of density used in step 8. Remember to use different shades for the colors of the front and side exterior walls against the reference line.

寒色系の窓ガラスの着色手順
Coloring process for windows using cold system color

寒色系での着色方法も、暖色系とは色が異なるだけで、まったく同様です。暖色系の場合と同じ空の色から始まり、ビリジャンやプルシャンブルーの単色か混合色に、少量の寒色ニュートラルを混ぜた淡い色から全体的な着色をして、着色段階が進むにつれて、寒色ニュートラルをさらに加えていき、第７段階からニュートラル・ブラックを加えて最暗の色をつくります。明るい人物のシルエットや照明は暖色系と同じです。

There is only one difference between coloring using cold system colors and that using warm system colors: the colors used. The rest of the method is entirely the same. Start using the sky color in the same way as applied to the warm system colors. Mix small amounts of cold neutral colors to a single viridian or a Prussian bule（or a mixture of the two）, and begin by painting the entire perspective in lighter colors. As the painting progreses, start adding more cold neutrals to the colors. Adding neutral black to the color used in step 7 will produce the darkest color. Bright silhouettes of the people and lighting should be expressed in the same manner as employed with the warm colors.

第1段階 Step 1

第2段階 Step 2

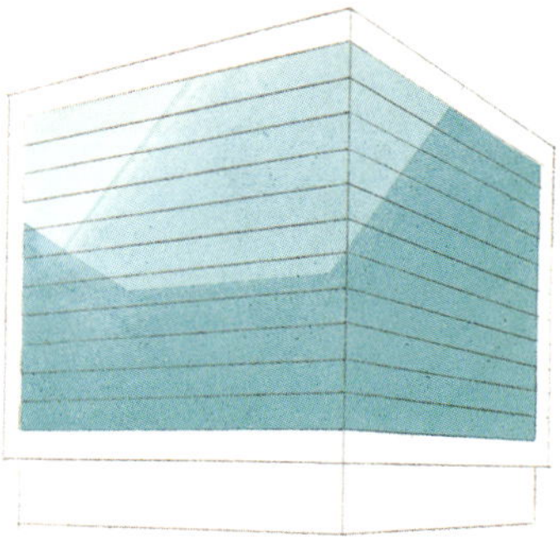

第3段階 Step 3

第4段階 Step 4

第5段階 Step 5

第6段階 Step 6

第7段階 Step 7

第8段階 Step 8

第9段階 Step 9

仕上り Final step

C.1階ロビー及び店舗の表現着色 Presentation and coloring of ground floor lobby and shop

カウンターのあるロビー
Coloring process for lobby with a counter

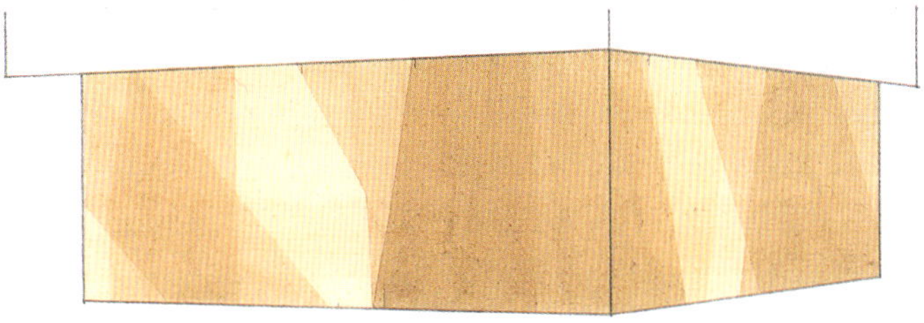

第1段階 Step 1

比較的淡い色で重ね塗りして大まかなガラス面全体の濃淡着色をします。色はイエロー・ディープにバーント・アンバーを少し加えた色から着色し始めます。

Lay relatively light colors with a rough touch to express the shade of the entire glass area. Begin applying a mixture of deep yellow with small amounts of burnt umber.

第2段階 Step 2

カウンターや人物、室内の備品等をいろいろな色の濃さで描き込みます。この段階では、バーント・アンバーの他、暖色ニュートラルも混ぜた色にします。

Paint the counter, people, furniture and interiors using a variety shades. Add warm neutrals to the burnt umber in the colors in this step.

第3段階 Step 3

部分的に色相の違った色を着色しますが、出来るだけ明るく下地着色されている所を選びましょう。

Although colors of different hues should be used for different portions of the painting, try to concentrate these different hues in areas with bright underpainting.

飲食関係の店舗
Restaurants and other eating places

第1段階 Step 1

カウンターのあるロビーの着色手順と同様に。

Make it in the same way as described above in Step 1 of "Coloring process for lobby with a counter".

第2,3段階 Steps 2 and 3

室内をはなやかにする為に、人物や物品のシルエットを多く描き込みます。

To present the interior as brilliantly as possible, draw as many people and interior elements as possible.

第4段階 Step 4

ブラインドを描き入れる場合、その部分を暖色ニュートラルの入った暗い色で着色しておきます。

When drawing the blind louvers, use dark colors with warm neutrals added.

第5段階 Step 5

白に暖色系の色を加えた明るい色を水でうすめて、ブラインドを描き込みます。

Finish painting the louvers using diluted whites with warm system colors added.

D.窓ガラスの着色実例 Coloring example of windows

マンションの窓ガラスの着色手順
Coloring process for windows of condominiums

第1段階 Step 1

まず、空の色を着色します。空の色は、ビリジャンに白を加えて水でうすめ、p.58の［絵の具の濃さ加減］で述べた❸程度の濃さにします。

Spread colors over the sky portion first. The color for the sky should be produced by adding white to viridian and thinning it with water until it reaches degree-❸ as explained in "Depth of colors" on p.58.

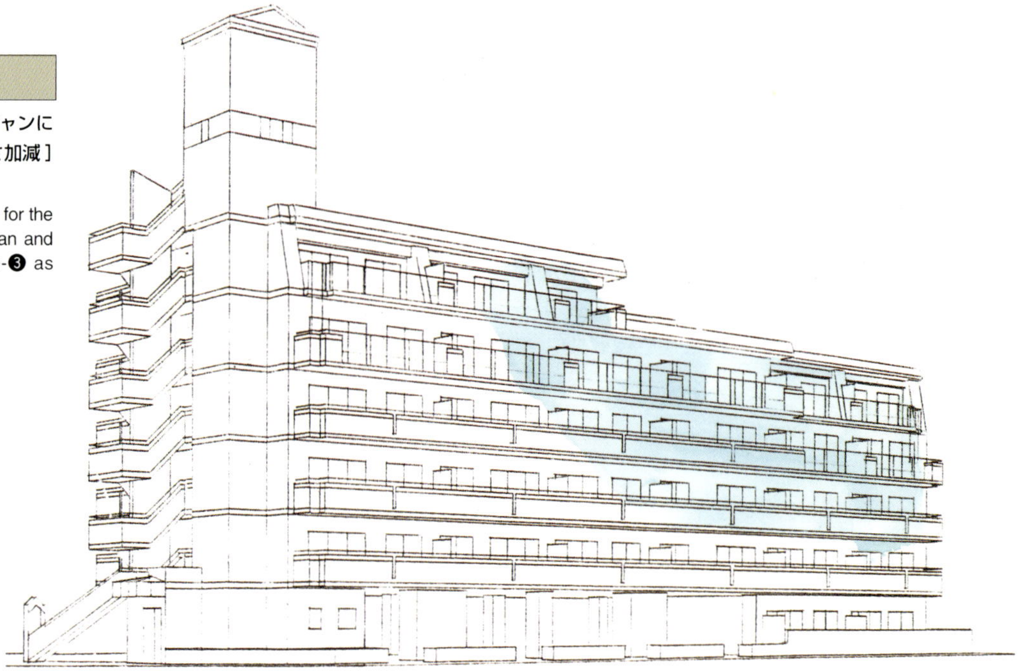

第2段階 Step 2

イエロー・ディープにバーント・アンバーを加えた❷程度の濃さの絵の具で全体的な窓の着色をして、一部は空の色と重なるようにします。住宅の場合と違って、マンションの場合は窓が多くて小さいので、必ず、窓ガラスの色が上階の窓ガラス面の下場に重なるように重ね塗りすることが必要です。その後、その色に暖色ニュートラルを加え、❸程度の濃さにして、基準線寄りの窓ガラスを見本のように暗くしておきます。

Color the entire window using a deep yellow mixed with burnt umber of a degree-❷ shade, overlapping part of the sky color with this color. Since many of the windows of the condominium tend to be smaller than windows in residential houses, always remember to lay colors so that the color of the glass overlaps the colors of the lower ends of the windows of the upper floor. Then add warm neutral colors over them to attain a degree-❸ shade, painting the window panes closer to the reference line in darker colors, as shown in the sample.

第3段階 Step 3

第2段階の色で目線（HL線）に近い部分の窓ガラス面を暗く着色します。

Using the color used in step 2, render the window pane near the eye level line (horizontal line) in dark colors.

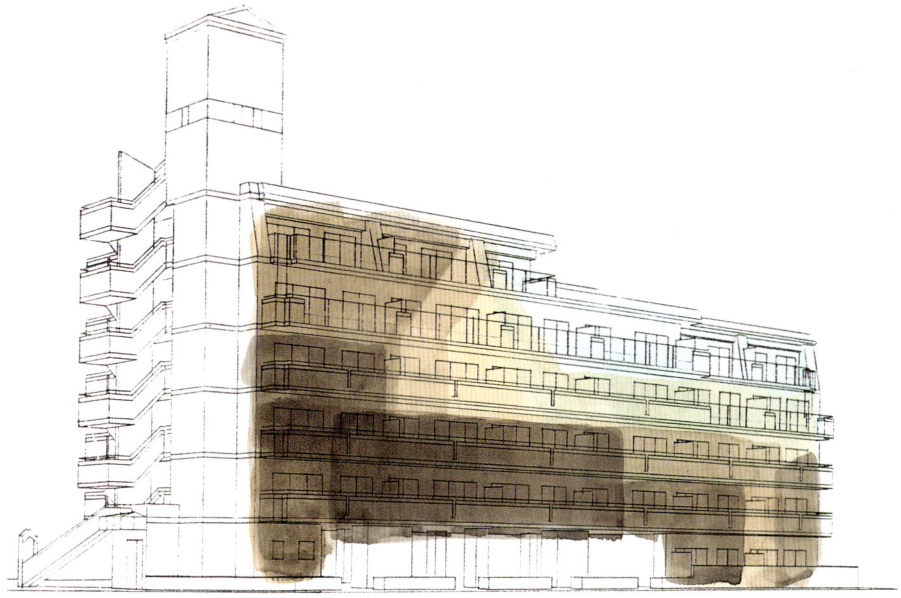

第4段階 Step 4

第3段階の色に、さらに暖色ニュートラルを加えて❹程度の濃さにして見本のように、目線に近いところに暗い面を描き入れて窓ガラスの深みを表現します。

Add the warm neutral color to the color used in step 3 so that it reaches a degree-❹ shade and paint the darker area around the eye level line to express the depth of the window panes.

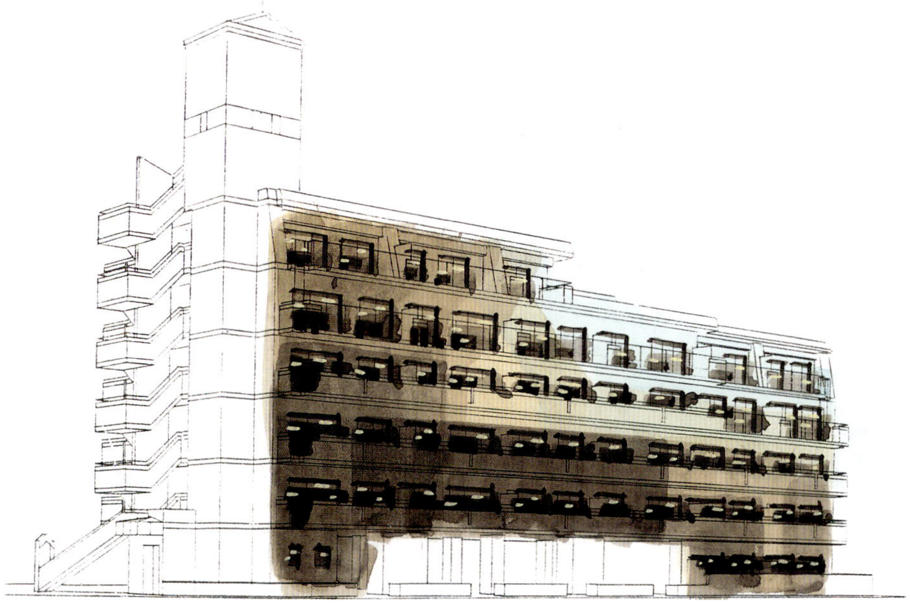

最終段階 Final step

仕上りに近づいたら、住宅の窓ガラスの表現を加えますが、その描き込みは、目線に近い程、多くしなければなりません。部屋の側壁の影や、奥の壁の暗い面や、置物の暗いシルエットを描き込み、イエロー・ディープに白を加えた明るい色で照明を描き入れ、サッシの影を太めに描き加えます。最後に、不透明色でサッシを描けば仕上ります。

As you draw nearer to the final step, render the details of the window panes. Spread more colors over areas closer to the eye level line. Paint the shade on the side wall in the room, the dark area on the back wall, and the dark silhouette of the ornaments. Next, paint the lighting using a bright color produced by adding white to deep yellow, rendering the shade of the aluminum sashes a bit wider. Finally, paint the aluminum sashes in opaque colors.

●下塗り着色の目安例（第１～４段階）Example of criteria for underpainting（Steps 1 through 4）

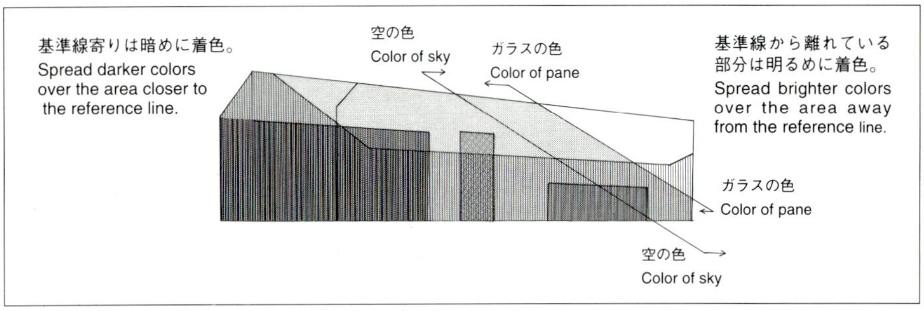

マンションの場合、窓が多いので下塗りでのガラス面の濃淡表現は、テナントビルと同様に考えてよいのですが、全体的な濃淡着色の後、各窓に室内の雰囲気をシルエットで表現着色します。色づかいは、一般的に暖色系が多いです。

Since the condominium has a lot of window panes, the same coloring idea applied to the tenant building can be considered when expressing the shade of the surfaces of the windows. But since this is a condominium, it's better to express the atmosphere of the interiors of the rooms in the reflected silhouettes on the window panes after coloring in all of the shaded areas. The colors used for this process are usually warm system colors.

●全体的な下塗り後の各窓ガラスの表現（最終段階）

Detailed expression of each window pane after the entire underpainting over the window area has been finished（Final step）

マンションの窓ガラスの着色例
Coloring example of condominium window

空の色の部分を多くして、ガラス面の反射を強調した着色例

Coloring example where the portion using sky color is wider and the reflection on the glass is stressed.

空の色の部分（光の反射面）を少なめにした着色例

Coloring example where the portion（area where light is reflected）using sky color is reduced

暖色系のガラス着色
Coloring of window panes using warm system colors

見本のパースのように、外壁色が暖色系の場合は、ガラス面の着色も暖色系ですると色調がまとまります。

As shown in the sample perspective, if the exterior wall is painted with warm system colors, it is better to color the glass in the same color system so that a good color balance can be achieved.

寒色系のガラス着色
Coloring of window panes using cold system colors

外壁色がグレー系や寒色系の場合は、寒色系のガラス表現をすると建物との調和がとれます。

If the exterior wall is expressed by gray system colors or cold system colors, it is better to color the window pane in the same color system so that a good color balance can be achieved.

住宅の窓ガラスの着色手順
Coloring process for windows in residential houses

第1段階 Step 1

空の色は、ビリジャンと白でつくり、見本のように着色し、ガラスの色と重なる部分の色は筆でぼかしておきます。窓ガラスの色は、イエロー・ディープにバーント・アンバーを加えて［絵の具の濃さ加減］❷程度の水っぽい色にして、空の色のぼかした部分に重ねてガラス面全体を着色します。この時、余分な絵の具は筆で吸い取っておくか、外壁面にはみ出させて、水ぼてがガラス面に出来ないようにします。

Mix the color for the sky by mixing viridian and white, and then spread it over the sky area as shown in the sample. The portions overlapping with the color of the window panes should be shaded off using a paintbrush. The color for window panes should be produced by adding burnt umber to deep yellow, and diluting it fairly heavily, attaining a degree-❷ shade as described in "Degree of color shade." Color the entire glass so that the color can be overlapped with the shaded off sky color. Soak the excessive colors with a paintbrush, or spread them towards the exterior wall to prevent the watery colors from dropping onto the surface of the glass.

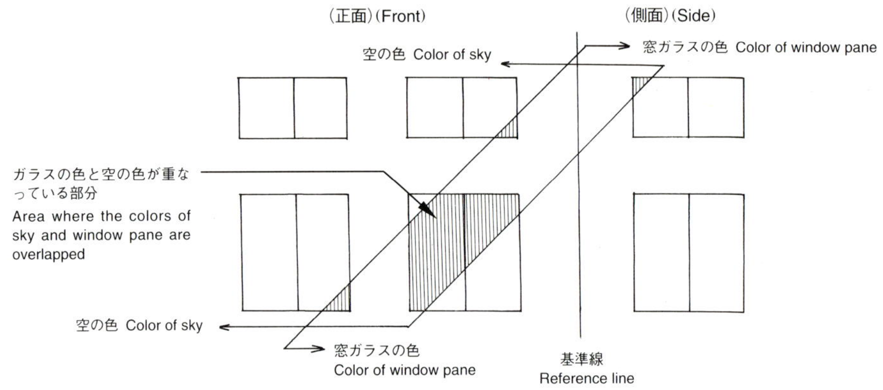

第2段階 Step 2

第1段階の色に、さらにバーント・アンバーを加えて❸程度の濃さにして、2階の窓ガラスのうち、正面側の基準線寄りにある窓ガラスの一部にかかるように、側面のガラス面全体を再度重ね塗りして暗くします。その後、同じ色で、正面の2階のガラス面に、室内の側壁と奥の壁を低めに図のように描き加えます。また、同時に、1階正面のガラス面には、部屋の奥行きを強調する必要があるので、図のような表現で着色します。

Thicken the color produced in step 1 until it reaches level -❸ thickness by adding burnt umber, and spread the color over the area near the reference line so that part of the window pane is covered with it. Lay the color over all of the side windows again to darken them, and then draw the side and back walls of the interior on the surface of the front glass on the second floor so that they appear short, as shown in the example. At the same time, paint the front glass of the first floor. Since it is necessary to stress the depth of room during this process, paint and color it as shown in the sample illustration.

2階のガラスの色のパターン
Color pattern on the windows of the second floor

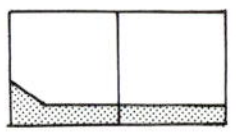

天井面を明るくする。
Make the surface of the ceiling bright.

1階のガラスの色のパターン
Color pattern on the windows of the first floor

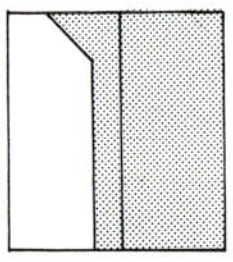

室内の奥行きを強調するために、基準線寄りを暗くする。
Make the area closer to the reference line darker to stress the depth of the room.

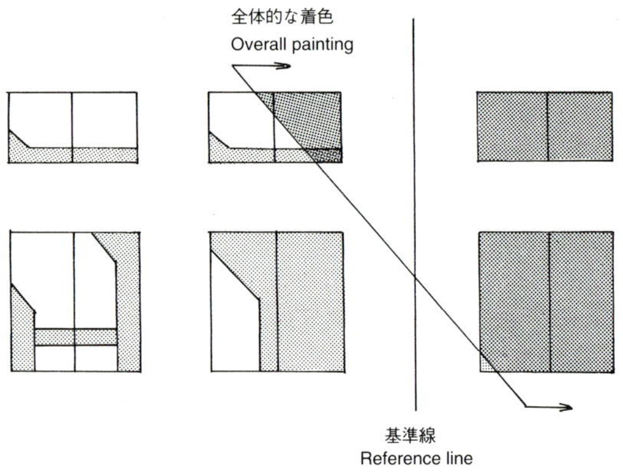

第3段階　Step 3

さらに、ガラス面に深みをもたせる為に、第２段階でつくった色に、暖色ニュートラルを加えて❹程度の濃さの色をつくり、２階の正面の基準線側の窓ガラスを、また、１階の窓ガラスはより奥行を強調する為に、図のように暗くします。他方、側面のガラス面には、部屋の内に出来る影を描き加えて暗くします。

To provide depth in the glass surface mix a color of level-❹ thickness by adding warm neutrals to the color produced in the 2nd step. To express the depth of the room, make the front window of the second floor facing the reference line darker than the side window pane of the first floor, as shown in the sample. Paint the shade created inside the room on the side window pane to make it darker.

基準線寄りを暗くし、また、２階のガラス面より１階のガラス面をより暗くします。

Make the area closer to the reference line darker, and make the glass surface of the second floor darker than that of the first floor.

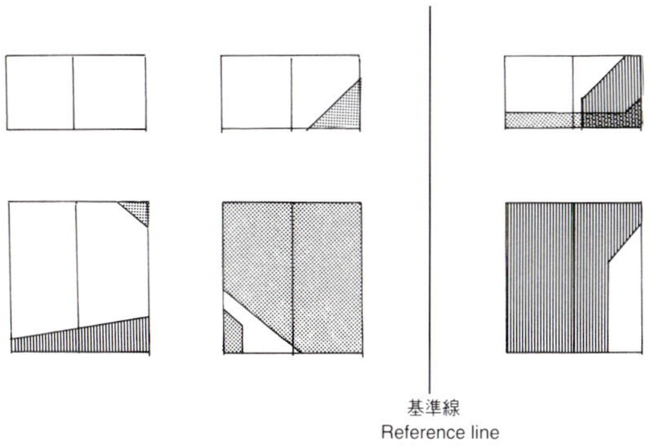

最終段階　Final step

第３段階の色に、さらに暖色ニュートラルを加えて❺程度の濃さにして、各窓ガラス面に出来る室内の影を強調したり、また、奥の壁面にいろいろな大きさのシルエットを何度も重ね塗りして暗くします。特に、１階のガラス面には、いろいろな四角い形の面で、シルエットを重ね塗りすると透明感のあるガラス表現が出来ます。その後、各ガラス面に、家具等のシルエットを描き込み、イエロー・ディープに白を加えた色で、照明や、家具のハイライトを描き加えます。サッシの影は❻程度の濃さで太めに描き入れます。

Mix a color of level-❺ thickness by adding warm neutrals to the color produced in the 3rd step and use it to stress the shade of the inside the room reflected on the window pane, and make the back side wall darker by repeatedly layering silhouettes over it. If you lay many silhouettes with squares of various sizes on the window glass of the first floor, the final expression of the window pane will have a clear feeling. Then silhouette the furniture and other elements on each window pane, and lay a series of colors produced by adding white to deep yellow to highlight the expression of the lighting fixtures and furniture. Draw the shade of aluminum sashes wider with a color of degree-❻ thickness.

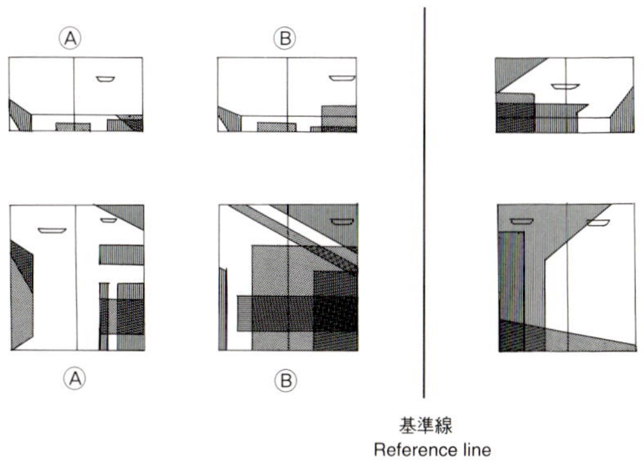

基準線に近い窓や側面の窓、及び１階の窓には、暗いシルエットを多く描き込み、また、ⒶよりⒷのガラス面に多くの暗いシルエットを描き込むとよいでしょう。また、１階はHL線（目線）に近いので、２階の窓ガラスよりも暗くします。

Paint as many dark silhouettes as possible on the window closer to the reference line and on the side window panes, as well as on the window panes of the firstfloor. It is recommendable to draw darker silhouettes on the Ⓑ-side glass than on the Ⓐ-side glass. As the firstfloor is closer to the horizontal level (eye line level), make it darker than the window pane of the second floor.

■住宅が多数並んでいて、住宅の下図が小さな場合 If there are many residential houses and small drafts of the main house

細かいシルエットは省き、ガラス面の濃淡着色を簡略化して大まかな表現でよいでしょう。

It is recommendable to eliminate the detailed fine silhouette and simplify the shade on the glass surface to express the rendering with a rough touch.

■窓ガラス面に出来る光の反射を表現する場合 Case of light reflected on the window pane

下の図は、ガラス面に反射される光の入れ方を図示していますが、特に、白の絵の具の濃さに注意して下さい。白を比較的薄く水で薄め、平筆にたっぷりふくませた後、濡れ雑巾で余分な絵の具を吸い取り、溝引き定規とボールペンの背（ガラス棒よりも引き易い）を使って、スピーディに描き込みます。この時、「カスレ」たりしないように注意します。特に、室内にフスマがある場合には、その上に光の反射を加えると効果的でしょう。

Observe how the illustration described below shows the light reflecting on the window pane, and pay extra attention to the thickness of the white. Dilute the white to a fairly thin consistency, pass a fairly wet brush over the surface, soak up the excessive colors with a wet dusting cloth, and quickly draw the perspective using a special ruler for fluting（more convenient than a fluting rod）and the back of a ball-point pen. Take care that none of the lines become blurred during this drawing process. If a sliding door is built inside the room, the reflection of the light over the sliding door will make the perspective more effective.

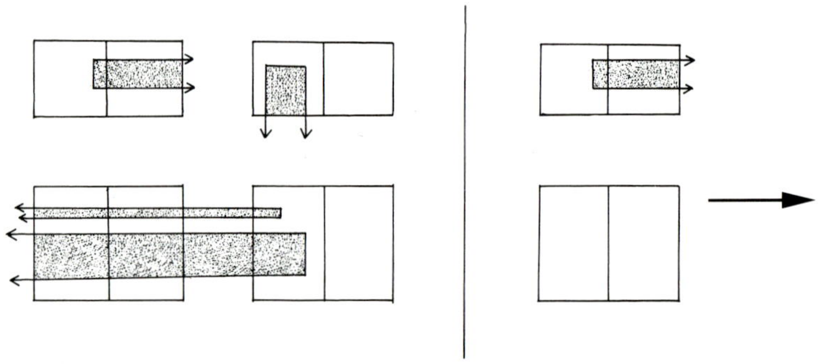

作品例
Sample of works

店舗のガラス面の着色手順
Coloring process for windows of a showroom

店舗のガラス表現は、はなやかで、明るくなければなりません。空の色の部分を多くし、ガラスの濃淡表現の着色は、比較的淡い色で、多めにするとよいでしょう。人物等のシルエットの濃さも、いろいろ変えると自然なにぎわいが表現されます。

The showroom's glass should be expressed gorgeously and brilliantly as well. Make the space painted with sky color larger, and express the shade of glass using relatively ample amounts of slightly lighter colors. Silhouetting the people and the other elements in colors of different densities will produce a natural gorgeous feeling in the perspective.

第1段階 Step 1

まず、空の色から着色し始めます。住宅の場合と同様に、重なる部分の空の色はよくぼかしておきます。[絵の具の濃さ加減] ❷～❸の濃さで、イエロー・ディープと若干のバーント・アンバーの混合色を、見本のように、床面・天井面・奥の壁面を重ね塗りします。

To begin, color the sky. Just as with residential houses, adequately shade off the color over the portion of sky where many colors are overlapped. Lay colors of level-❷ to-❸ thickness as described in "Depth of colors". Mix the colors by blending yellow with a slight amount of burnt umber, and spread them over the surfaces of the floor, ceiling and back wall, as shown in the sample.

第2段階 Step 2

さらに、バーント・アンバーを加えながら暗い色で、店舗の奥行を表現する為に、基準線寄りを暗くします。その後、その色にイエロー・ディープを加えた、少し鮮やかな色を❷程度の濃さで、ガラス面がさびしくならないように、棒グラフ状の帯を何度も重ね塗りして描き加えます。

To express the depth of the showroom, make the area closer to the reference line darker by applying a color with further portions of burnt umber. Then, overlay a series of bar-graph-like stripes using a moderately vivid color of a level-❷ thickness so that the glass surface does not appear too simple.

第3段階 Step 3

第2段階の色に、バーント・アンバーと暖色ニュートラルを加えた暗い色を❹程度の濃さで、床と奥の壁の境目に横長の帯を描き入れて、奥行を強調します。

To stress the depth of the showroom, draw a horizontal boundary strip between the floor and back wall using a dark color of level-❹ thickness produced by adding burnt umber and warm neutral.

第4段階 Step 4

最後に、第3段階の色に暖色ニュートラルを加えて、暗い人物やテーブル、棚等を細かく描き込み、にぎやかな感じにします。その後、イエロー・ディープに白を加えた明るい色で、照明や明るい人物、家具や備品等のハイライトを描き入れ、はなやかにします。

To add a gay atmosphere to the perspective, paint the details of the darker people, table and similar elements using colors produced by adding warm neutral colors to the color produced in step 3. Finally, paint the lighting, bright people, furniture and fixtures in bright colors produced by adding white to deep yellow, highlighting the perspective for a gorgeous effect.

カーテンウォールの着色手順
Coloring process for curtained wall

■熱線ガラスの場合 Heated glass

第1段階 Step 1

プルシャンブルーとビリジャンの混合色に白を加えて空の色をつくり、「カスレ」がないように着色します。この時、着色する前に、ガラス面全体を水で濡らしておくと絵の具がよく伸びてむらなく着色出来ます。さらにプルシャンブルーとビリジャンの緑がかった色に寒色ニュートラルを加えて、彩度をおさえたガラスの色を［絵の具の濃さ加減］❷程度に濃くして、ガラス面の下場半分ぐらいを着色し、空の色と接する部分は、画面上で混ぜ合わせてぼかします。ミラーガラスの場合は、このガラス色のかわりに、白そのままの色で下場半分を着色し、空色と接する部分は、画面上で混ぜ合わせて自然な色の流れにします。この時の白は、濃くしてはいけないので、化粧品の乳液よりも少し水っぽい感じにして、よく伸ばしながら着色します。

Add white to a mixture of Prussian blue and viridian colors to spread the paint over the canvas carefully so that it doesn't become blurred. Before spreading the colors over the canvas, it is recommendable to wet the entire glass area with water so that colors can be well and uniformly spread. Produce greenish Prussian blue and viridian colors of a level-❷ thickness as described in "Depth of colors" by adding cold system neutral. Start coloring from the lower half of the glass surface and shade off the area where the sky colors meet the glass by blending them on the canvas. For mirror glass, color the lower half of the glass areas with white instead of the colors used for painting the glass, and attain a natural flow of color by mixing the colors used for the area meeting the sky color directly on the canvas. Since the white shouldn't be excessively thick during this process, dilute the white color until its a bit more watery than cosmetic milk lotion and spread the color well.

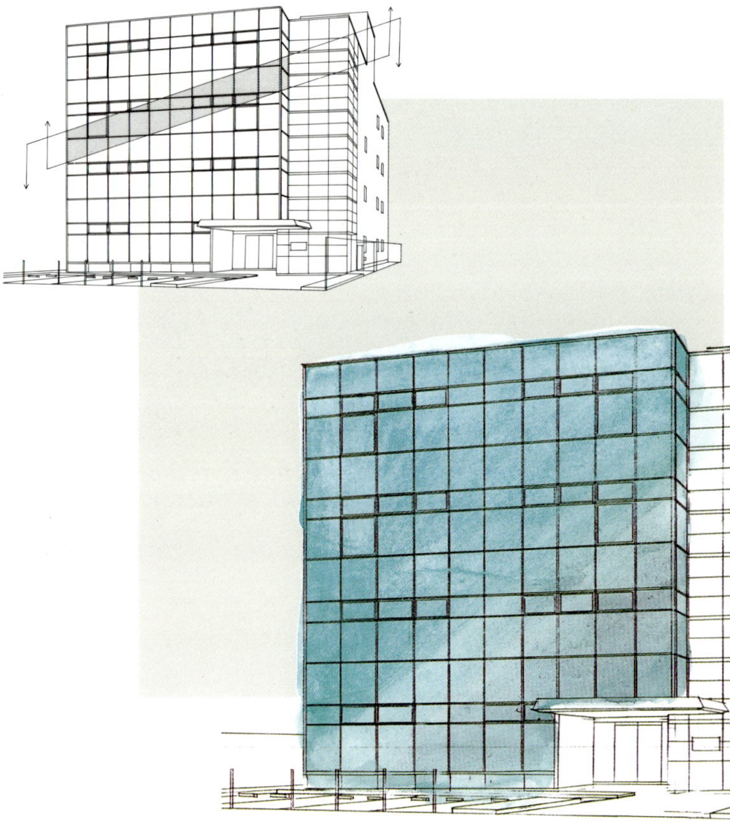

第2段階 Step 2

雲は、白っぽくした色を、化粧品の乳液よりも水っぽい濃さにして、丸筆で描き入れますが、省略することも多いです。目線に近い部分は、他の建物の映り込みもかねているので、タテ長やヨコ長の面で描き入れます。色は、ガラスの色にさらに寒色ニュートラルを加えながら❸❹❺❻の濃さで暗くしていきます。暗い色を重ね塗りする過程で、水っぽさがガラス面に出来ないように注意し、もし出来るようであれば、後で、より暗い色を重ね塗りする部分まで引き伸ばしておくと、次の重ね塗りで目立たなくなります。他の建物の映り込みや暗い面は、出来るだけ低くおさえた方が実在感が出ます。

Paint the clouds using the white color diluted to a more watery consistency than cosmetic lotion using a round paintbrush. The clouds are often eliminated. The area closer to the eye line level should be lengthened slightly in the vertical and horizontal directions since the rendering includes the expression of shade of other buildings reflected on the curtained wall. Make the colors used for painting in this step progressively darker as you move to thickness levels of ❸,❹,❺ and❻ by adding cold system neutral colors to the glass color. When laying the dark colors, do not allow the window panes to get too watery. If it cannot be avoided during this step, spread these colors over the areas which will receive the additional overlay of darker colors later. At a later point the watery colors will be overlapped and hidden by the subsequent colors. Make the reflection of other buildings and the darker areas as short as possible to express the feeling of their existence.

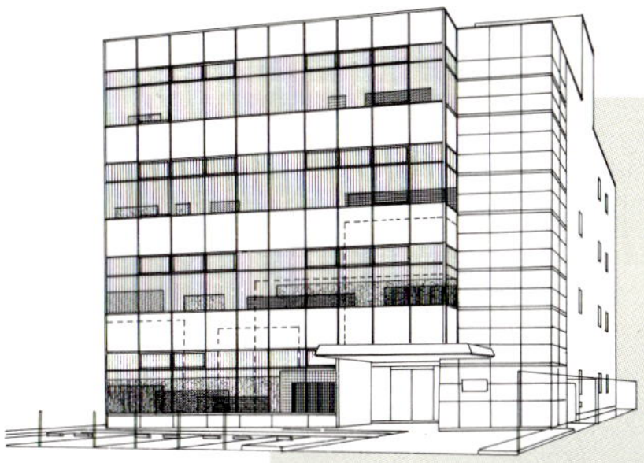

第3段階 Step 3

テナントビルの着色と同様に、室内の奥の壁や柱、ロッカー等のシルエットを描き入れます。寒色ニュートラルを多く加えた❺程度の濃い暗い色で、下の階から着色し、階高が高くなるにつれ、水で淡くして着色するとよいでしょう。(「暖色系の窓ガラスの着色手順」p.59参照)

The silhouettes of the wall of the back room, the pillars and lockers should be painted in the same manner as applied to the rendering of the tenant buildings. It is better to paint using darker colors of a level-❺ thickness with a lot of cold system neutral colors mixed in, and to thin the colors with progressively greater amounts of water as the height of the floor progresses.(See "Coloring sequence for window with warm a feeling of warm color" on p.59)

最終段階 Final step

サッシの影を少し太めに描き、サッシを描き入れると仕上ります。

Render the shade of the aluminum sashes widely, and finish the perspective by painting the sash.

■ミラーガラスの場合 Mirror glass

カーテンウォールのガラス面の着色で、空色の後にガラスの色を下場半分に着色することは、熱線ガラスの場合に説明しましたが、ミラーガラスの場合は、ガラスの色でなく白で着色します。その場合、白の絵の具は濃すぎないように注意します。そうして下塗りが出来たら、他の建物の映り込みを描き入れます。従って、熱線ガラスとミラーガラスの違いは、ガラスの色で下塗りするか、白でするかの違いの他、第3段階の着色がミラーガラスの場合、必要ない点です。

It has already been explained that the glass surface of curtained walls for heated windows should be colored starting from the lower half of the glass after coloring the sky. For mirror glass, color with white instead of glass color. Make sure that the white doesn't become too thick during this process. After the underpainting has been finished, draw the reflection of other buildings. The difference between the heated glass and the mirror glass is the color used for the underpainting, i.e., glass color or white color; for mirror glass, step 3 coloring won't be necessary.

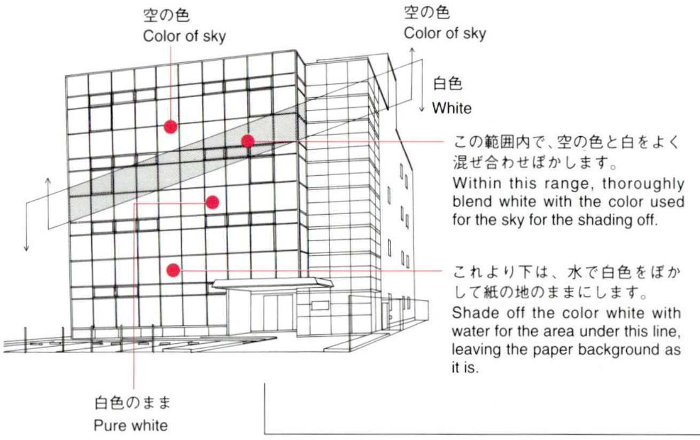

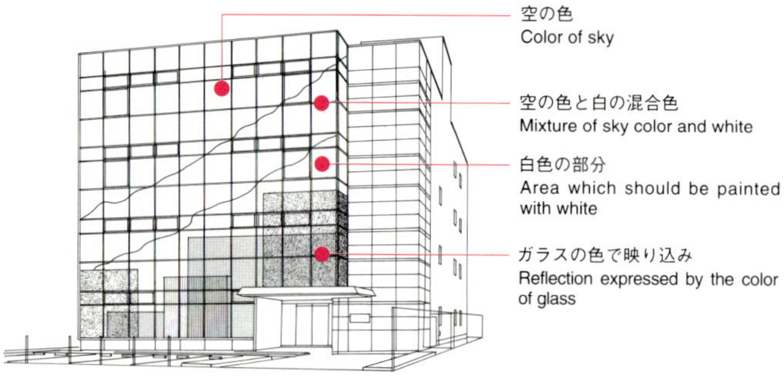

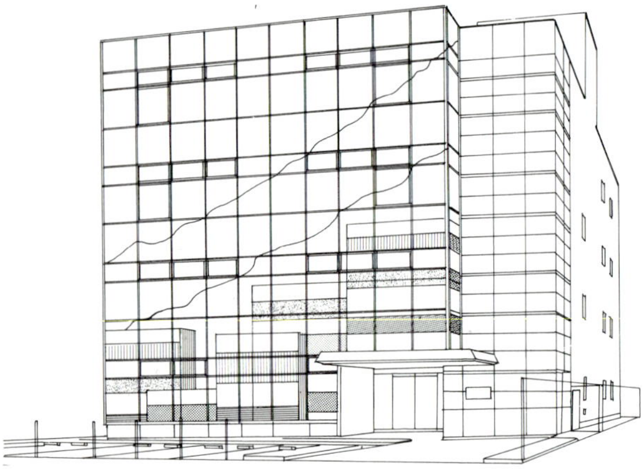

ミラーガラスの表現例
Example of mirror glass coloring

エアーブラシによる着色
Coloring with an airbrush

筆塗りによる着色
Coloring with paintbrush

E. 不透明水彩絵の具による窓ガラスの着色 Coloring of windows using opaque watercolors

不透明水彩絵の具による窓ガラスの着色も、透明水彩絵の具による着色と全く同じです。p.59で説明した［テナントビルの表現着色］を再度見て下さい。ただ、不透明水彩絵の具であるため、透明水彩絵の具より絵の具の伸びがよくなく、また混色による色のにごりがあるので、その点に注意して着色しなければなりません。

従って、その欠点を補う手法として、まず、画面をあらかじめ湿らせておくことと、バーント・アンバーを加えて暗い色をつくる場合には、イエロー・オレンジを加えて彩度を上げるようにします。

下塗り段階である第１, 2, 3 段階では、画面の湿りを利用して、それぞれの明るさの違う色が接する部分をよく画面上で混ぜ合わせて、自然な色の流れにします。

第 4, 5, 6, 7, 8, 9 段階での着色は、重ね塗りによるガラス面の質感表現ですので、前の段階で着色した絵の具がよく乾いてから着色します。また、不透明水彩絵の具であることから、着色する絵の具が濃すぎないように注意して下さい。

色づくりは、透明水彩絵の具の場合と同じで、その時の色に白を加えればよいでしょう。

The process used to color the windows with opaque watercolors is quite similar to the process used to color them with clear watercolors. Refer to "Coloring of tenant buildings" explained in p.59 again. The only difference is that the opaque watercolors do not spread well compared to clear watercolors, and the colors have a tendency to cloud when mixed. Keep this tendency in mind when using opaque colors.

A good method to use to compensate for this shortcoming is to moisten the canvas well in advance, and increase the chroma by adding yellow and orange colors the burnt umber when producing the dark colors. In the underpainting steps of 1, 2 and 3, blend the colors in the area where the different bright colors meet on the canvas utilizing the moisture applied to the canvas in advance. This allows you to produce a natural flow of colors.

As the purpose of coloring in steps 4, 5, 6, 7, 8 and 9 is to express the texture of the window glass by overlapping the colors, it is not recommendable to lay additional colors until the previously laid colors have dried sufficiently. And as the colors are opaque watercolors, take care that they don't become excessively thick.

The method to produce the colors is almost exactly the same as that applied using clear watercolors. The only difference is the addition of the color white.

不透明水彩絵の具による着色手順
Coloring process using opaque watercolors

第１段階 Step 1

第１, 2, 3 段階の下塗り段階ですが、あらかじめ画面を水で濡らしてから着色し、それぞれ暗さの違う色が接する部分は、よく混ぜてぼかします。色は、透明水彩絵の具の場合と同じですが、白が加わるだけ色がにごり易いので、透明水彩絵の具・第１段階でのガラス色に白の他、イエロー・オレンジを加えておくとよいでしょう。

This step is one of the underpainting steps. Moisten the painting in advance before applying the colors, and shade off by mixing the colors well on the portions where colors of different darknesses meet. Though the colors are entirely same as those mixed with clear watercolors, they tend to cloud when the white is added. It's good, therefore, to add yellow orange and white in addition to the glass color in step 1 for clear watercolors.

第２段階 Step 2

第２段階の着色からは、前段階の絵の具がよく乾いてから進めます。暖色ニュートラルが多く加わるので彩度が下りすぎて、にごらないように、絵の具の混合を調節して下さい。

Start coloring in this step after the colors have been well dried. Since many warm neutral colors are included, adjust the mixing ratio of the colors so that their chroma won't be lowered excessively or cloud up when they are mixed.

第３段階 Step 3

さらに、暖色ニュートラルを加えた暗い色で重ね塗りして、他の建物のシルエットを描き入れます。その後は、透明水彩絵の具の場合と同様に、室内の奥の壁の着色に入ります。

Lay the dark colors produced by adding warm neutrals and paint in the silhouettes of the other buildings. Next, follow the same procedures used for the coloring with clear watercolors, and color the back wall of the room.

第4段階 Step 4

室内の奥壁の着色

Color the back wall of the room.

第5段階 Step 5

室内の影の着色

Color the shade inside the room.

第6段階 Step 6

家具のシルエット着色

Color the silhouettes of the furniture

第7段階 Step 7

人物のシルエット着色

Color the silhouettes of the people.

第8段階 Step 8

照明の着色

Color the lighting fixtures.

第9段階 Step 9

ガラス面の影の着色

Color the glass surfaces.

最終段階 Final step

外壁面にはみ出した色を洗い出すか、白で下塗りした状態

Wash out the extended colors over the exteriorwall and underpaint using the color white.

F. エアーブラシによる窓ガラスの吹き付け着色
Spraying the colors over the windows with an airbrush

エアーブラシによる着色は、筆塗り着色の場合と全く逆になります。つまり、最も暗い部分から吹き付けるので、透明水彩絵の具の場合での第７段階から始め、６,５,４,３,２,１段階へと吹き付け着色を進めます。

The procedure using an airbrush is basically the same as the procedure using a paintbrush, but in reverse. The coloring is started from the darkest portion, so the first step corresponds to step 7 in the procedure using clear watercolor. The coloring should be carried out in sequence, beginning with step 6 and finishing with step 1.

暖色系での吹き付け着色手順
Color spraying process with warm system colors

第１段階 Step 1

室内の柱やロッカー等のシルエットを、最も暗い部分からマスキングフィルムを取り外しながら吹き付けます。色は、筆塗りの場合と全く同じです。

Spray the colors over the silhouettes of the pillars and lockers in the room by peeling off the masking film from the darkest portions first. Use exactly the same colors as those used for the brush coloring.

第２段階 Step 2

室内の影を吹き付けますが、階高が高くなるにつれ、淡くなるようにします。この点についても、筆塗りと全く同じです。

Spray the shade inside the room. Make the colors lighter as the floor gets higher. This step is also the same as that employed in the brush coloring procedure.

第３段階 Step 3

室内の奥壁を吹き付けます。階高が高くなる程、淡く吹き付けます。

Spray over the back wall inside the room. Make the colors lighter as the floor gets higher.

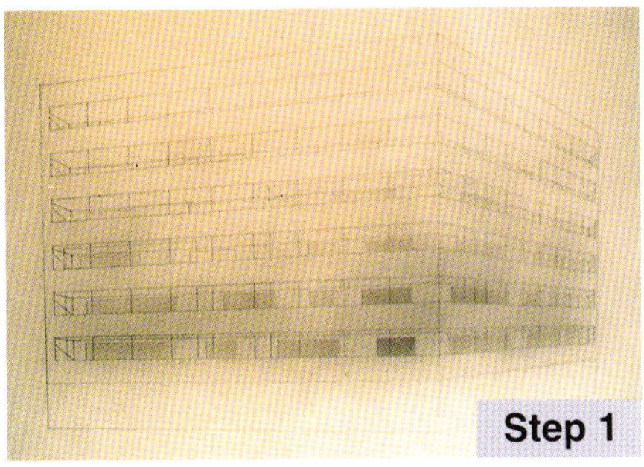

第４段階 Step 4

窓ガラスの全てのマスキングフィルムを外し、ガラス面全体の濃淡表現をします。この見本では、他の建物の映り込みのシルエットは省いてありますが、あれば、よりガラスの深みが表現出来ます。

Remove all the masking film covering the window pane to express the shade of the entire glass surface. Though the silhouette of the other buildings reflected is eliminated in this example, the depth of the window pane can be more sufficiently expressed if the silhouette is painted.

第５段階 Step 5

マンガニーズブルーで空の色を吹き付けます。

Spray manganese blue over the sky portion.

第６段階 Step 6

照明を描き入れ、ガラス面の影やサッシの影を入れます。

Draw the lighting and then draw the shade on the window panes and the shade of the sashes. brush coloring procedure.

寒色系での吹き付け着色手順
Coloring process by spraying cold system colors

吹き付け方法も、全く筆塗りと同じですが、暖色系の吹き付けと同様、筆塗りと全く逆の順番で進めます。最も暗い部分から吹き付け、空の色で終ります。この見本では、他の建物の映り込んだシルエットが表現されています。

The color spraying method is entirely the same as that used for brush coloring , but just as in the warm color spraying, the steps in the procedure are reversed. Start spraying from the darkest portions and finish up with the sky portion. In this sample, the silhouettes of the other buildings reflected is expressed.

照明と影を描き入れると仕上ります。

Finish by drawing the lighting and shade.

■外観パースと鳥瞰パースでの窓ガラスの表現の違い
Difference of expression of windows in exterior perspectives and birds-eye view perspectives

外観パースの窓ガラスの表現では、建物の下部になる程、暗く着色しますが、鳥瞰パースの場合は、それとは逆に、建物の上部になる程、暗く着色します。これは、視点に近い所のコントラストが強いという空気遠近法による解釈から来る表現であるからです。

In exterior perspectives, window panes are rendered in darker colors as the level gets lower. In birds-eye perspectives, they get darker as the height of the buildings increase. This is because the air perspective method, in which the contrast gets stronger as the areas get closer to the viewpoint, is used.

●外観パース
Exterior perspective

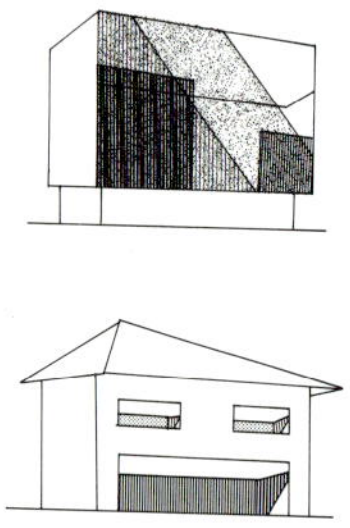

●鳥瞰パース
Bird's-eye view perspective

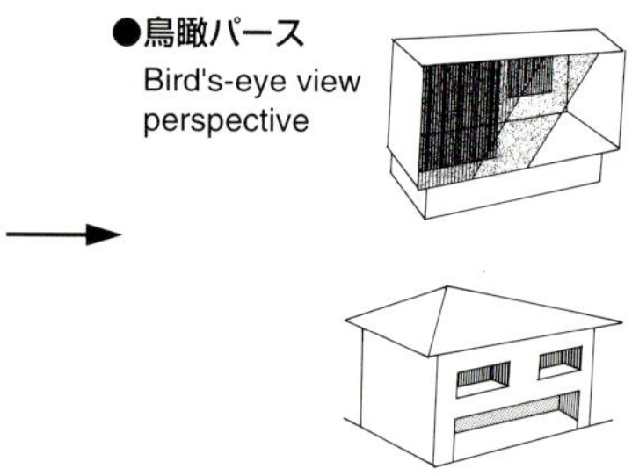

2. 外壁面の描き方 How to paint exterior walls

外壁の着色で、一番重要なことは、正面壁と側面壁の色を同じ彩度(色みのあざやかさ)の色にすることです。もし、彩度が異なると、その建物の材質及び色調が違ったものになってしまいます。明るい面としての正面と、少し暗くなる側面は、明るさ(明度)の違いはあっても、一般的には、同じ材質のものが使われ、同じ色のものでデザインされています。それは光の影響によって異なった色に見えるだけで、明るさの違う色にすぎません。

また、影についても同様で、彩度は同じでなければなりません。いいかえれば、影も光の関係で生じるもので、同じ色のものであることには変りありません。従って、外壁の正面、側面壁、及び、影の色は、同じ彩度をもち、単に明るさだけが異なるにすぎません。

着色の手順として、筆塗りの場合は、明るい色の外壁面から始め、暗い色の影へと描き進めます。なお、暗い色は、少々、濃くてもかまいませんが、白の多く入った明るい色は、あまり濃くしないで、二度塗り、三度塗りするときれいな仕上りになります。

この時、はじめに着色した絵の具が、よく乾いてから重ね塗りすることが大切です。同時に、下図の鉛筆の線を残さず、その上から着色してかくすことも大切です。

また、建物によっては、外壁面の着色の前に、外壁面にはみ出した窓ガラスの色を、平筆にきれいな水をふくませて洗い落すと、外壁面の重ね塗りの回数が少なくて済み、より速く、きれいに着色出来ます。従って、外壁や窓のデザインが平坦で単純な場合や、窓の数が少ない場合は、はみ出した窓ガラスの色を洗い落した方が、速くて効率的でしょう。

そこで、外壁面の着色に慣れていない初心者は、複雑な建物であっても、はみ出した窓ガラスの色を洗い落しておく方がよいでしょう。

The most important point to remember in coloring the exterior wall is to present both the front and side exterior walls in the same chroma (vividness of colors.) A difference in color vividness would bring about the difference in the exterior wall material and color hue. Even if there is a slight difference in brightness of color between the color in the front exterior wall and that in the side wall, the construction material and design is usually the same in both walls. The colors in the front and the side exterior wall look different to people only because of the light; the only real difference in the colors is their brightness.

The same thing can be said about the shade expression, and the colors used to express the shade should have the same vividness. In other words, as the shade is created due to the effect of light, there is no difference in the color itself. Therefore, the colors in the front and side exterior walls and those in the shade portion should be the same in vividness, and differ only in brightness.

As the sequence of coloring, start coloring over the surface of the bright exterior wall and then move to the shade portion with darker colors. Never mind if the darker colors are mixed rather thickly, but make sure that the bright colors with the generous portions of white mixed in are thicker, and that they are spread over the previous colors two or three times to obtain a clear finish.

During the above step, the trick is to overlap the colors after the previously laid colors have completely dried. At the same time, it is also important to hide the pencil lines from the drafting stage with overlapping colors.

Depending on the building, the colors used to paint the window panes and extruded into the adjacent exterior wall should be wiped off using a flat paintbrush soaked with clean water. This will reduce the number of times colors will have to be overlapped over the exterior wall, thereby allowing you to finish the clean rendering more quickly. If the exterior wall and windows have a flat and simple design, or if there are only a few windows, the rendering can be finished more quickly and effectively if you wipe out the extended window pane color before starting the overlapping.

For beginners who have less experience in coloring exterior walls, it is advisable to wipe off the extended colors in even the complicated building

before starting the overlapping of colors.

着色手順
Coloring procedures

❶正面の壁面………指定された色から判断して純色(チューブの色)に白、黒を加えてつくる
❷側面の壁面………正面の色よりも、明度を2度(p.85参照)程度下げた色
❸正面壁の影………正面の色よりも、明度を3度程度下げた色
❹側面壁の影………正面の影の色よりも、明度を2度程度下げた色
❺軒裏、屋根、手すり、建物に付随する細かい部分

— 全て同彩度

↓

路面の着色(外構)

↓

点景(植栽、人物、車等)

❶ Front exterior walls .... Judging from the designated colors, mix the colors by adding white and black to pure colors (just after being squeezed out of the tube).
❷ Side exterior walls .... mix colors which are two degrees (see p.85) lower in brightness than the colors used for the front exterior wall.
❸ Shade on the front exterior walls .... Produce colors which are three degrees lower in brightness than the colors used for the front exterior wall.
❹ Shade on the side exterior walls .... Produce colors which are two degrees lower in brightness than the colors used for the shade on the front exterior wall.
❺ Coloring in detailed portions such as the eaves, roof, spandrel and other small areas of the building

— Use colors of the same chroma

↓

Color the surface of the road (exterior landscape).

↓

Color elements such as plants, people and cars.

正面の壁面の着色
Coloring of front exterior walls

指定された色になるように、純色に白・黒を加えて、彩度・明度を合わせます。色が正しく調合されたら、水を加えながら、化粧品の乳液を目安にして、それよりも少し水っぽくしてから、平筆にたっぷりふくめ、パレット上で余分な絵の具を筆から取り除き、最上階から順次、下の階の壁面へと着色します。そして、その着色した絵の具が乾いたら、窓ガラスの色や、壁面に着色した外壁色の色むらがなくなるまで、同じ濃さの色を2、3回程度、重ね塗りします。ここで大切なことは、たっぷり筆にふくめた絵の具が、ぼてぼてにならないように、余分な絵の具を取り除き、着色する時に、塗り始めた部分の絵の具が盛り上がらないようにすることです。

Match the chroma and brightness of the color by adding white and black to pure colors so that the designated colors can be produced. After the proper color matching has been finished, dilute the colors with water until they become a bit more watery than cosmetic milk lotion. Soak the colors into a flat paintbrush generously and remove the excessive colors from the brush on the palette. Begin by coloring from the exterior wall of the top floor, and then move to the exterior wall of the lower floor. And after such colors have been dried, lay colors of the same thickness two or three times until all mottling can be removed from the surface of the exterior wall.
The trick here is to remove excessive amounts of color that has soaked into the brush before coloring to prevent the colors from swelling at the starting point.

側面の壁面の着色
Coloring of side exterior walls

正面壁に着色した色よりも、明度を2度程度下げた同じ彩度の色（黒を加えて暗くした分だけ純色を加えて彩度をもどした色）をつくり、正面壁と同様に重ね塗りします。

Produce colors which are two degrees lower in brightness but the same in chroma (colors in which chroma is resumed by the degree it is darkened through the addition of black and pure color), and lay the colors over the side exterior wall in the same manner as applied to the front exterior wall.

壁面の色の変化表現
Expression of change in the colors of exterior walls

色の遠近感（空気遠近法）を表現する為に、基準線より離れた部分は、明るい色（もとの色に白と純色を加えた色）で重ね塗りして明るくします。つまり、視点から離れた所は、色みをおさえて明るくするのです。その場合、明るい色の着色は、一定の方向性を守って着色します。

To express the perspective in colors, brighten the portions closer to the reference line by laying bright colors (produced by adding white and pure color to the original color) there. Express the area far away from the viewpoint more brightly by avoiding the use of heavy colors. In this case, use bright color and keep the direction of coloring consistent.

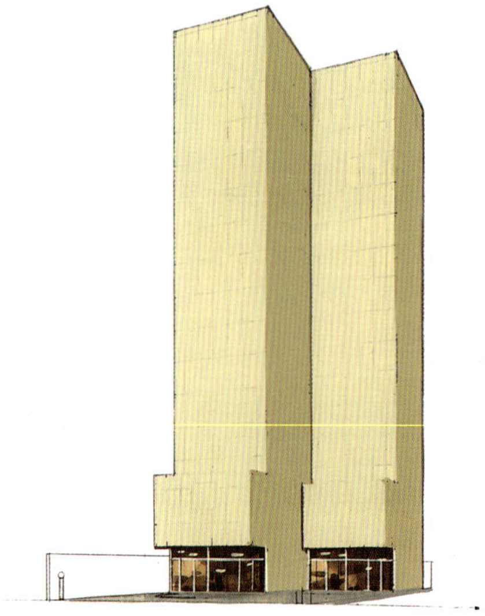

下塗り状態
Underpainting condition

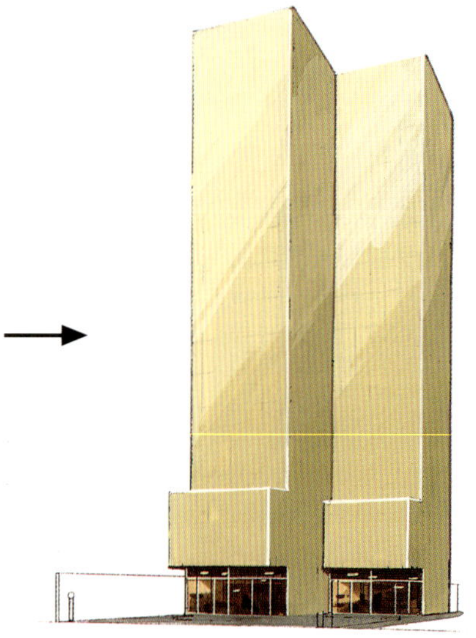

色の変化を加えた状態
Condition to which color change has been added

正面壁の影の着色
Coloring the shade of the front exterior walls

正面壁の色に、黒と純色を加えて、明度を3度程度下げた色で、指定された色の暗い色（同じ色みの暗い色）をつくり、外壁面の絵の具よりも濃いめにして着色します。また、壁面が目線に近づくにつれて、影の遠近感を表現する為に、影の色も暗くしていきます。その場合、前に着色した影の色に、黒と純色を加えながら暗くすると彩度が合わせ易いでしょう。さらに、その上に、色の変化を明るい色、暗い色で重ね塗りして描き加えます（上図参照）。

Produce the designated dark colors three degrees lower in brightness by adding black and pure colors to the colors used for the front exterior color, making them thicker than the colors used for the exterior wall. Use a darker color for the shade than that used for the exterior wall so that the perspective in the shade can be expressed. During the step, if you make the color darker by adding the black and the pure color to the colors previously used for expressing the shade, it will be easy for you to match the chroma of the colors. Lay the bright and dark colors further to express the change in color. (See upper two photos)

側面壁の影の着色
Coloring of shade in the side exterior walls

正面の影を塗り終えたら、その余った影の色に黒と純色を加えて暗い色をつくり（明度差2度程度）、上層階から順次、下の階の影へと着色します。この場合も、黒が入った分だけ彩度も下がるので、純色を加えながら彩度を合わせなければなりません。また、正面壁の影と同様に、階高によって影の色も変えると同時に、同じ階の影であっても、明るい部分、暗い部分といった、色の変化を重ね塗りで表現します（上図参照）。

After the shade on the front exterior wall has been finished, produce the dark colors (which has two degrees difference in brightness) by adding black and pure colors to the colors remaining on the palette after being used for the shade expression, and start coloring the shade from the top story to the lower stories. As the chroma of the color will be reduced by the degree of black added, it is necessary to add pure colors during this step to match the chroma. As with the coloring of the shade on the front exterior wall, change the color of the shade as the level of the floor changes, and lay the colors so that changes in color can be expressed for the brighter and darker portions even on the same floor. (See upper two photos)

軒裏の着色
Coloring the eaves

下塗り状態
Underpainting condition

色の変化を加えた状態
Condition to which change in color has been added

軒裏は、光が地面から反射されていることを考え、影よりも明るく着色します。
従って、影の色に白と純色を加えて、影よりも明るくした色で着色します。また、軒裏の色の変化は、基本的に、垂直方向に影の色の変化に合わせて描き入れればよいでしょう。そのことは、光の反射が地面からおこることに関係しています。

Since the eaves receive light reflected from the ground, color them more brightly than the shade.
Therefore, lay colors which are brighter than the color used for the shade and are produced by adding white and pure colors to the shade color. To express the change in color on the eaves, try to match the change in color of the shade in the vertical direction. This is related to the light reflected on the eaves from the ground.

影と軒裏の色の変化の入れ方
〈How to express change in the colors of shadows and eaves〉

外壁面の色の変化とその方向性
Change in color on the surface of the exterior wall and the direction of coloring

正面壁と側面壁の明度差（２度）
Difference in colors applied to the front and side exterior walls (by two degrees)

影の色の変化及び明度差（２度）
Change in colors of the shade and difference in brightness of color (by two degrees)

明度は異なるが彩度は同じ
Brightness differs but chroma is the same.

軒裏の色の変化とその方向性
Change in color on the eaves and the direction of coloring

明度は異なるが彩度は同じ
Brightness differs but chroma is the same.

ハイライト（白っぽい線）と引き締め線（暗い線）の入れ方
How to express the highlights (whitish lines) and tension lines (dark lines)

ハイライトは光があたると思われる場所（下図の赤線）に入れ暗い色の引き締め線は光があたらない影との境（下図の青線）に入れるのが基本です。つまり物体の上場の角にハイライトの白っぽい線を描き加え、下場の角には暗い締めの線を描き加えます。

In principle, express areas where ample light is reflected as highlights (red line in the illustration below), and express dark areas where no light is reflected as tension lines (blue line in the illustration below). That is to say, draw whitish lines over the corners of objects as highlights, and draw dark lines under the corners of object as tension lines.

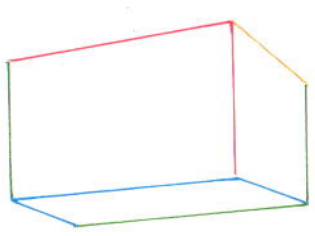

赤　線…ほとんど白に近い明るい色
黄　線…明るさを弱めた明るい色
青　線…黒っぽい暗い色で少し太く
黄緑線…少し暗い色で細く
Red line ... Line drawn in a bright near-white color
Yellow line .... Line drawn in a color of slightly reduced brightness
Blue line .... A slightly wider line drawn in a blackish dark color
Yellow-green line .... Fine line drawn in a with a slightly darker color

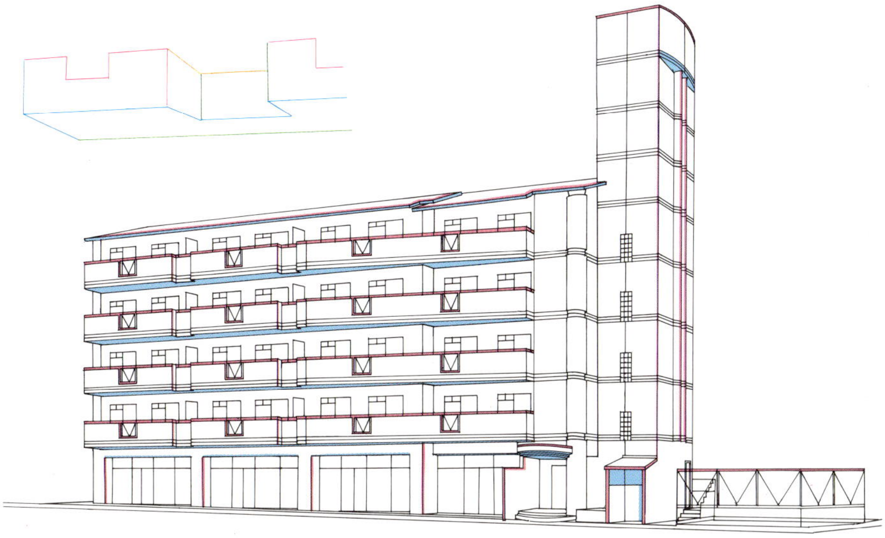

A. 外壁色の色づくり Producing colors for exterior walls

一般的な外壁色の調合
General matching of colors for exterior walls

		外壁 Exterior wall	影 Shade	窓ガラス window pane
白っぽい建物 Whitish building	暖色系 Warm system colors	イエロー・オーカー十白十ごく少量の黒 Yellow ocher + white + black in small amount	多めのイエロー・オーカー十白十バーント・アンバー、暖色ニュートラル Yellow ocher in ample amount + burnt umber, warm neutral colors	イエロー・オーカー十バーント・アンバー、暖色ニュートラル Yellow ocher in ample amount + burnt umber, warm neutral colors
	寒色系 Cold system colors	少量のプルシャンブルー十白十ごく少量の黒 Prussian blue in small amount + white + black in small amount	プルシャンブルー十白十黒 Prussian blue + white + black	プルシャンブルー十ビリジャン十寒色ニュートラル Prussian blue + viridian + cold neutral colors

暖色系
Warm system colors

寒色系
Cold system colors

		外壁 Exterior wall	影 Shade	窓ガラス window pane
グレー系色の建物 Gray-system-colored building	暖色系 Warm system colors	イエロー・オーカー十白十セピア Yellow ocher + white + sepia	イエロー・オーカー十白十黒十セピア Yellow ocher + white + black + sepia	ビリジャン十寒色ニュートラル、ニュートラル・ブラック Viridian + cold neutral colors, neutral black
	寒色系 Cold system colors	少量のイエロー・オーカー十白十黒多め Yellow ocher in small amount + white + black in a bit ample amount	イエロー・オーカー十白十より多めの黒 Yellow ocher + white + black in a bit more ample amount	プルシャンブルー十ビリジャン十寒色ニュートラル Prussian blue + viridian + cold neutral colors

暖色系
Warm system colors

寒色系
Cold system colors

	外壁 Exterior wall	影 Shade	窓ガラス window pane
ベージュ系の建物 Beige-colored building	イエロー・オーカー十白十セピア(またはバーント・アンバー) Yellow ocher+white+sepia (or burnt umber)	イエロー・オーカー十白十黒十セピア十バーント・アンバー Yellow ocher + white + black + sepia + burnt umber	暖色系で着色 Coloring with warm system colors

バーント・アンバー入りベージュ系
Beige system color to which burnt umber is added

バーント・アンバーなしのベージュ系
Beige system color without burnt umber

	外壁 Exterior wall	影 Shade	窓ガラス window pane
レンガタイル系の建物 Building with its exterior wall finished with brick tile	レッド・ディープ十イエロー・オレンジ十白十バーント・アンバー Deep red + yellow orange + white + burnt umber	レッド・ディープ十多めのバーント・アンバー十白十セピア(側面部の影には多く) Deep red + burnt umber in a bit ample amount + white + sepia (A bit ample for the shade on the side exterior wall)	暖色系で着色 Coloring with warm system colors

レッド・ディープ多めのタイルA
Tile "A" of heavier deep red color

イエロー・オレンジ多めのタイルB
Tile "B" of heavier yellow orange

AとBの中間色のタイル
Tile of color between tiles "A" and "B"

バーント・アンバー多めの外壁
Exterior wall of color containing a somewhat ample portion of burnt umber

有彩色と無彩色
Chromatic colors and achromatic colors

赤・橙・黄・緑・青・紫といった「色み」のある色を有彩色といい、白・灰色・黒のように「色み」のない色を無彩色といいます。有彩色は、「色み」(色相)・「あざやかさ」(彩度)・「明るさ」(明度)といった色の3属性をもっていますが、無彩色は、「明るさ」(明度)しかもっていません。しかも、有彩色は、この3属性によって、同じ色相であっても無彩色と違って彩度・明度によって違った色になります。

Colors which have color tone, i.e., red, orange, yellow, green, blue and purple, are called chromatic colors, colors with no color tone such as white and black are called achromatic colors.Although chromatic colors have three attributes, i.e., tone, chroma and brightness, achromatic colors have only brightness. Unlike achromatic colors, even chromatic colors of the same color tones can be developed into different colors by varying the chroma and brightness.

■色相 Color tone

色には赤・青・黄のように、幼児にも区別が出来、容易に理解される色名があります。これらの色は、非常にあざやかで、誰が見ても同じようなイメージを受ける色です。つまり、彩度が最も高い純色です。このような赤・青・黄といわれる「色み」を色相といいます。

Colors such as red, blue and yellow can easily be identified and understood even by children. These colors are quite brilliant; almost everyone in the world has the same image of them. These colors are mainly known for their great purity and very high chroma. The "colors" that these reds, blues and yellows have is called color tone.

■明度 Brightness

白色は、最も明るい色として一般的に認識され、反対に、黒色は、最も暗い色として認識されています。普通、明るい色をつくるには、誰もが白色を加えるだろうし、暗い色をつくる場合には、黒色を加えるでしょう。その根拠は、白は最も明るい色であり、黒は最も暗い色であると体験されているからでしょう。同じ純色であっても、白色や黒色、または、それらの中間的な灰色が加えられると、明るさの違った色になります。この明るさの違いを明度といいます。

White is generally recognized as the brightest color in the spectra, and black the darkest. Generally speaking, people who want to produce brighter colors do so by adding white, and people who want darker colors use black.

The reason for this may be that people know from experience that white is the brightest color, and black the darkest. Even the same pure can change in brightness if white, black, or gray, the intermediate color between black and white, is added. This difference in color brilliance is called the brightness of color.

■彩度 Chroma

同じ赤でも、派手な赤もあれば、くすんだ赤もあります。これは、純色の赤に他の色が混ざり合ったことによって、いろいろな「あざやかさ」の色になるからです。このような「あざやかさ」つまり、色みの強さを彩度といいます。

Even in the red group based on the same red color, there are several types of reds ranging from brilliant red to dark red. This is because the red can be developed in different chroma by varying the ratio in the mixture of pure red and other colors. This brilliance of color, or the strength of its tone, is known as the chroma.

■暖色と寒色 Cold system and warm system colors

一般的に、暖かみや柔らかさを感じさせる赤・橙・黄等の色は暖色といわれ、他方、寒さやさびしさを感じさせる青・緑・青紫系の色は寒色といいます。絵の具で区別すると下のようになります。

In general, the colors red, orange and yellow, all of which give a warm and soft feeling, are called warm system colors, while blue, green and blue-purple, which tend to convey a cold and cheerless feeling, are called cold system colors. The classification of colors into warm and cold system colors are shown below.

色名	分類	Color	Classification
イエロー・オーカー	暖色系	Yellow ocher	Warm system colors
イエロー・レモン	暖色系	Yellow lemon	Warm system colors
イエロー・ディープ	暖色系	Deep yellow	Warm system colors
イエロー・オレンジ	暖色系	Yellow orange	Warm system colors
レッド・ディープ	暖色系	Deep red	Warm system colors
カーマイン	暖色系	Carmine	Warm system colors
ウルトラマリン・ディープ	寒色系	Ultra-marine deep	Cold system colors
コバルトブルー・ティント	寒色系	Cobalt blue tint	Cold system colors
プルシャンブルー	寒色系	Prussian blue	Cold system colors
マンガニーズブルー	寒色系	Manganese blue	Cold system colors
ビリジャン	寒色系	Viridian	Cold system colors
グリーンペール	寒色系	Green pale	Cold system colors

概して、暖色系の色は膨張して見え、寒色系の色は後退して見える性質もありますが、建築物で見ると、安らぎの場としての住宅には暖色系の色が多く使われ、他方、能率的な行動が要求される仕事場になるビル等では、寒色系の色が多く使われています。

Generally speaking, the warm system colors looks swelling and expanding, while cold system colors seems depressed. From the stand point of architectural design, buildings which have been designed as places for comfort and rest employ many warm system colors, while buildings designed to be serve as a base for efficient business activities employ many cold system colors.

[純色と白・灰色・黒の混合による変化]
Color variation made by mixing pure colors with white, gray or black

下表は，純色に無彩色の絵の具(白・黒・灰色）を加えた場合の彩度・明度の変化を示しています。
白色や黒色，あるいは，この２つの色を純色に同時に混合すれば，明度は，それらの無彩色の明るさによって変化するだけでなく，混合される無彩色の量の多少に応じて彩度も低くなっていきます。反対に，純色(絵の具のチューブの色）を加えて混合すると，その純色の量によって彩度は高くなっていきます。
従って，下表のように，白・黒・純色の混合量によって，彩度，明度の異なる色をいろいろつくり出すことが出来ます。

The below-mentioned chart shows the changes in chroma and brightness when achromatic colors(white, black or gray) are added to pure colors.
If either white or black is added to a pure color, or if both white and black are simultaneously added to the pure color, the brightness of the achromatic colors will affect brightness of the pure color, and the amount of achromatic color will affect the chroma of the pure color. On the other hand, if the pure color is added to another pure color, the chroma of the pure color added can be increased by the amount of the pure color to which it is added.
Therefore, you can produce various colors which have different chroma and brightness by adjusting the amounts of white, black and pure colors, as shown in the following table.

●白黒の混合量と彩度の変化 Relationship between amount of white or black added and variation of chroma

白・黒・灰色の混合 Mixing of white, black and gray colors →	全て彩度を下げます Chroma will be always reduced.
純色の増量 Increasing the pure color →	全て彩度を上げます Chroma will be always increased.

●白黒の混合量と明度の変化 Relationship between amount of white and black color mixture and variation of brightness

白の混合 Mixture of white →	明るくなります(明度が上がります) Brightness will be increased.
黒の混合 Mixture of black →	暗くなります(明度が下がります) Brightness will be decreased.

灰色の混合 If gray color is mixed,

- 純色の明るさより明るい灰色の場合 → 明るくなります(明度が上がります)
  If the brightness of the gray is higher than that of the pure color with which it is mixed → Brightness will be increased.
- 純色の明るさより暗い灰色の場合 → 暗くなります(明度が下がります)
  If the brightness of the gray is darker than that of the pure color → Brightness will be decreased.
- 純色の明るさとほぼ同じ明るさの灰色の場合 → 明るさは変わりません(明度は変わりません)
  If the brightness of the gray is almost the same as that of the pure color → Brightness remains unchanged.

●彩度・明度の変化と白黒混合量の関係 Relationship between change in chroma/brightness and amounts of white and black

彩度を変化させずに Without changing the chroma,

- 明度を上げる → 純色と白の混合
  The brightness will be increased if pure color and white are mixed.
- 明度を下げる → 純色と黒の混合
  The brightness will be decreased if pure color and black are mixed.

明度を変化させずに Without changing the brightness

- 彩度を上げる → 純色の混合
  The chroma will be increased if pure color is mixed.
- 彩度を下げる → 同じ明るさの灰色の混合
  The chroma will be decreased if gray color of the same brightness is mixed.

彩度を上げて With the chroma increased,

- 明度を上げる → 多めの純色と白の混合
  The brightness will also be increased if the white is mixed with a somewhat generous portion of pure color.
- 明度を下げる → 多めの純色と黒の混合
  The brightness will be decreased if the black is mixed with a somewhat generous portion of pure color.

彩度を下げて With the chroma decreased,

- 明度を上げる → 白の混合
  The brightness will be increased if the white is mixed.
- 明度を下げる → 黒の混合
  The brightness will be decreased if the black is mixed.

彩度の合わせ方
How to match the chroma

彩度を計るスケールのようなものはありませんが、肉眼的に推測することは出来ます。
まず、必要な彩度の色が決まると、それと同彩度の色をつくるには、決められた彩度の色に、調合した色を試し塗りして重ね合わせます。そうした上で、それらの色を見比べて、色みの強さが同じように感じられるかどうかで判断すれば、肉眼的に見て、同彩度の色をつくることが出来ます。もし、見比べてみて、色みが弱いようであれば、純色を加えるようにし、反対に、色みが強すぎるようであれば、白と黒を加えて加減すればよいでしょう。

There is no scale which can measure the chroma, but it can be visually measured.
Once the color having the required chroma has been decided, lay the mixed color over the color having the decided chroma to produce a trial color of similar chroma. After that, try to compare the colors. If you can assess whether the strengths of the tones of the colors are similar or not, you will be able to produce a color having the same chroma which can be visually identified. If you find that the strength of the color tone of the two colors does not seem sufficient, add the pure color. conversely, if the strength of the color tone seems strong, add white and black to adjust the strength.

明度の合わせ方
How to match the brightness

右図は、実際上の色がもつ明度の計り方を示しています。調合した色を試し塗りした後、その上に、下に示したモノクロトーンの明度スケールを重ね合せて、目を細めて見ることによって、その境界がはっきりと見えるかどうかで、その調合した色の明度を引き出すことが出来ます。もし境界が、わからないように感じられたら、明度が合っています。
従って、求めようとする明度の色をつくるには、試し塗りした後、よく乾かしてから、モノクロスケールを重ね合わせて、明度の確認を行い、その境界が、はっきり感じられた場合、試し塗りした色の方が明るければ黒色を、暗ければ白色を加えればよいでしょう。
パース画の着色時には、下のモノクロトーンのスケールを切り抜き、外壁色の明度合せに使うことをおすすめします。

The LH side chart shows how to measure the brightness that the color actually has. After laying the mixed color as a trial, superimpose the below-mentioned monochrome brightness scale over the color. If you can clearly see the boundary line when you narrow your eyes, the brightness can be considered proper. If you cannot see the boundary line, the brightness is not proper.
Therefore, to produce the color of the required brightness, dry the color up after the trial painting has been finished, and then superimpose the monochrome scale over the color to confirm its brightness. When the boundary line can be clearly seen, add black if the trial color seems brighter, and add white if it seems darker.
When coloring the perspective, cut out the following monochrome tone scale and use it to adjust the brightness so that it matches the brightness of the color of the exterior walls.

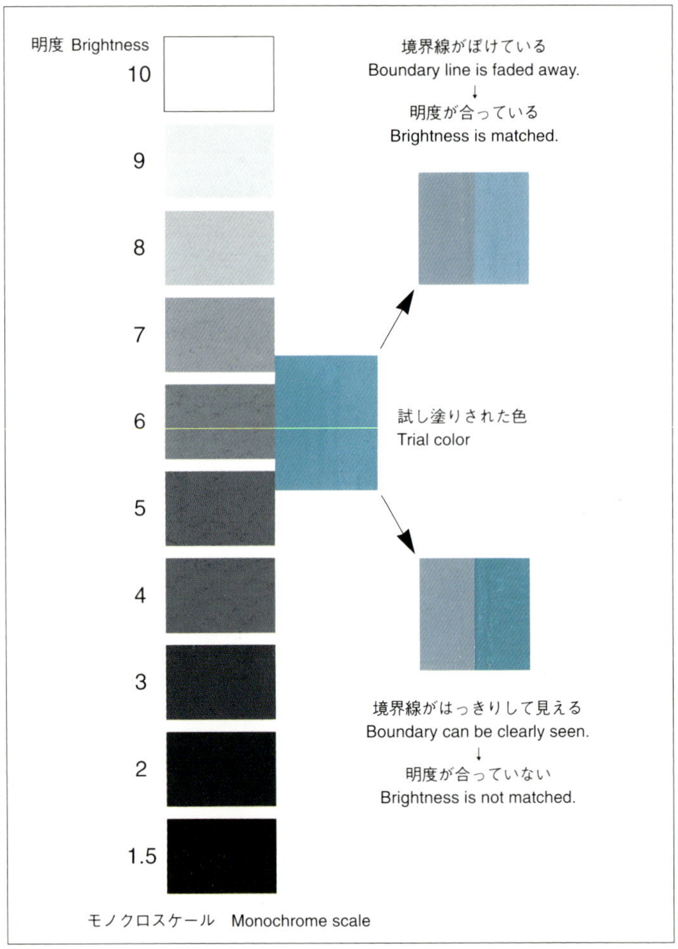

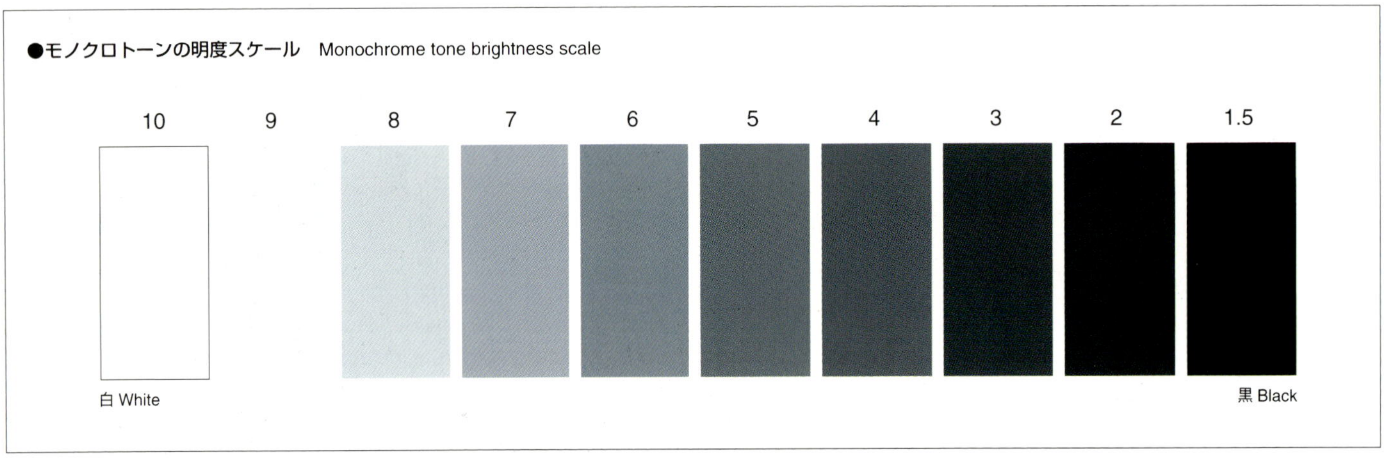

B. 透明水彩絵の具による着色 Coloring of clear watercolors

淡彩パースでの外壁面の着色は、白っぽくて淡い色から着色し始めると同時に、大きな面から小さな面へと着色を進めます。また、側面壁のように、正面壁よりも明度を2度程度暗い色にする場合は、いっきに暗く着色せずに、重ね塗りすることによって暗くしていく方がよいでしょう。また、淡い色での外壁面の着色で、窓ガラス面に色がはみ出しても、気にしなくてよいでしょう。それは、窓ガラス面の着色過程で目立たなくなります。

なお、きれいな仕上りを得るには、大きな筆に、たっぷりと絵の具をふくませて、伸ばすように出来るだけ速く着色しなければ、色むらやシミが出来易くなるので、注意して下さい。

色づくりに関しては、基本的に、暖色系の色にはバーント・アンバーや暖色ニュートラル、さらにはニュートラル・ブラックを加えて、他方、寒色系の色には寒色ニュートラルやニュートラル・ブラックを加えて彩度をおさえたり、暗い色をつくるようにします。

従って、下に示した「ニュートラル化した色の一覧表」の色の調合をよく見て練習しておくとよいでしょう。

When coloring the exterior wall of the building in the light color perspective, start coloring with whitish light colors in the larger areas, and then progress to the smaller areas. For areas like the side exterior wall, which should be finished in colors about two degrees darker than the colors used for the front exterior wall, it's better to darken the tone by laying many colors rather than directly applying dark colors from the beginning. Don't be overly concerned if the colors are spread over the adjacent window panes when you are coloring the exterior wall with lighter colors. These spreading colors will later be hidden during the coloring of the window glass.

To finish the rendering more beautifully, spread the colors as quickly as possible using a thick paintbrush soaked with ample colors. Slow brushstrokes might result in 'smearing or mottling of the perspective.

When mixing your colors, try to add burnt umber, warm neutrals, or an even more neutral black to the warm color system, and add cold neutrals or neutral blacks to the cold system colors to reduce the chroma or produce darker colors. In doing this, it's recommendable to make a practice of referring closely to the color mixture shown in the following "Schedule of neutralized colors."

透明水彩絵の具による色づくり
How to produce colors using clear watercolors

■ニュートラル化した色のつくり方 How to produce neutralized colors

●ニュートラル化した色の一覧表 Schedule of neutralized colors

暖色系 Warm system colors		トーン段階 Tone gradation	紫（カーマイン＋コバルトブルー） Purple (Carmine+ cobalt blue)	カーマイン Carmine	イエロー・ディープ Deep yellow	レッド・ディープ Deep red	オレンジ Orange	イエロー・オーカー Yellow ocher
	A	純色のみ Only pure color						
	B	純色＋バーント・アンバー Pure color + burnt umber						
	C	純色＋バーント・アンバー＋暖色ニュートラル Pure color+ burnt umber+warm neutral						
	D	純色＋ニュートラル・ブラック Pure color + neutral black						
	E	純色＋ニュートラル・ブラック＋暖色ニュートラル Pure color + neutral black + warm neutral						

寒色系 Cold system colors		トーン段階 Tone gradation	グリーン・ペール Pale green	グリーン・ペール＋ビリジャン Pale green+ viridian	ビリジャン viridian	プルシャンブルー Prussian blue	コバルトブルー・ティント Cobalt blue tint	青紫（カーマイン＋プルシャンブルー） Blue purple (Carmine+ Prussian blue)
	A	純色のみ Only pure color						
	B	純色＋寒色ニュートラル少なめ Pure color + a bit of cold neutral						
	C	純色＋寒色ニュートラル多め Pure color + ample amount of cold neutr						
	D	純色＋ニュートラル・ブラック Pure color + neutral black						
	E	純色＋ニュートラル・ブラック＋寒色ニュートラル Pure color + neutral black + cold neutral						

■ニュートラル化した色の使い方 How to apply neutralized colors

一覧表で示したように、ニュートラル色の加え方によって、純色の彩度・明度を変えることが出来ます。
基本的には、寒色系の色には寒色ニュートラルを、暖色系の色にはバーント・アンバーや暖色ニュートラルを加えることで、彩度・明度を変えることが出来、ニュートラル・ブラックの混合は、不透明な色にせずに、黒を加えたような暗い色をつくる場合に使われます（「ニュートラル化した色の一覧表」を参照)。
下表は、矢印の方向で、色を組み合わせた場合の微妙な色の配色を示しています。つまり、一つの色だけの配色による変化と、複数の色の配色による変化の違いを表しています。

As shown in the schedule, you can change the chroma and brightness of pure colors by varying the neutral colors that you mix in.
Basically you can change the color chroma and brightness by adding the cold neutrals to cold system colors, and by adding burnt umber or warm neutrals to warm system colors. The neutral black mixture is used to produce blackish dark colors without making them opaque.（See "Schedule of neutralized colors."）
The following table shows the fine color scheme produced when combining the colors in the direction of the marked arrow. The difference between the change made by a single color scheme and that made by a plural color scheme can be observed.

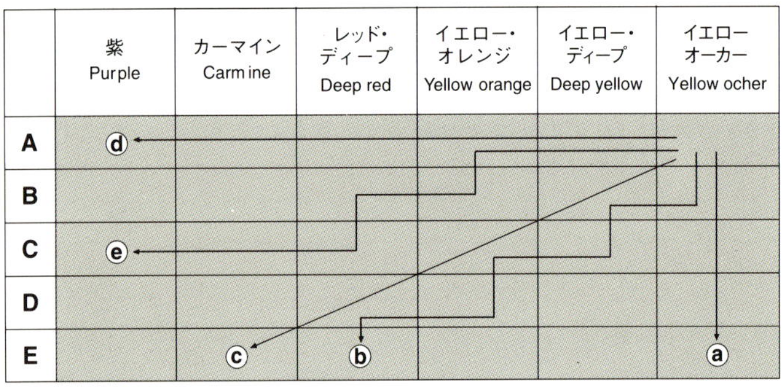

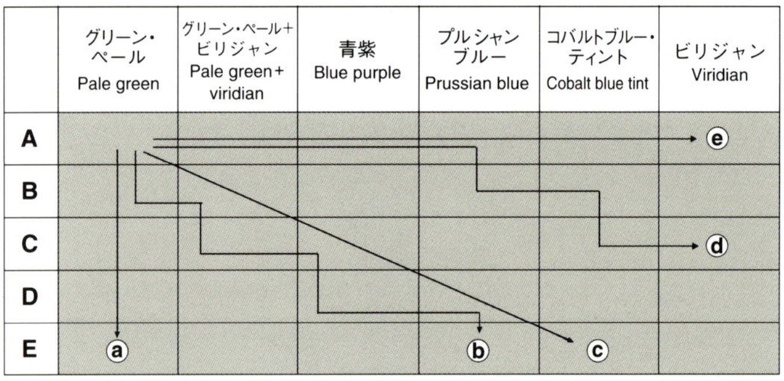

ⓐの方向 In the direction of ⓐ

一色だけで暗い色へと移るグラデーション表現で、非常に落ち着いた感じのグラデーションになります。

Expression of gradation of a single color to darker colors. Quite a calm gradation can be produced.

ⓑの方向 In the direction of ⓑ

多くの色を使いながら暗い色へと移るグラデーション表現ですが、となり合った色を使いながら暗い色へと移るので自然な暗さのグラデーション表現になります。しかも、多くの色を使っているので、はなやかな感じがします。

Expression of gradation of plural colors to darker colors. Since the colors used to express the gradation are adjacent to each other, a very natural gradation to dark colors can be expressed. In addition, since many colors are used, a gay and bright atmosphere can be produced.

ⓒの方向 In the direction of ⓒ

色数の多いグラデーション表現であるため、かなり、はなやかな感じがします。

Since many colors are used in this expression of gradation, a fairly gay and brilliant atmosphere can be produced.

ⓓの方向 In the direction of ⓓ

明暗のグラデーションはありませんが、色の変化が自然で、はなやかに見えます。

Though this is not a gradation of color shade, the change in color is quite natural and looks gay and brilliant.

ⓔの方向 In the direction of ⓔ

色数を少なくしたグラデーション表現であるが、自然な明暗が表現出来る他、大きな広がりがはなやかさのある暗い色に変っていきます。

Expression of gradation with a limited number of colors. While facilitating expression of natural brightness,a large expanse changes into a dark,brilliant color.

■白っぽい建物や淡い色の建物の着色 Coloring whitish colors and light-colored buildings

外壁面の着色は、窓ガラス面を気にせずに建物全体を着色し、側面壁は、少し暗い色で重ね塗りします。影も一度に暗くせず、重ね塗りで暗くしていくと色の変化をも表現出来ます。次に、窓ガラス面の着色に入ります。窓ガラスの着色は、空の色から始め、「1. 窓ガラスの描き方」で説明したように着色しますが、出来るだけ、外壁面にはみ出さないように着色していくと同時に、色むらが出来ないように、乾かしながら進めます。また、絵の具の水ぼてが出来るようであれば、窓の下場や、暗く着色する部分に出来るように、絵の具を伸ばしながら着色します。そうすれば、後の暗い色の着色によって、目立たないようになります。

When coloring the exterior wall, begin by coloring all of the building except for the window panes, and then spread an additional layer of slightly darker colors over the side exterior wall. When coloring the shade, express the changes in color by laying many colors repeatedly, instead of making the area dark all at once. Then color the window panes. When coloring the window panes, begin by coloring the sky portions, laying the colors as shown in "1. How to color windows." Try to keep the colors from spreading over the exterior wall during this process, and eliminate mottling by waiting until the previously laid colors are dry before painting over them. If the colors are smeared by excessive water in the brush, spread the smeared colors well. By doing so, you can conceal the smears in the subsequent layers of color.

■濃い色の建物や色みの強い建物の着色 Coloring buildings with dark colors or strong-toned colors

白っぽい建物の場合と違って、窓ガラス面に色がはみ出してはいけません。後に説明する「着色のコツ」の方法で、窓ガラス面を避けて外壁面だけを着色します。もし、窓ガラス面にはみ出した場合は、きれいな水を平筆にふくめて、洗い落しておきます。

Never spread the colors over the window panes as you would to color a whitish building. Begin by coloring the entire surface of the exterior wall except for the window portions. Utilize the method later explained in the "Trick to applying fine coloring." If any colors are accidentally spread over the window panes, wipe them off using a brush soaked with clean water.

[透明水彩絵の具による着色のコツ]

Tips for coloring with clear watercolors

透明水彩絵の具は、速く紙に吸収され易いので、すばやく着色しないと色むらや色カスレがおきます。そのような欠点を避けるには建物の壁面をいっきに塗り上げようとせず、まず、色の変化の方向性（光の方向性）を決めて、その方向性で部分的に、順次、前の着色した部分に重ならないように、少しすき間を開けながら塗り上げていくと、きれいに着色出来ます。従って、色の濃い建物や、室内の壁面は、特に、この方法で着色しないと色むらや色カスレが出来て失敗し易いでしょう。
そうした結果、より色みを濃くしたければ、その上から再度同様の方法で、先に着色した絵の具が完全に乾いてから、「継ぎ目」や「すき間」を目立たないようにする為に、その上から少し濃いめの色を重ね塗りします。この作業を、建物の基準線寄りにくり返すと、壁面の色の変化も自然に表現出来ます。
もしそのようにしても色むらが目立つ場合は、着色した絵の具が乾いてから、小さな丸筆を使い、その部分に点のようなものを淡めの色でたくさん描き込むことによって、全体としての色あいと濃さを調節します。

Since clear watercolors are likely to soak into paper quickly, apply the coloring as quickly as possible to avoid mottling or blurring, and make sure not to color the exterior wall surface all at once. Decide the direction of the coloring first, and then spread colors one by one, allowing a small space between previous layers and newer ones so that none of the colors overlap. This will allow you to finish clear perspectives.
It is especially helpful to follow this method of coloring for dark-colored buildings or the dark-colored surfaces of interior walls. Otherwise mottling and blurring are likely to be generated.
If you want to finish the perspective in darker colors, apply additional layers of slightly darker colors than before, making sure to wait until the previously laid colors have completely dried to conceal the "color overlap" or "gap" in the same coloring method initially employed.
If this step is repeated around the area closer to the reference line of the building, the exterior wall can be expressed with a natural touch.
If mottling is still found after this step, wait until the previously spread colors have dried and draw a lot of light-colored dots over the affected area using a small round paintbrush to adjust the color tone and thickness in the perspective as a whole.

外壁面を濃く着色する場合
When coloring the exterior wall in heavier colors

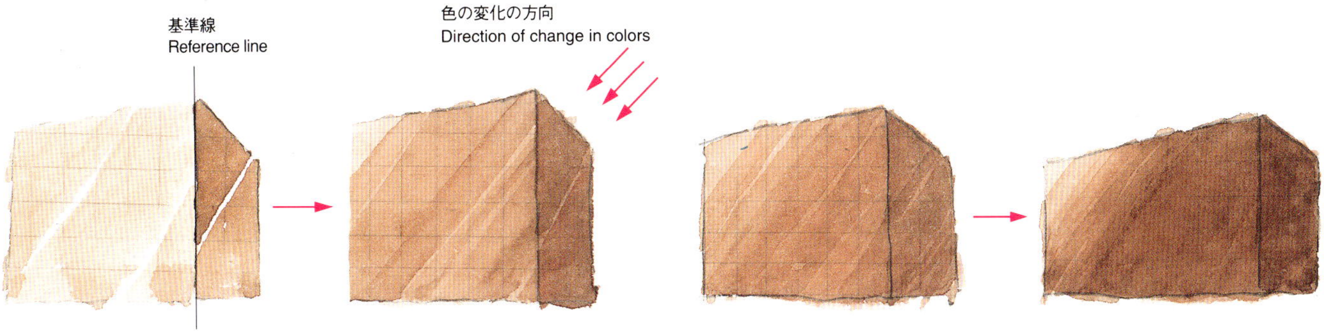

さらに、色の濃さを強くするには
In addition, to make the colors heavier

基準線寄りに同じ作業をくり返します
Repeat coloring over the area closer to the reference line.

色むらをぼかす方法
How to shade off the mottling

白っぽい部分や濃い部分の「色むら」のある状態
Condition of the mottling seen on the whitish or dark areas.

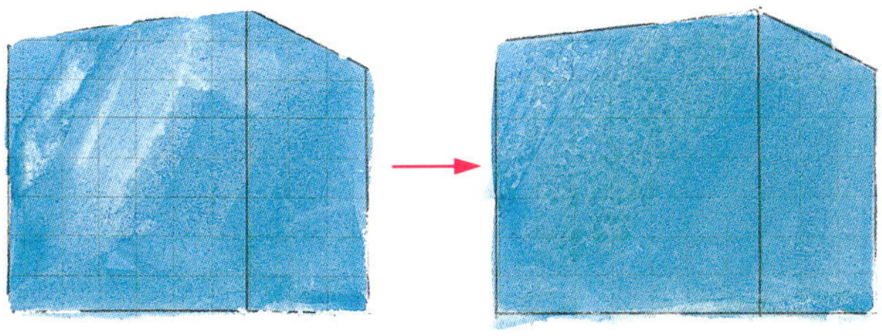

白っぽい部分に丸筆を使って点のようなものを描き込み、同じような濃さに見えるようにした上で、さらに淡い色を重ね塗りしてぼかした状態
Paint many dots over the whitish area using a round paintbrush. Once a similar color thickness is expressed, lay the lighter colors over them to shade off the area.

着色例
Coloring example

着色実例
Coloring example

建物全体を着色しながら重ね塗りで色の変化を表現しています。

Changes in colors can be expressed by overlaying the colors while coloring the entire building.

その後、側面のみを少し暗い色で重ね塗りして暗く表現しています。

After that, lay slightly darker colors only over the side exterior wall to express the darkness on the side wall.

作品例
Sample of work

C. エアーブラシによる吹き付け着色 Spraying colors with an airbrush

エアーブラシによる吹き付け着色には、先に説明したように、下塗りした上に吹き付けるものと、直に吹き付けるものがあります。
下塗りした上にエアーブラシで吹き付けるパースは、あらかじめ窓ガラスの着色（筆塗りでもエアーブラシ着色のどちらでもかまいません）を済ませてから、外壁の下塗りをして、その下塗りの絵の具が乾いてから、マスキングをします。マスキングが出来ると、各々のパートをデザインカッターで切り込み、絵の具を吹き付けていきます。同じ面の色の変化は、吹き付け時間を長くしたり、より暗い色を部分的に吹き付けることで表現出来ます。
直吹きパースの場合は、下塗りがないので目安になる色がありません。そこで、必ず試し吹きをして色の確認をしなければなりません。吹き付け着色は、下塗りパースと同様にしますが、特に、同系色の暗い部分から吹き付けるようにすると、マスキングの回数を減らすことが出来て、速く着色出来ます。
いずれの場合であっても、吹き付ける絵の具は、筆塗りパースの場合よりも、やや水っぽくした方が、ピース（吹き付け器具）の絵の具づまりがなくて吹き付け易いでしょう。また、直吹きの場合の窓ガラスの吹き付けは、あらかじめ、下図のコピーに、明るくする部分や暗くする部分を鉛筆でスケッチしておき、そのスケッチを見ながら、最も暗い部分からマスキングフィルムをはがしながら吹き付けると速く着色出来ます。
また、吹き付け具合は、本書の第2章の「エアーブラシパースの着色」を、再度復習して下さい。特に、マスキングフィルムが貼り付いている場合の色は、吹き付けた部分が白く見えていてもかなりの色が吹き付けられていることを、念頭におかなければなりません。もし、自信がなければ、常に、吹き付けた部分に、白い紙を重ね合わせて、その紙の白さとの比較で吹き付けた色の濃さを確認すればよいでしょう(p.30の上段2枚の写真を見比べて下さい)。
エアーブラシによる吹き付け着色の特長は、色の濃淡変化が、自然な流れで極端に表現されることにあります。従って、色みの強い壁面であっても、白っぽい淡い色から、実際上の濃い色への濃淡変化をもつように吹き付けます。次ページの見本は、同一面の吹き付けでの色の濃淡表現を示しています。明るい部分は、吹き付け量を少なくして白っぽく、他方、建物の基準線寄りは、暗い色で吹き付けて、濃い目に着色します。なお、見本の色は、最も代表的な建物の外壁色と、その調合を示しているので参考になるかと思います。

As explained earlier, there are two ways of spraying colors with an airbrush: spraying the colors over the underpainting, and spraying directly over the canvas without any underpainting.
When airbrushing over the underpainting in your perspective, begin by spreading the underpainting over the window glass(either a normal paintbrush or airbrush will do）, underpaint the exterior wall, and apply the masking after the underpainting dries. After masking has been completed, use a design cutter to cut it away from the area where the next colors are to be airbrushed on. Changes in color in the same areas can be expressed by adjusting the spraying time or by partially spraying the darker colors.
When directly airbrushing the perspective without underpainting, there is no underpainted color to which the subsequent coloring should refer. Accordingly, you have to carry out a trial spray in advance to confirm the colors you are going to spray. The steps followed are the same as those for spraying over the underpainted colors, but it is recommendable to start by spraying with darker colors of the same color system so that you won't have to mask as frequently and can finish the process a little more quickly.
In either case, try to soak the colors you use in a bit more water than those used for finishing the perspective with a paintbrush. With wetter colors, the color will not clog in the piece (a spraying device) and you will be able to spray more smoothly. When spraying directly over the windows, you can finish more quickly if you sketch the bright and dark portion on the canvas with a pencil beforehand, peel the masking film away from the areas where coloring is necessary, and spray them.
Review the section "Coloring with an airbrush" in Chapter 2 to learn how to spray the colors properly. Take note that fairly large amounts of color have already been sprayed on the areas covered with the masking film, even if the sprayed portion tends to look white. If you don't have confidence in proper coloring in this step, confirm the density of the colors by putting a white paper over the area sprayed with color and compare it with the white. (Compare the two photos shown at the top of p.30)
Changes in the shades of the colors can be expressed with an extremely natural touch in perspectives prepared using an airbrush. Therefore, even for color shades, begin by spraying with whitish light colors and finish up by expressing the changes in the shades with heavier dark colors. Samples shown next page the difference in color shades sprayed on the same surface. The bright area is expressed using a small amount of whitish colors, while the dark area closer to the reference line of the building is expressed by spraying a fairly thick coat with dark colors. The representative colors of the exterior wall of the building in the sample and their color mixtures are shown.

エアーブラシによる壁面の吹き付け例
Example of airbrushing colors over exterior wall

暖色ニュートラル+バーント・アンバー
Warm neutral + burnt umber

暖色ニュートラル+バーント・アンバー
+イエロー・オーカー少し
Warm neutral + burnt umber + a bit of yellow ocher

暖色ニュートラル+バーント・アンバー
+イエロー・オーカー多め
Warm neutral + burnt umber + ample amount of yellow ocher

ニュートラル・ブラック+イエロー・オーカー多め
Neutral black + ample amount of yellow ocher

ニュートラル・ブラック
+イエロー・オーカー少なめ+プルシャンブルー
Neutral black + a bit of yellow ocher + Prussian blue

ニュートラル・ブラック
Neutral black

実際の着色で、見本の色と一致しない外壁色が要求される場合は、この見本の調合を参考にして、調合比を変えるか、または、「ニュートラル化した色の一覧表」を参考にして、色の調合を変えれば、ほとんどの色がつくれるはずです。

When it is necessary to spray a color which does not match the sample color in the actual coloring, change the ratio of the color mixture referring to the sample mixture, or change the mixture of colors referring to "Schedule of neutralized colors" In this way, you will be able to produce almost all the colors.

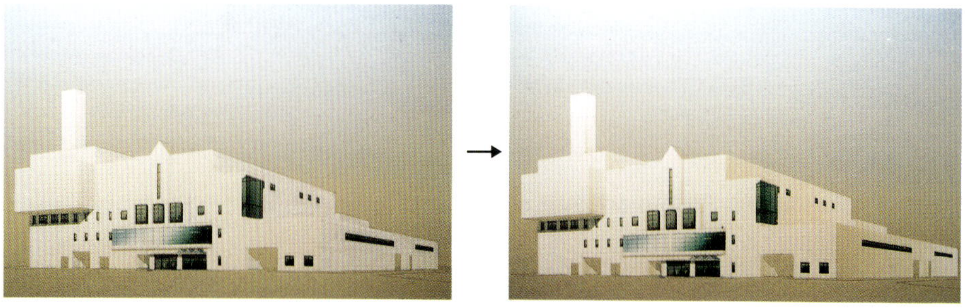

下塗りエアーブラシパースによる吹き付けで表した濃淡表現
Color shade expressed on the perspective by airbrushing over the underpainted colors

直吹きエアーブラシパースによる吹き付けで表した濃淡表現
Color shade expressed on the perspective by directly spraying the colors over the canvas without underpainting

3. 室内パースの描き方 How to paint perspectives of room interiors

室内パースは、透明水彩絵の具着色であっても、不透明水彩絵の具着色であっても、大きな面から小さな面へ、また、白っぽくて淡い色から暗い色へと着色します。具体的には、白っぽくて淡い色の大きな壁面から着色し始め、順次、天井、床へと着色し、家具や置物、照明器具は後廻しにします。

When preparing interior perspectives, move from the larger areas to the smaller areas beginning with whitish lighter colors and progressing to the darker ones, regardless of whether your using clear or opaque watercolors. Specifically, start coloring from the large whitish light-colored area and then move to the ceiling and floor areas, finishing the rendering by coloring the furniture, ornaments and lighting fixtures.

透明・不透明水彩絵の具による描き方
How to paint perspectives using clear or opaque watercolors

室内パースの着色過程については、第2章を再度確認して下さい。なお、不透明水彩絵の具で描く場合は、絵の具の濃さを、外観パースの場合よりも、やや濃いめにして、下図の輪郭からはみ出さないように、さらに絵の具が盛り上がらないように、よく伸ばしながら着色するときれいに仕上ります。
色の変化は、室内の奥に向かうほど、暗くしていくと、室内の奥行きが表現され易いでしょう。また、着色の方法は、もとの色を若干暗くした色で重ね塗りする方法をとるとよいでしょう。ただし、床面に関しては、室内の安定感を表現する為に、奥よりも手前の方を暗く表現した方が迫力のあるパースに仕上ります。天井面については、圧迫感が出ないように明るめに仕上げることが望ましいでしょう。

For the suitable coloring process to use in preparing interior perspectives, refer to Chapter 2 again. When rendering using opaque watercolors, make the colors a bit heavier than those used for coloring the exterior wall. Spread them so that they don't run out from the outline as shown in the illustration below, and spread them thoroughly so that there are no raised areas.
You can express the depth of a room by darkening the color tone towards the end of the back wall. When laying colors over previously laid colors, try to choose darker colors than those laid previously. When painting the floor, however, you should make the floor closer to you darker so that a stable and impressive expression of the room can be achieved. It is best to finish the ceiling a bit brighter to avoid giving the room a stuffy or pressurized atmosphere.

■側面壁の奥の方を、重ね塗りで少し暗くし、床面は、手前の方を暗く着色した基本的な淡彩パース
Fundamental light-colored perspective where the back side of the side wall is darkened by overlaying colors and the floor in the foreground is rendered darker

まず、壁面全体を淡い色で着色し、側面壁は重ね塗りで、色の変化と暗さを表現しています。その後、天井面も淡い色で下塗りして、部分的に溝引き定規を使って垂直方向に重ね塗りして変化を出しています。
床面は、少し暗めに下塗り着色した上で、側面壁同様に、重ね塗りで暗い色の変化を入れてあります。

Color the entire interior wall with light colors first, and lay the colors over the side wall to express the shift and darkness in colors. After that, underpaint the ceiling with light colors, laying the colors partially in the vertical direction using the scale to express the changes in the colors. When coloring the floor, underpaint the darker colors first, and then lay the colors in the same manner employed in coloring of the side wall to express the change in colors.

特に、天井面を明るく着色し、床と柱を暗めに着色することで、建物の重量感を表現したパース
Perspective in which the ceiling is colored bright, while the floor and posts are painted darker to express the massiveness of the building.

天井面、壁面、ガラス面を透明水彩絵の具仕上げで床面のみ不透明水彩絵の具の暗い色で仕上げげた、安定感のあるパース
Perspective in which the ceiling, wall surface and window glass are finished using clear watercolors, and the floor is finished with darker opaque watercolors to give an impression of stability.

エアーブラシによる描き方
How to paint the perspective using an airbrush

エアーブラシのみで描き上げる場合は、暗い部分から吹き付け着色をします。筆塗り着色と全く反対であることについては、外観パースの着色で説明しました。ただし、下塗りエアーブラシ仕上げの場合は、筆塗りと同様に進めればよいでしょう。なお、エアーブラシのみでの着色については、第2章の着色過程を参考にして下さい。

If you want to finish the perspective using only an airbrush, start spraying over the darker portion first. It has already been explained in the chapter on preparing exterior perspectives that this process is exactly the same as the process employed in coloring with a brush, but in reverse. When using an airbrush for finishing the underpainting, however, take the same steps you would use in coloring with a brush. For details on coloring using only an airbrush, refer to the coloring process explained in Chapter 2.

作品
Sample of work

床と木製のドアや家具類のみ下塗りエアーブラシ仕上げで、他は透明水彩絵の具だけで着色したパース画
Perspective in which only the underpainting of the floor, wooden doors and furniture are finished using an airbrush, and the rest is finished using clear watercolors.

エアーブラシのみで吹き付けたインテリアパースで、基本通りに、壁面の奥を暗く着色し、床面は、手前を濃いめの色で吹き付け着色したパース画
Perspective finished with airbrushed colors in which the surface of the wall is colored dark, while the floor in the foreground is sprayed in darker colors according to the principle.

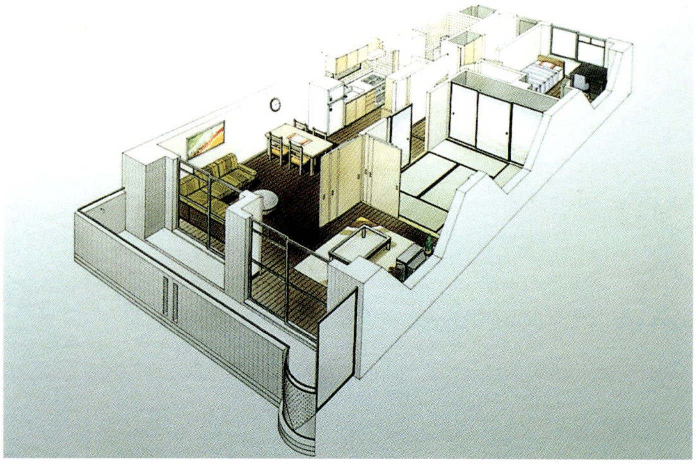

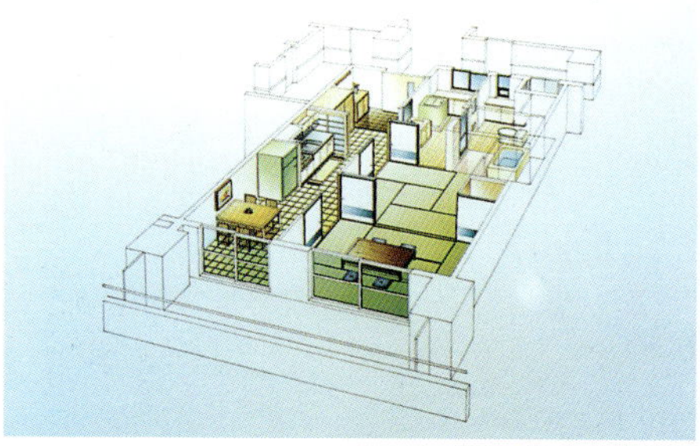

エアーブラシによる室内鳥瞰パース
Bird's-eye view perspective of interior finished by airbrush.

4. 影の描き方 How to paint the shadows

実際の建物は、朝・昼・夜のそれぞれに違った表情の影をもっています。季節によっても、夏は強いコントラストの影をもち、冬は弱いコントラストの影をもっています。
一般的に、平面上に立体図として表現されるパース画では、特別な要求がない限り、そのような強い、また、時間的制限のある影は表現せずに、立体としての建物の形や色彩が、最もよく説明出来るような影を表現することが大切です。従って、実際とは少し違っていても、立体としての凸凹が誰にでも簡単に理解されるような影を入れなければなりません。
原則的には、建物の最も大きく見せたい面の影は浅く、それに対して、側面になる面には深い影を入れます。そうすれば、建物のデザインや、色彩、材質等の表情を損ねることなく立体の表現が出来るでしょう。
影の入れ方としては、まず、より大きく見せたい面を正面としてとらえ、最も手前に出来る影を比較的浅く決め、奥に向かうにつれて影を深くしていきます。光は建物の基準線上の角に向かうものとして考え、下の図のように最初に出来る影を45°程度に定め、あまり深くならないように途中で直線の影に変え、正面から側面に変わる地点で再び45°よりやや小さめの角度で斜めの影にし、次の正面の影で直線のより深い影にしていく方法をとります。
ただし、側面になる面の距離が長い場合は、影が深くなりすぎますので、立体的に見て、適当な位置で直線的な影にします。また、下の図の○印の所のようにバルコニーの出を強調する為には、影をA点よりA′点までに延長してもかまいません。
なお、鳥瞰パースの場合は、正面の影を特に浅くして、側面の影も浅めになるように決めなければ、影ばかりの壁面になってしまうので、注意して下さい。

The shadow of the actual building changes in the morning, daytime and nighttime, and also from season to season; in summer the shadow has a strong contrast, while in winter it is weak.
Since the depth of perspectives is finished on flat canvases, it is generally better to avoid the time-consuming process necessary to render strong shadows unless a special request has been made for that. Instead, it is important to draw a shadow which can effectively express the color of the building and its shape as a three dimensional object. The shadows on the perspective must convey the three dimensionality of the building strongly to all viewers, regardless of whether that entails straying a bit from the way that they actually appear. In principle, draw the shadow on the areas where you wish to express a large scale and lightness, and make the shadow on the side wall somewhat heavier. By doing so, you can faithfully express the design of the building, the colors, and the texture of the construction materials in full detail.
The secret to draw the shade is to start drawing the areas that you want to make large from the front, while painting the shadows cast in the foremost foreground and in the back in heavier colors. Since the light travels towards the corners on the reference line, choose the 45-degree-angle shadow as the first to be rendered, straightening it out before it becomes too wide. Next, draw a diagonal shadow at an angle of slightly less than 45 degrees at the point the shadow changes from the front to the side wall, and then draw the straight and wider shadow at the front.
Since the shadow tends to become too long over the side wall which has a large area, straighten the shadow at the point where it can most effectively convey three dimensionality. And like the portion marked by the circle, you can extend the shadow from point A to A' so that the projection of the balcony can be specially stressed.
For bird's-eye view perspectives, render the shadows on the front wall and side wall in light colors. Otherwise, too many shadows will be rendered on the surface of the wall.

影の基本的な入れ方
How to paint the shadows : Basic principles

●影の入れ方の基本 Basic method used to

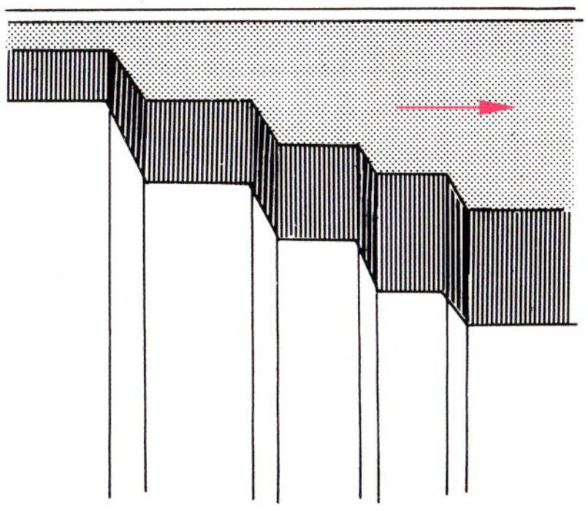

奥に入り込むにつれて影が深くなる。
The shadow becomes deeper as it advances towards the back.

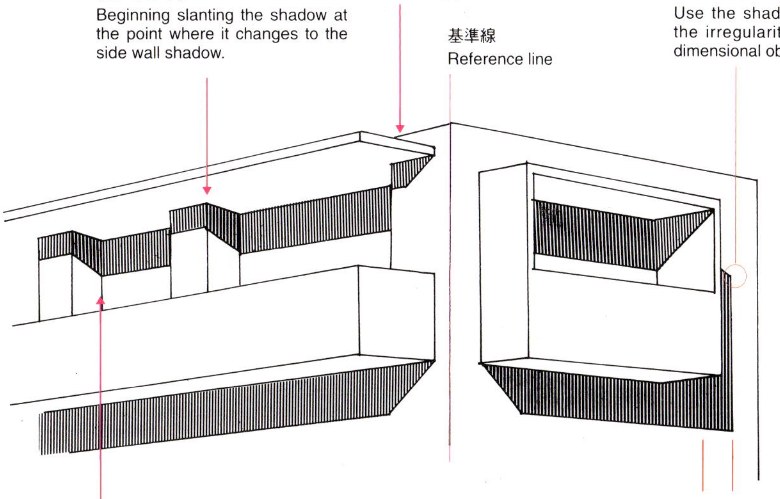

■鳥瞰パースの影 Shadows in bird's-eye view perspective

階高が低層に向う程、影の幅を細くするだけでなく、全体的に影面積を小さく表現します。又、出窓の影はⓐのように強調した方が、立体感が表現され易いでしょう。

Narrow the width of the shadow as the height of the floor is increased and make the area of shadow smaller as a whole. Stressing the shadow in a manner similar to shadow a of the balcony will help you to express the three dimensionality of the perspective.

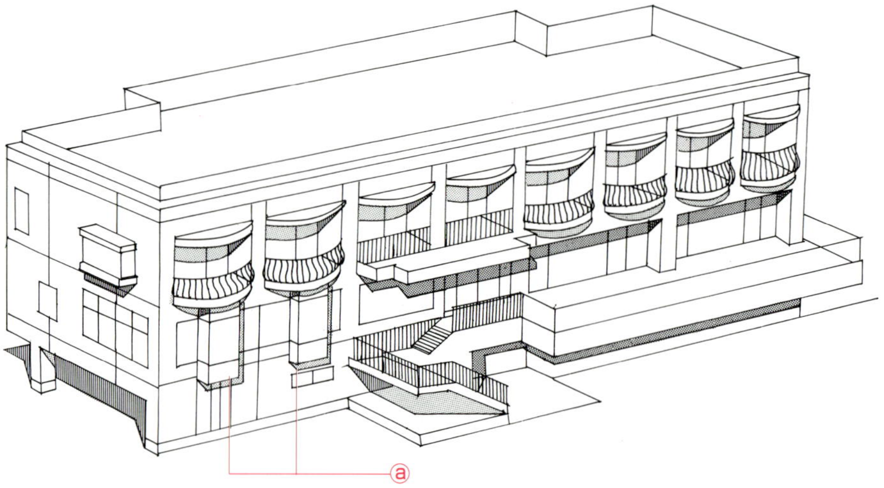

■住宅の半鳥瞰パースの影 Shadows in the bird's-eye view perspective of residential houses

目線が高いので奥にある影は浅くなっていきます。
Since the eye level is high, the shadow in the back is drawn light.

影が深くなりすぎないように影を上げます。
Narrow the width of the shadow so that it doesn't become too deep.

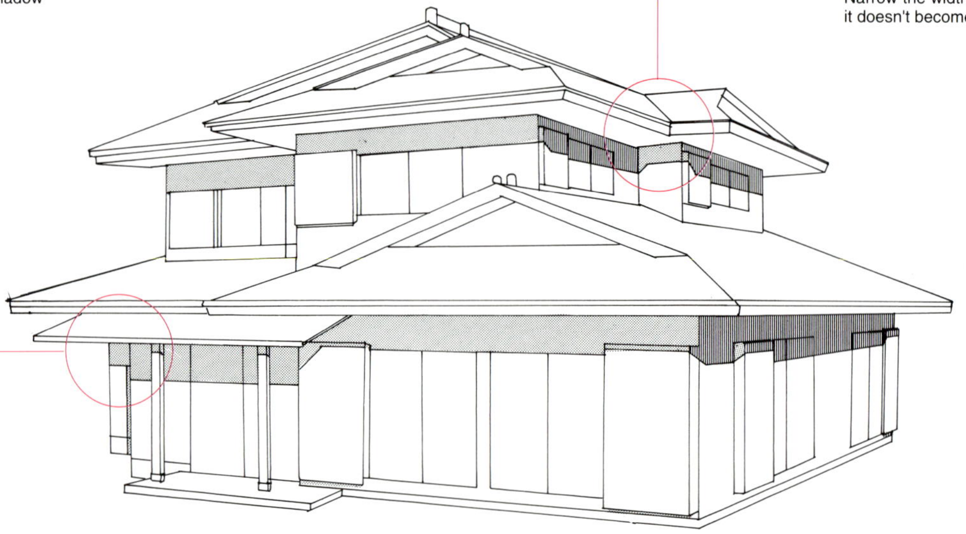

■外観パースの影 Shadows in exterior perspectives

5. 夜景の描き方 How to paint night scenes

夕方や夜に町に出て見ると、窓には室内の光が漏れて黄みがかった暖かい雰囲気が感じられ、建物の色は無彩色に近くなっていることに気づくことがあります。太陽光線が少なくなるにつれて、電灯の光以外は、見えにくくなってくるからですが、夜景パースを描く場合も、この現実に沿って、建物の窓ガラス面は明るく、壁面は暗く表現します。
また、夕方の町の風景は、太陽が夕陽となり、季節によって、赤茶・青紫系の町をつくり出します。そこで、パース画の表現も、夕方か夜かの違いの他、その季節感をどのように表すかによって、変える必要があります。
従って、夜景パースを描く場合、まず、暖かい季節か寒い季節かを決め、さらに夕方か夜かを決めてから、着色に入ります。
一般的には、パース画全体の色調で季節感を表し、夕方の建物は、形と色が比較的はっきりと解るように表現し、夜の建物は、建物と空との境界が解る程度まで暗く表現します。

If you take a stroll in the street at twilight or nighttime, you can often see yellow light reflecting off of the surfaces of the windows, and this helps to create a warm atmosphere. You can also notice that the colors of buildings tend to become achromatic. This is because as the sunlight fades away, it becomes difficult for the eye to perceive anything but the illumination of the electrical lights. When drawing night scene renderings, therefore, take this into account, making the window panes of the buildings brighter, and the exterior walls dark.
Depending on the season, the coloring of the town at twilight can vary between reddish browns to bluish purples. When preparing the rendering of the town, therefore, the colors you use should be selected on the basis of whether you want to depict a twilight or nighttime scene, or if you want to express the season.
Accordingly, if you wish to draw a nighttime perspective, confirm that the season is warm or cold, and confirm that it is twilight or nighttime before starting coloring.
Generally speaking, the feeling of the season can be expressed by the tone of colors used for the overall perspective. At twilight, the outline of the building should be expressed so that the shape and color can be identified relatively clearly. The outline of the building at nighttime should be expressed in colors sufficiently dark to make the boundary between the sky and the outline of the buildings recognizable.

夜景の描き方
How to paint night scenes

第 1 段階 Step 1

まず、季節感から、空の色を青系、紫系、赤茶系のうち、どの系統にするかを決めます。その後、決められた系統の色を基調にしながら、夕方のパース画では比較的明るめに、夜のパース画では暗めに空の色を着色します。
もし、季節感の指定がなければ、青系のカラーボードを使うと速く着色できるでしょう。つまり、紙の色の青みを利用して、不透明水彩絵の具で着色すれば、空の下塗りを省くことが出来るからです。

To begin with, decide whether you want to use a blue, purple, or reddish brown color system. Based on the color system you select, color the sky in relatively bright colors for twilight perspectives and in relatively dark colors for night scenes. If the season is not designated, you can finish quickly if you use the bluish color board. In other words, you can exclude the underpainting of the sky if you use opaque watercolors and the bluish color of the color board.

第 2 段階 Step 2

窓ガラス面を不透明水彩絵の具で着色します。
暖色系の場合、イエロー・ディープに白を加えることによって、不透明な絵の具にして、窓ガラス面全体の下地着色をします。さらに、イエロー・オレンジとバーント・アンバーを加えた色でガラス面の濃淡表現をし、さらに、暖色ニュートラルを加えて家具等の暗いシルエット着色をします。ただし、昼間のガラス面と違って、全体的に明るめに着色することに努め、最暗色での着色は最小限に留めるようにします。

Color the window glass using opaque watercolors.
When applying warm system colors, lay underpaint over the entire window glass area with opaque colors produced by adding white to deep yellow. Express the shade of the glass surface with the colors produced by adding further yellow orange and burnt umber, and then color the dark silhouette of the furniture and similar elements with a color blended by adding a warm neutral. Unlike the window glass at the daytime, however, try to color the window relatively brightly, avoiding the use of darker colors as much as possible.

第 3 段階 Step 3

完全な夜景の場合を除いて、一般的な夜景では、建物や点景の着色は、昼間と同じように描き上げます。夕焼けの場合は、夕焼けの空の色調で、外壁面を着色します。あまり夜景であることに気がとられると、着色方法が難しくなり、きれいに仕上がらないので注意して下さい。

The coloring of buildings and incidental elements in perspectives of normal night scenes should be painted just as they are in day scenes. If you want to paint a blazing sunset sky, color the exterior wall of the building in the same color used for the sky. If you are too conscious about the night scene, you might find it difficult to color the scene as you would like and have trouble in achieving the desired clarity in the finish of the rendering.

第 4 段階 Step 4

建物と点景が仕上がると、エアーブラシを使って、青系の空ならプルシャンブルーで、紫系の空なら、ウルトラマリン・ディープとカーマインの混合色である紫系の色で、赤茶系の空ならカーマインとバーント・アンバーの混合色で、建物の周りを空と同時に吹き付けて、建物の輪郭をぼかします。特に、夜景の場合は多めに吹き付けて、かなりぼかすようにします。

After the building and incidental elements have been finished, spray Prussian blue over the bluish sky. Use a mixture of ultra marine deep and Carmine over purple system color skies and a mixture of Carmine and burnt umber over reddish brown system color skies. Spray the same color over the area surrounding the building to shade off the outline of the building. If you are preparing a rendering of a night scene, spray the colors generously to sufficiently shade off the colors.

最終段階 Final step

最後に、白だけを使って、星を描き加えたり、窓ガラス面の照明を入れます。その後、特に強調したい照明等にエアーブラシを使って、白を吹き付けることで明りの光を表現します。もちろん、この時点で、建物のハイライトも描き入れます。

Finish up by painting the stars in the sky using only whites, and render the lighting reflected on the window panes. Next, airbrush more whites over the lighting and other highlights to stress the lightness of the lighting system. You should also paint in the highlights of the building at this stage.

夜景パースの着色過程 1
Coloring process No.1 for night scene perspectives

青系の色で空を着色してから、ガラス面を寒色系の透明水彩絵の具で仕上げ、昼間の建物と同じ要領で着色します。青色のカラーボードを使った場合は、ガラス面を不透明な絵の具(透明水彩絵の具と白を混ぜる)にして描き上げます。

After coloring the sky in bluish colors, finish the glass surface of the windows with clear watercolors of the cold system, using the same procedure to color them as applied to the daytime building perspective. When the bluish color board is used, paint the surfaces of the windows with opaque colors (mixture of clear watercolors with white).

点景も昼間のパースのように描き上げた後、エアーブラシで建物の輪郭をぼかして、強調したい照明等を白で吹き付けて仕上げます。

After painting the incidental elements in the same manner as applied to the daytime building perspective, shade off the outline of the building using an airbrush, and spray white over the lighting which you wish to process as the highlight.

黄色みにライトアップした夜景の場合、建物の外壁は昼間の建物の要領で、黄色みのある色で着色します。

When drawing the perspective of lit-up yellowish night scenes, color the exterior wall of the building with yellowish colors in the same way as applied to the preparation of the daytime building perspective.

空の色と合わせて、プルシャンブルーで建物の輪郭をぼかした後、白とイエロー・ディープの混合色で、建物の一部の窓や池に照明の光をエアーブラシで着色します。その後、白だけで、さらに光を強調して仕上げます。

After shading off the outline of the building and the sky with Prussian blue, spray the colors over the light of the lighting system besides the building and window pane using an airbrush. Next, finish the perspective by highlighting the light using only white.

(資料)海外旅行の雑誌より
(Source) From a magazine on overseas traveling

夜景パースの着色過程 2
Coloring process No. 2 for night scene perspectives

普通のキャンソンボードのグレーを使い、空の部分にプルシャンブルーを吹き付け、次にコバルトブルーにカーマインを加えた紫系の色を吹き付けます。その後、デッド・ディープに白とイエロー・オレンジを加えた不透明な色で下の方を吹き付けた後、赤みのある色で濃淡着色して空を仕上げます。次に建物の窓ガラス面をイエロー・ディープに白を加えた色で着色して、建物の外壁の着色に移ります。夕焼けであることから、外壁面は正面側を暗く着色します。正面壁を暗く着色しおえると側面壁の着色に入りますが、側面壁の下地色の上から白っぽい不透明色（純色に白を加えた色）で、空との境目を集中的に吹き付けて仕上げます。

Spray Prussian blue over the sky portion using an ordinary gray Canson board, and then spray a purple system color mixed by adding Carmine to cobalt blue. After spraying the lower portion with an opaque color produced by adding white and yellow orange to dead deep, finish the sky by shading with a reddish color. Color the window panes of the building with a color produced by adding white to deep yellow, and then color the exterior wall of the building. To express the blazing sunset sky, apply dark colors over the front exterior wall. Next, spray the whitish opaque color（a color produced by adding white to pure color）over the underpainted colors of the side exterior wall, applying the paint more thickly over the boundary between the exterior wall and the sky.

周囲の建物を窓ガラス面も含めて、エアーブラシを使って暗くして、中心の建物を浮き上がらせます。その後、街路樹の着色や点景の着色に入ります。

Airbrush the colors over the areas adjacent to the building and the window panes in sufficiently dark colors to allow the building to clearly come out. Next, color the street trees and other incidental elements.

点景の着色が終ったら、白の入った明るい不透明色でライトアップの表現をして仕上げます。

After you have finished up with the incidental elements, express the lit-up areas with a mixture of bright opaque color and small portions of white.

夜景の作品例
Sample of night scene perspectivse

PACHINKO TAIGA

6. 効果的な構図 Effective composition

建物が仕上り、点景を描き入れる段階で、一番大切なことはいかに効果的に点景を描き込むかということです。画面全体を見て、間延びせずに、建物を中心にまとめることが重要です。
従って、出来るだけ車や人物、植栽等の点景は基準線上から離して、建物を中心にしてシンメトリーに見えるように配置します。そして、車を建物の両端に少し重なるように描き入れ、植栽や人物も建物からあまり離れた位置には描き入れないようにします。これは、建物を中心にした安定感のある構図にまとめ上げることの他、パースの目的である建物に焦点を合わせる為でもあります。

"The most important thing in finishing the people, cars and other incidental elements in building perspectives is to paint them effectively." These elements should be drawn taking the entire perspective into consideration.They should be never be finished like dull, processed, secondary elements functioning only to support the main object.
Therefore, draw the people, cars, and plants as far away from the reference line as possible,and compose them so that they work together in symmetry around the main building. Have the cars superimpose a bit over the building, and place the people and plants in areas fairly close to the main building. People, cars, plants and other incidental elements are used in perspectives to add stability to the composition and focus the viewer's attention on the main building.

●よい例 Good example

建物を中心にしてまとまっている。
The focus of this perspective is placed strongly on the main building.

●悪い例 Bad example

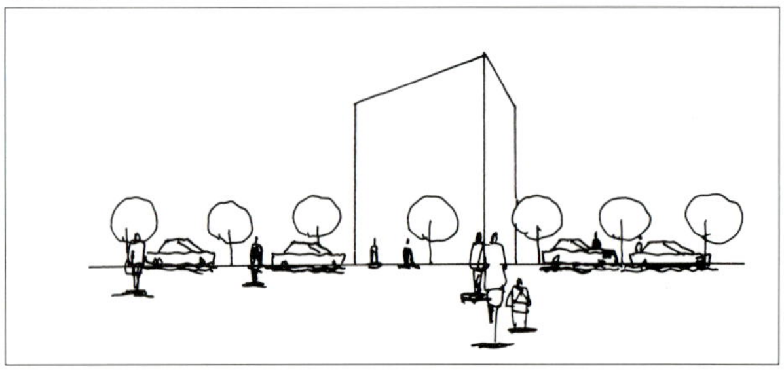

点景が間延びして、まとまらない上、基準線上に人物があるのはよくない。
The dull incidental elements have been rendered without consideration of the balance of their locations, and they even appear on the reference line.

まとまりのある構図例
Example of perspective in which the incidental elements are well balanced in the overall composition

第4章

点景の実際

Chapter 4

How to effectively draw the incidental elements

点景の表現方法

How to paint the incidental elements

建物が描き上がったら、路面、植栽、車、人物など点景を描き加えます。
点景は建物の実在感を表現するのに必要なもので、その表現次第で、パースそのものが良くもなれば悪くもなります。
点景の描写能力は、建物の描写とは異なり、絵心の有無が関係するでしょう。これまでのパース画では、点景は補助的な役割として、比較的簡単な表現だけでよいとされていました。従って、路面や植栽、車、人物の描き方もかなりデフォルメされ、特徴だけをとらえて描かれていました。
しかし、新聞、雑誌、パンフレット等のマス・メディアで見られる最近のパース画は、点景の表現もよりリアルなものになり、はなやかさがあります。それは、パースそのものの目的が、主に、説明図的なものであった時代から、一般大衆の目を惹き付け、自分のものにしたいと思わせるような夢のあるものでなければならない時代へと変わってきたからです。
そこで、よりリアルな点景の描き方の例を示しておきます。

1. 路面の描き方 How to paint road surfaces

路面の描き方は、アイレベルで描かれた外観パースの場合と、高い位置から見た鳥瞰パースの場合では、その表現方法が異なります。

A. 路面の着色過程 Coloring process for road surfaces

透明水彩絵の具による路面着色
Coloring road surfaces with clear watercolors

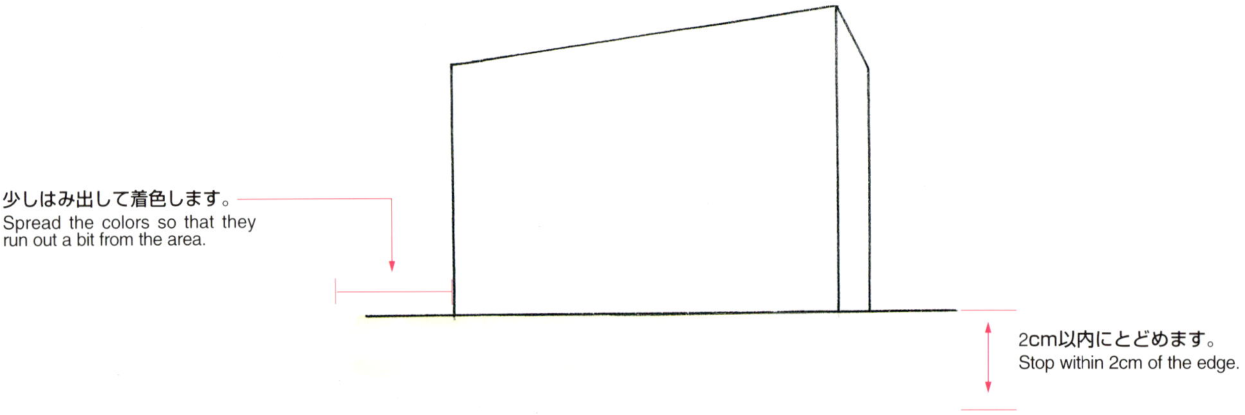

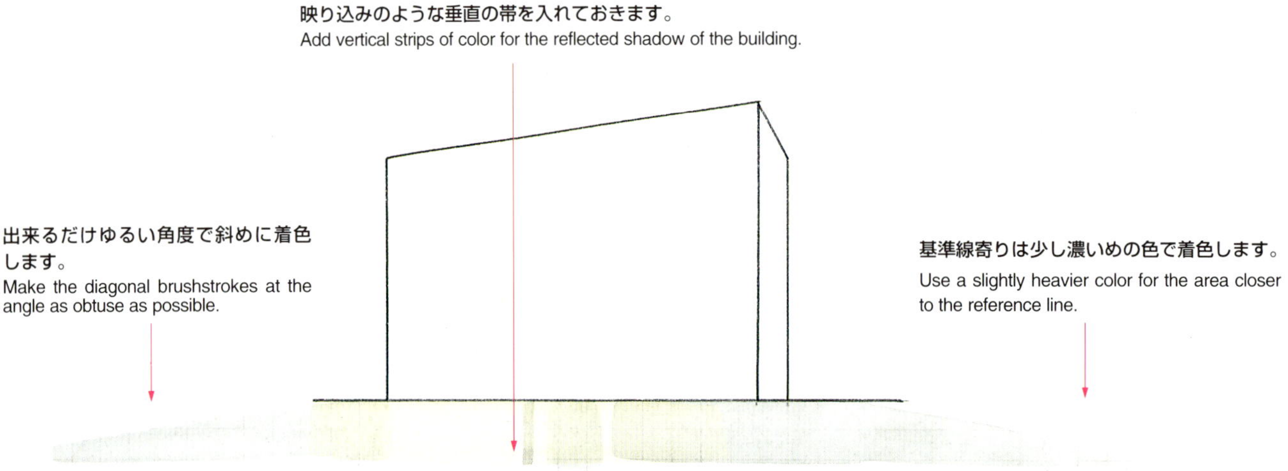

After the building has been finished, it is time to start with the surface of the roads, plants, cars, people, and other accessory elements in the perspective.
Since one of the primary functions of these elements is to add reality to the main building, how they are handled is very important to the overall success of the perspective.
Painting the incidental elements requires a very different kind of skill than that needed to draw the buildings in perspectives; it may require a more painterly touch. Traditionally, these elements have been considered secondary in perspectives and expressed in a relatively simple manner. Their expression has often been fairly deformed as a result of this, with only their base attributes rendered.
However, the incidental elements appearing in recent perspectives in mass media such as newspapers, magazines and pamphlets have been rendered more realistically than in the past, and also have tended to have a gay atmosphere. The era when incidental elements were added to support the main perspective has gone; now, their main role is to attract the general public, and to stir them to act upon the dreams that the perspectives invoke within them.
Some examples of how to paint realistic interests are shown here.

Road surfaces are rendered differently in exterior perspectives and bird's-eye view perspectives. In the former they are prepared based on the eye-level position; in the latter, a much higher position.

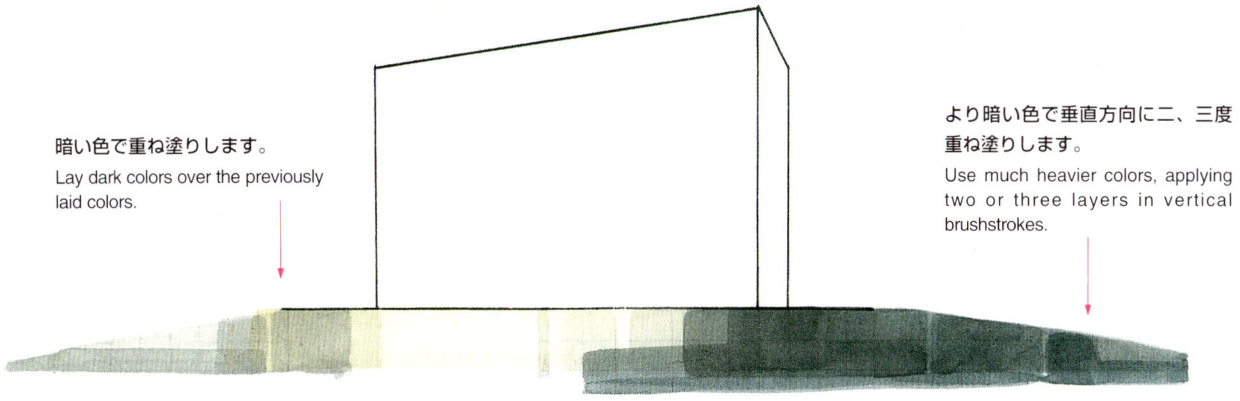

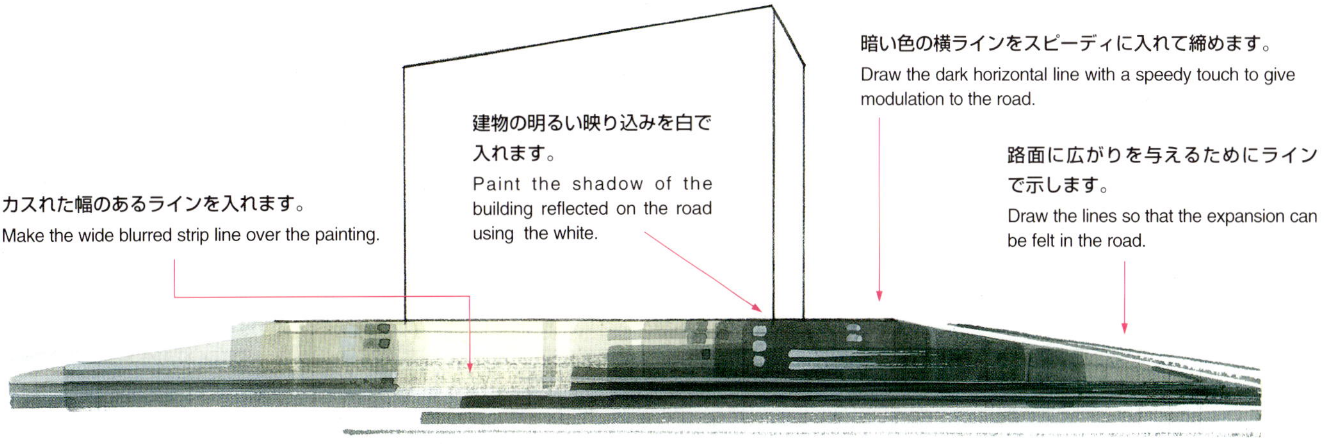

第1段階 Step 1

イエロー・オーカーを水で淡くして建物の下を見本のように着色した後、その両端を寒色ニュートラルを淡めにした色から重ね塗りします。ただ、基準線寄りは濃いめの色で重ね塗りすることが大切です。また、帯状に着色される色の幅は2cm程度に留めておくと構図的にまとまります。

After spreading the underpainting of yellow ocher thinned with water over the building area as shown in the example, lay thinned cold neutral colors over both ends. It is important to apply thicker layers of colors over the areas nearer to the reference line. Keep the width of the strips within 2cm at most to maintain the balance of the composition.

第2段階 Step 2

さらに、寒色ニュートラルを濃くして、基準線寄りの道路を暗くしておきます。なお、前回の重ね塗りされた色を少しずつ濃くして重ね塗りすることを忘れないようにして下さい。

Darken the surface of the road near the reference line by making the cold neutrals heavier. When laying the colors, always remember to apply slightly darker colors over the previous layers.

第3段階 Step 3

道路面の遠近感を強調するために、基準線寄りをより暗くしましょう。その後、着色された色が、不自然な濃淡表現になったなら、見本のように、丸筆で淡い色の垂直線を加えるとよいでしょう。

To stress the perspective of the road surface, color the portion near to the reference line dark. If the shade of colors becomes unnatural, adjust the colors by adding light vertical lines using a round brush as shown in the example.

第4段階 Step 4

下地着色が終れば、最も暗い色を平筆3号につけ、よくしぼってから、左から右へとカスれた幅のあるラインをスピーディに描き加えます。その後、丸筆を使って、手前の方に、暗いラインをスピード感のある線で見本のように描き入れると車等の動きが表現出来ます。

After the underpainting has been finished, swiftly paint in the blurred wide strips of dark colors. Move from the LH to the RH side, and use a flat No. 3 brush that has been soaked with color and completely squeezed out. Next, draw the dark lines in the foreground. If you use a speedy touch for this step you can obtain a very nice expression of the movement of the cars and other elements, as shown in the example.

最終段階 Final step

さらに、平筆で乳液程度の濃さの白をよくしぼった上で見本のように建物の下にスピーディに重ね塗りします。これは省いてもよいが、建物の映り込みや、太陽の反射の表現になるので、練習して加えて下さい。

Finally, mix a white with the approximate thickness of cosmetic milk lotion and use a flat brush to spread it over the area below the building, as shown in the example. Although this step can be skipped, the technique that it employs is very useful for rendering reflections of buildings and sunlight, so it is recommendable to make it a practice.

［表現力アップのワンポイント］ Key Points for Enhancing Expression

●暖色系の着色 Coloring of warm system colors

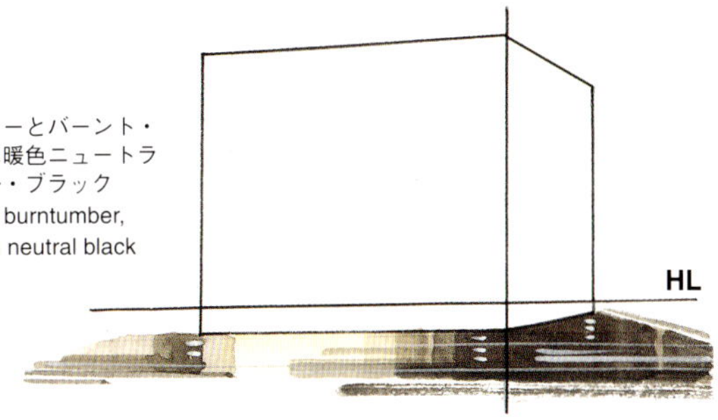

イエロー・オーカーとバーント・アンバー、さらに暖色ニュートラルにニュートラル・ブラック
Yellow ocher and burntumber, warm neutral and neutral black

●寒色系の着色 Coloring of cold system colors

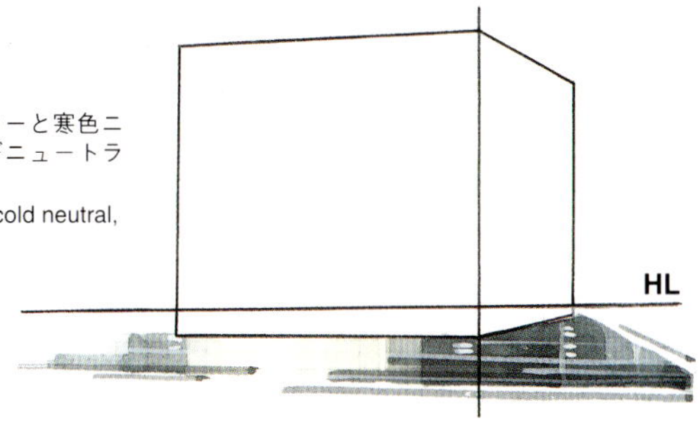

イエロー・オーカーと寒色ニュートラル、及びニュートラル・ブラック
Yellow ocher and cold neutral, and neutral black

不透明水彩絵の具による路面着色
Coloring road surfaces with opaque watercolors

着色手順の基本は透明水彩絵の具と同様ですが、透明水彩絵の具のような透明感のある表現は出来ません。その反面、不透明水彩絵の具の特徴として重量感のある表現には適しているでしょう。
明るい色は、イエロー・オーカーに白と黒を加えた明るいグレーで、暗い色や最暗色は、黒を多く加えた色で着色します。絵の具の濃さは、あまり水っぽくしない方がよいでしょう。着色方法は、透明水彩絵の具の場合と同じ要領で、イエロー・オーカーに白を加えた明るい色から着色し始め、生乾きのうちに、その両端を、少し暗い色で重ね塗りして、その絵の具が乾いたら、さらに暗い色で重ね塗りしながら暗くしていきます。

Though coloring procedures for opaque watercolors are the same in principle as those using clear watercolors, it is impossible to imbue the rendering with the same degree of clarity of expression using opaque colors. However, opaques are quite suitable for expressing a sense of massiveness when it is necessary in a perspective.
Use a gray mixed by adding white and black to yellow ochers to cover the brighter portions of the perspective, and then add more black to the same gray to color the darker and darkest portions. To keep the proper density of color, avoid adding to much water when you are mixing them. Use the same procedures to apply the opaque colors as you would for clear watercolors. Start with the brighter colors mixed by adding white to yellow ocher, and then apply relatively dark colors over both ends before the previously laid colors are completely dry. After these additional colors are dry, darken the rendering by overlaying more dark colors.

エアーブラシによる路面着色
Coloring road surfaces with an airbrush

明るい部分や、暗い垂直的な面の表現を、別に用意した下図のコピーにデッサンして決めておき、路面全体をマスキングした後、全ての垂直面を切り込みます。それから、コピーのデッサンを見ながら、最も暗くする面から明るくする面へと、順次マスキングフィルムをはがしながら、路面の色（透明でも不透明でもかまいません）を吹き付けていきます。
このようにすれば、吹き付ける回数の多い所は暗く着色されて、垂直的な面の濃淡表現が簡単に出来るでしょう。

Decide the expression of bright and dark vertical areas by making a sketch on a separate sheet of paper in advance. After masking the entire road surface, cut all the vertical area and spray the colors（either clear or opaque colors will do）over the surface by peeling off the masking. Refer to the sketch to determine the sequence of this step, starting with the darkest area and progressing to the brighter ones. By this method, the portions sprayed frequently become darker, readily expressing the shade in the vertical areas.

B. アイレベルでのアスファルト道路の表現 Expression of asphalt roads at eye level

透明水彩絵の具や不透明水彩絵の具による着色、あるいは、エアーブラシによる吹き付け着色であっても、道路の表現方法は同じです。アイレベルでの路面は、建物を見ている人から見て、水平面であるので、下の図のように垂直的な濃淡表現がなされています。また、その垂直的表現のなかに空気遠近法的表現をしなければならないので、基準線寄りや、画面の手前の部分を暗く着色し、遠く離れた部分は明るく着色した方がよいでしょう。

When expressing the road at this level, there will be no big differences between the use of clear watercolors, opaque watercolors, a paintbrush, or an airbrush.
Since a person looking at a road from the eye level basically sees it as horizontal, the vertical shade can be expressed as it is shown in the illustration below. Since it is necessary to employ the air perspective method in the vertical expression, you should color the areas close to the reference line and the area in the foreground dark, and keep the area away from the reference line bright.

垂直的な表現
Vertical expression

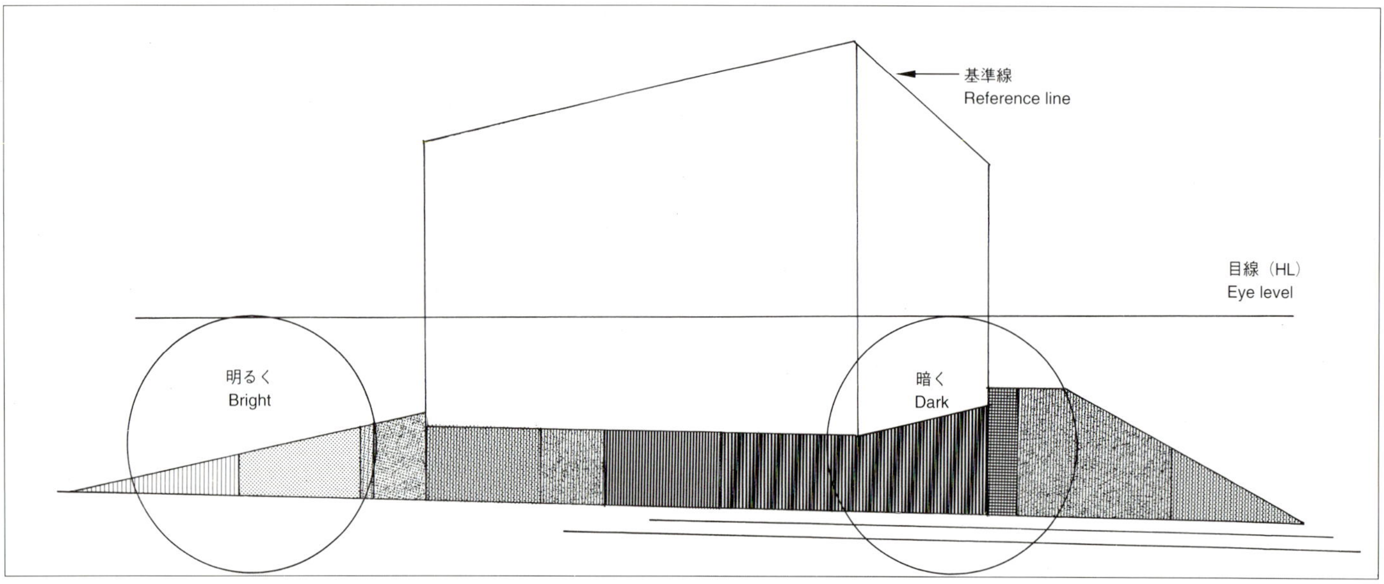

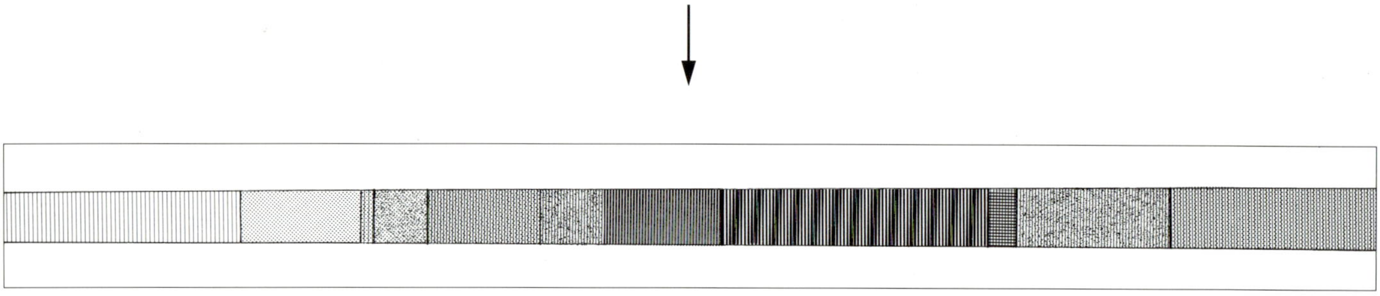

C. 鳥瞰パースでのアスファルト路面の表現 Expression of asphalt road surfaces in bird's-eye view perspective

鳥瞰パースの路面は、見ている人から見て、対面方向になり、路面全体が建物と同一面で見えることから、外観パースのような垂直的表現はしません。つまり、建物が道路面に映り込むというより、建物と連続した面で見えます。そこで、色の自然な濃淡変化で着色しなければなりません。その上で、基準線より離れている所は明るく、反対に、基準線に近い所は暗く着色します。また、アイレベルの場合にみられる色の濃淡による強いコントラストは避けて、全体的に明るく着色することが望ましいでしょう。

In bird's-eye view perspectives the road is located opposite to the person preparing the perspective; since the entire surface of the road can be seen on the same plane as the building, the vertical expression employed in exterior perspectives cannot be used. In other words, there is no reflection of the building on the roads, and the roads themselves can be seen on the plane continuing from the building. Therefore, the roads should be expressed by the natural changes in the shade of the colors. Apply brighter colors to the area away from the reference line, and darker colors to the area closer to the reference line. It is recommendable to avoid creating any of the strong contrast often expressed by the shades of the colors in renderings prepared based on the eye level, and to use bright colors for all of the road portions.

丸筆でスキ間をあけて徐々に細めのラインで焦点に合わせてぼかします。
After making the space using a round brush, gradually hade off using fine lines that match the focus.

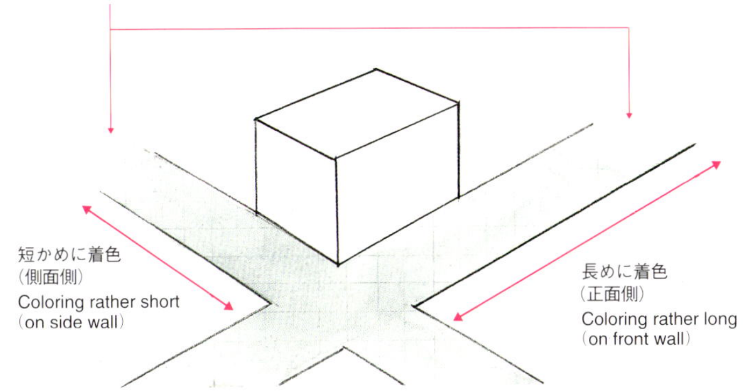

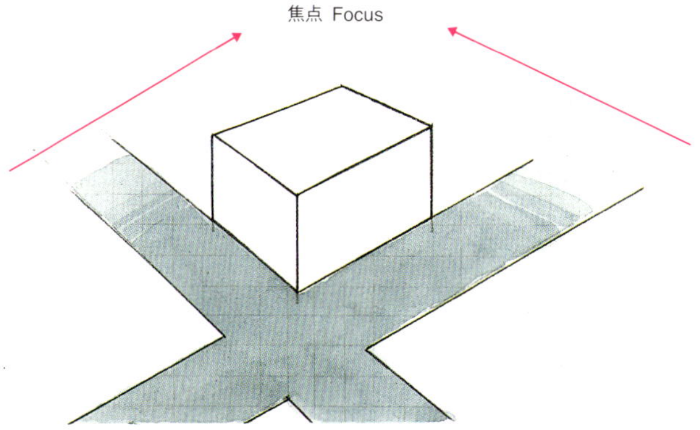

手前の方は、重ね塗りで徐々に暗くするが、色の濃さが自然に変わるように、ラインを焦点に合わせ丸筆で描き加えながらぼかします。
On this side, darken gradually by overlapped coation, but in order that the color shade can gradate naturally, match the line to the focus point, then with a round-tipped brush, shade off the color while adding the drawings.

●明るく仕上げた道路 Road finished in bright colors

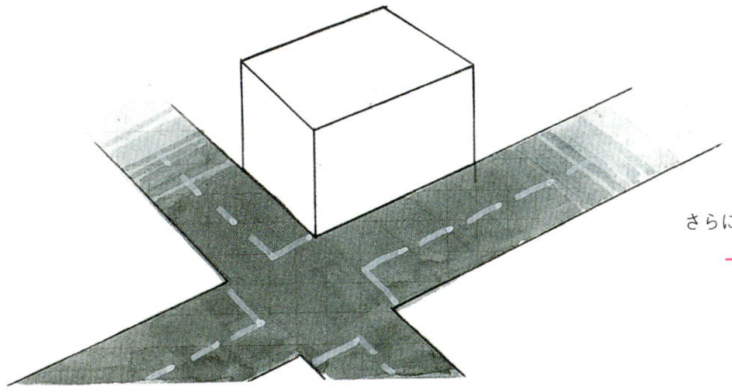

さらに暗くする場合は

●暗く仕上げた道路 Road finished in dark colors

建物より少し越えた位置から暗くします。
Start coloring the area a bit after the building dark.

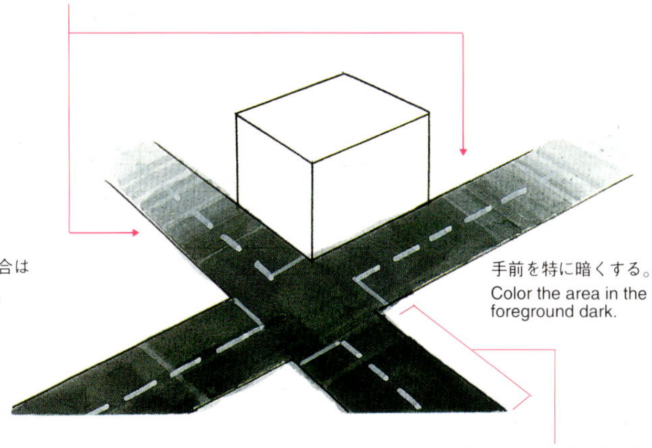

このあたりの暗い色も全て焦点に合うように着色します。
Paint a dark color around this area so that it can match the focus.

不透明水彩絵の具による筆塗り仕上げも、エアーブラシ仕上げも、同様に着色すればよいでしょう。ただ、エアーブラシの場合は、線描でぼかさず、吹き付けを弱くしてぼかして下さい。

Follow the same coloring steps for both brush finishing and airbrush finishing with opaque watercolors. There is only one difference between these two finishing techniques: With airbrushing, the shading off of colors should be achieved by spraying colors lightly instead painting lines.

作品例
Sample of work

透明水彩絵の具で基本通りに仕上げた道路
Road finished following the basic technique using clear watercolors

エアーブラシで仕上げた鳥瞰パースの路面
Road in a bird's-eye view perspective finished using an airbrush

2. 植栽の描き方 How to paint plants

街路樹や植込みとしての高木、中木、低木の描き方には、これといった決まりはありませんが、特に、色づかいには注意しなければなりません。つまり、絵の具のチューブから直接取り出したままの彩度の高い色は避け、必ず、他の色を混ぜたり、ニュートラル化した色（色みをおさえた色）で着色しないと漫画的なものになります。着色手順としては、中暗色から着色し始め、暗い色、それから明るい色へと描き進み、最暗色で、植栽の光のあたらない部分を描き込むと、速く立体的な植栽の表現が出来ます。

Although there are no special rules for drawing tall trees, medium-sized trees and shrubs on the street, you have to take care in coloring them. It is very important to avoid using colors with a high chroma that have been just squeezed from their tubes; if you forget to mix the colors or neutralize them, the trees that you finish may end up looking like cartoons.
Start coloring using medium dark colors, and then move to darker colors and then brighter colors. If you draw the area in the trees where no light is reflected with the darkest colors, a quick three-dimensional expression of plants can be achieved.

A. 木の描き方 How to paint trees

低木の描き方
How to paint shrubberies

中暗色で全体を着色します。色は、グリーン・ペールに若干のバーント・アンバーを加えた色に白を混ぜた不透明色をつかいます。それから下半分ぐらいの部分を少し暗い色で帯状に着色します。暗いグリーンはプルシャンブルーを加えるとよいでしょう。

Color the tree portions entirely with medium dark colors. The colors used should be somewhat opaque, mixed by adding white and a bit of burnt umber to a pale green. Color the lower half of the trees with strips of dark colors. It's recommendable to use a Prussian blue to produce the dark greens.

❶

下塗りされたグリーンの最上部に、明るい葉を連続的に描き加えます。この時、中暗色がなくならないように注意します。大体、植栽の上端 3 分の 1 程度に描き加えるとよいでしょう。

Continuously draw the bright leaves of the trees over the top of the green underpainting. Be careful not to let the medium dark colors disappear during this process. It's generally better to put additional colors over the upper third of the painted trees or so.

❷

最後に、暗い色で植栽の暗い部分に連続的な点を描き込み、立体感を出します。

Next, continuously paint over the dark portions of the trees to reproduce the feeling of depth.

❸

❹

❶まず、低木の形を決め、ビリジャンとイエロー・ディープに白を加えた色で全体を着色します。
❶After finishing up with the shape of shrubbery, cover the entire area with a blend of white added to viridian and deep yellow.

❷ビリジャン多めのイエロー・ディープに、バーント・アンバーを加えて下半分を着色します。
❷Paint the lower half of the trees in a blend of burnt umber added to a deep yellow containing a generous amount of viridian.

❸イエロー・ディープにグリーン・ペールを少々加えた色に白を混ぜて、ハイライトの葉を描き加えます。
❸Paint the leaves at the tops of the trees with a blend of white added to small amounts of pale green and deep yellow.

❹ビリジャン多めのイエロー・ディープ入りの色に、バーント・アンバーを加えた暗い色で、光のあたらない影の葉を描き込んで立体的にします。
❹Try to express three dimensions of the trees by painting the shaded portions of the leaves in dark colors produced by adding burnt umber to a deep yellow containing a generous amount of viridian.

中木の描き方
How to paint medium-sized trees

中暗色で全体的に着色した後、小さな丸筆を使い星の形で、暗い色、明るい色、最暗色を描き入れます。低木と違って、帯状に着色せず木の葉を描くように、少しちりばめて描き込むとよいでしょう。色は、低木と同じように調合すれば出来ます。

After coloring all of the trees with medium dark colors, paint star shapes in bright and dark colors using a small round brush. The stars shouldn't be rendered as they were in the shrubbery; instead painting them in strips, they should be somewhat scattered.

まず、鉛筆で上のような下図を入れ、その上に描き加えていきます

To begin with, sketch out the area in pencil. Try to end up with something similar to the sample shown above. Next, add the others.

❶ビリジャン＋イエロー・ディープ＋白
Viridian + deep yellow + white
↓
❷ビリジャン多めのイエロー・ディープ
Deep yellow containing an ample amount of viridian
↓
❸さらにバーント・アンバー入りの色
Color containing burnt umber
↓
❹イエロー・ディープ＋プルシャンブルー＋バーント・アンバー
Deep yellow + Prussian blue + burnt umber
↓
❺イエロー・ディープ＋グリーン・ペール＋白
Deep yellow + pale green + white
↓
❻イエロー・ディープ＋白
Deep yellow + white

高木の描き方
How to paint tall trees

丸筆を使い星を描きながら形づくります。まず中暗色で全体的な形を造り、明るい色は、あまり連続させずに上端の方に多く、中暗色の中にも部分的に描き加えます。最暗色での描写は、出来るだけ大小のかたまりで下端に描き込みます。
木の枝や幹は、出来るだけ細く描き、影は平行に描くと自然に見えるでしょう。色づかいは、低木の場合と同様にしてもかまいません。
平筆を使って描写する場合は、平筆の角で葉を形づけるとよいでしょう。

Draw the trees by drawing stars using a round paintbrush. To begin with, draw the entire shape with medium dark colors. Then apply bright colors generously to the upper portions of the trees without contacting the stars, and partially paint the stars in medium colors. Draw the darkest portion at the lower area as large or small lumps of leaves.
Add as much detail as possible to your rendering of the branches and trunk. If the shade is drawn in parallel, it looks natural. The coloring of the tree can be done in the same manner used for the shrubbery.
When using a flat brush to paint the trees, paint the leaves with a flat corner of the brush.

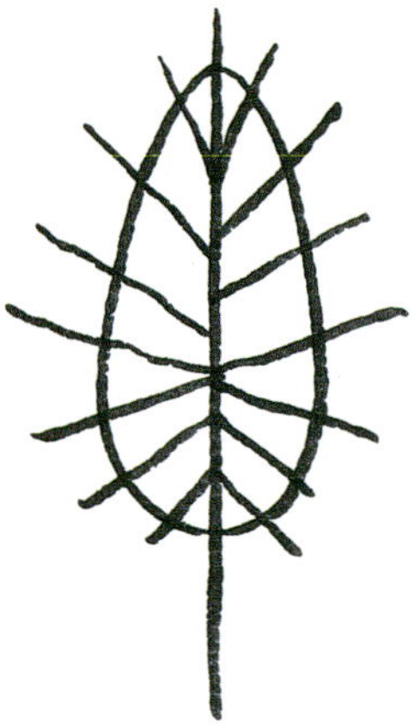

❶ビリジャン＋バーント・アンバー＋イエロー・オレンジ＋白
Viridian + burnt umber + yellow orange + white
↓
❷さらにバーント・アンバーを加えた色
Color with burnt umber added
↓
❸さらにプルシャンブルーを加えた色で上から下へと着色していきます。
Color the trees from top to bottom in colors with greater portions of Prussian blue mixed in.

まず、木の形を決め、その線上に星の形のグリーンを描き込みながら着色を進めて下さい。

To begin with, decide the shape of the tree as shown above, and draw the greenish stars over the line of the described shape.

❶（中暗部）ビリジャン＋イエロー・ディープ
(medium dark portion) viridian + deep yellow
↓
❷（明部）ビリジャン多めのイエロー・ディープ
(bright portion) deep yellow containing an ample amount of viridian
↓
❸（暗部）さらにプルシャンブルーを加えた色
(dark portion) color with further portions of Prussian blue mixed in

■いろいろな色による高木表現 Expression of trees with various colors

●明部 bright portion	ビリジャン＋グリーン・ペール＋白少々 Viridian + pale green + a slight amount of white	ビリジャン＋イエロー・ディープ＋白 Viridian + deep yellow + white	ビリジャン＋イエロー・ディープ＋白 Viridian + deep yellow + white
●中暗部 medium dark portion	ビリジャン＋プルシャンブルー＋白少々 Viridian + Prussian blue + a slight amount of white	ビリジャン多め＋イエロー・ディープ＋バーント・アンバー A generous amount of viridian + deep yellow + burnt umber	ビリジャン多め＋イエロー・ディープ A generous amount of viridian + deep yellow
●暗部 dark portion	ビリジャン少々＋プルシャンブルー Small amount of viridian + Prussian blue	ビリジャン＋イエロー・オレンジ＋バーント・アンバー Viridian + yellow orange + burnt umber	ビリジャン多め＋イエロー・ディープ＋バーント・アンバー A generous amount of viridian + deep yellow + burnt umber
●ハイライト highlight	グリーン・ペール＋白 Pale green + white	ビリジャン＋イエロー・ディープ多め＋白 Viridian + generous amount of deep yellow + white	イエロー・ディープ多め＋ビリジャン少々＋白／イエロー・ディープ＋白 A generous amount of deep yellow + a slight amount of viridian + white/deep yellow + white

●明部 bright portion	ビリジャン＋イエロー・オレンジ＋バーント・アンバー＋白 Viridian + yellow orange + burnt umber + white	ビリジャン＋イエロー・オレンジ＋白 Viridian + yellow orange + white	ビリジャン＋バーント・アンバー Viridian + burnt umber
●中暗部 medium dark portion	ビリジャン＋イエロー・オレンジ＋バーント・アンバー多め Viridian + yellow orange + generous amount of burnt umber	ビリジャン＋イエロー・オレンジ＋バーント・アンバー Viridian + yellow orange + burnt umber	ビリジャン＋プルシャンブルー＋バーント・アンバーの変化 Variation of viridian + Prussian blue + burnt umber
●暗部 dark portion	ビリジャン＋バーント・アンバー Viridian + burnt umber	ビリジャン＋バーント・アンバー Viridian + burnt umber	
●ハイライト highlight	ビリジャン＋イエロー・オレンジ＋バーント・アンバー＋白 Viridian + yellow orange + burnt umber + white	ビリジャン＋イエロー・オレンジ多め＋白 Viridian + a generous amount of yellow orange + white	

■ 平筆タッチの高木表現 Expression of tall trees with the flat paintbrush touch

●中暗部 ビリジャン＋プルシャンブルー＋白少々
Medium dark portion Viridian + Prussian blue + a slight amount of white

●暗部 ビリジャン＋プルシャンブルー多め
Dark portion Viridian + a generous amount of Prussian blue

●明部 ビリジャン＋グリーン・ペール＋多めの白で平筆の角をつかい、何度も白を増やして描き込みます
Bright portion Viridian + pale green + a generous amount of white Use the flat paintbrush and repeat drawing by increasing the amount of white.

●明部 グリーン・ペール＋イエロー・オレンジ＋白
Bright portion Pale green + yellow orange + white

●中暗部・暗部 グリーン・ペール＋イエロー・オレンジ＋プルシャンブルー＋バーント・アンバー少々
Medium dark portion Pale green + yellow orange + Prussian blue + a small amount of burnt umber

シチュエーションによる表現の違い
Different expressions by situation

戸外での木の表現　Expression of trees in the open

夜景での木の表現　Expression of trees in a night scene

ガラス越しの木の表現　Expression of trees seen through windows

建物から光のもれている場合の木の表現
Expression of trees reflecting light from a building

暖色系と寒色系の木の表現
Expression of trees using warm system colors

■基本色 Basic colors

●寒色系　ビリジャンかグリーン・ペール、または、その混合色に、イエロー・オレンジ、さらには、バーント・アンバーを加えます。

Cold system colors　Viridian or pale green, or a color produced by adding yellow orange and burnt umber to a mixture of the two.

●暖色系　グリーン・ペールとイエロー・ディープ、または、イエロー・オレンジの混合色に、バーント・アンバーを加えます。

Warm system color　Pale green and deep yellow, or yellow burnt umber added to yellow orange

■最暗色 Darkest color

●寒色系　ビリジャンとバーント・アンバーの混合色

Cold system color　Mixture of viridian and burnt umber

●暖色系　バーント・アンバーとセピアの混合色

Warm system color　Mixture of burnt umber and sepia

効果的な最近景の木の表現
Effective expression of trees in the foreground

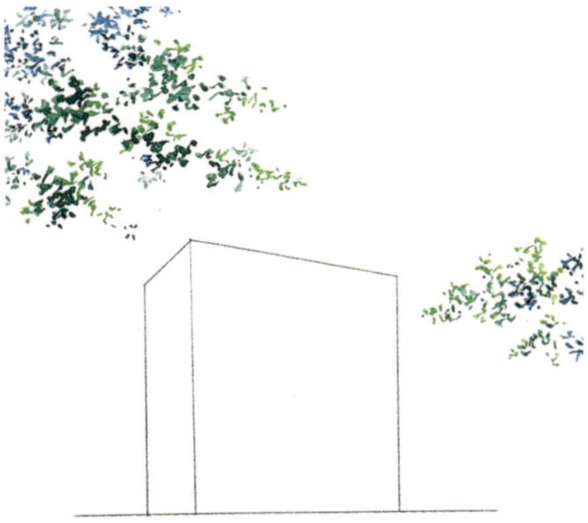

木の葉の形で表現
Expression of the form of the leaves

丸筆のタッチで表現
Expression using a round paintbrush

いずれの場合であっても、基準線側に多く描き入れ、反対側は少なめにすると効果的になるでしょう。

In either case, painting many trees in the area closer to the reference line and fewer on the opposite side will bring about an effective presentation of the rendering.

遠景としての木の表現
Expression of trees in the distance

●カエデの葉の形で表現
Expression of the form of the maple leaves

カエデの形
The form of the maple leaves

遠景の山や森を描写する場合、樹木の色の彩度に注意しなければなりません。比較的近い山や森の場合は、それ程、彩度を下げなくてもよいのですが、遠くにある山や森の場合は、彩度、明度共にコントラストを弱くして着色することが大切です。左の例は、透明水彩絵の具を使って、カエデの葉の形で描かれています。つまり、カエデの葉のかたまりで山や森を形づくり、上端は比較的明るい色で、下端は暗い色で描写するとよいのですが、より遠近感を出す為には、青みのある色を比較的淡くして上端に描き加えると効果的でしょう。

When drawing the mountains and forest in the distance, you have to pay attention to the chroma of the colors of the trees. Although it's not necessary to reduce the chroma when coloring the mountains and forest portions in the relatively short distance, it is important to reduce the contrast in both the chroma and brightness of those in the far distance. In the example shown on the RH side, the mountains and forest are drawn in the form of maple leaves. More precisely, they are drawn in a block of maple leaf coloring, with the upper areas rendered in lighter paints, and the lower areas in darker ones. To give the perspective a clearer expression, however, it is effective to color the upper part of the mountains using thinned-out bluish colors.

●杉の木の形で表現
Expression of the form of the cedar trees

杉の木の形
The form of the cedar trees

表現の方法は上と同じですが、杉の木の形で描写すると針葉樹の多い山や森の表現になります。また、遠景であることから、上の描写と同様に透明水彩絵の具で着色する方がよいでしょう。

The mountains and forest are expressed in the same way as they are in the form of maple leaves. If they are expressed in the form of cedar trees, however, the feeling of mountain and forest acicular trees can be obtained. Since the mountains and forest are located in the far distance, clear watercolors are the most suitable for coloring them, just as with the mountains rendered in the form of maple trees.

山・森の表現着色過程 1
Expression and coloring process for mountains and forests 1

カエデの葉の形での下地着色。
Underpainting in the form of maple leaves.

杉の木の形での下地着色。
Underpainting in the form of cedar trees.

平筆の角で、明るい葉と暗い葉を描き加えた状態。
Condition in which bright and dark leaves are drawn using a flat paintbrush.

平筆の角で「点を打つ」ように描くと の形の葉が出来ます。
If you "paint dots" on the canvas using the corner of a flat paintbrush,you express the leaves in an form.

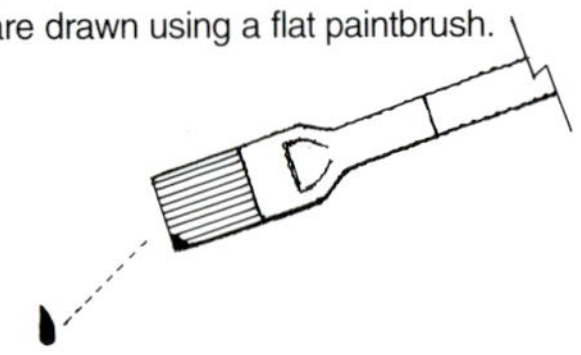

丸筆で、ハイライトや暗い影を描き加えて仕上げた状態。
Condition in which highlights and dark shadow are drawn using a round paintbrush.

平筆や丸筆で、いろいろな木を描き入れて仕上げた状態。
Condition in which various tress are drawn using flat and round paintbrushes.

作品例
Sample of work

大まかな色の変化の下塗りの後、平筆タッチで仕上げたパース画。
Perspective lightly finished with a flat paintbrush after underpainting in rough color.

山・森の表現着色過程 2
Expression and coloring process for mountains and forest 2

遠景の山と芝生を着色します。
Color the lawn and mountains in the distance.

明るい色でハイライトを入れます。
Paint the highlights in bright colors.

手前の森に明るい木や暗い木のシルエット(杉の木の変形)で下地着色します。
Underpaint the bright trees and the silhouette (a deviation of expression using cedar trees) of the dark trees in the forest in the foreground.

遠景の山をエアーブラシでぼかします。
Spray colors over the mountains in the distance to shade the color off.

森の木を暗い色で形づくります。同時に、低木も描き入れます。
Paint the forest in dark colors. At the same time, paint the shrubbery.

車を入れて仕上げます。
Paint the cars before finishing the perspective.

3. 車の描き方 How to paint cars

最近、車のモデルチェンジにより、丸みのある車が多くなっています。従来のパースは、あまり車種まで確認出来るような表現はせず、あくまでも、建物中心にその現実感を与える点景として描かれていました。
今日、パースそのものの目的が広がり、車の表現もそれにつれてよりリアルに描かれるようになってきました。特に、ベンツ等の高級外車は、施主自身が所有している場合も多く、建物に高級感を与える目的からも、パースの点景によく描かれています。

The recent models of cars are often designed to have a roundish exterior style. In traditional rendering the models of the cars drawn in the perspective cannot be identified. Since priority is given to the expression of the building, the cars and other incidental elements are utilized as auxiliaries to support the reality of the expression of the building.
But the perspectives of today are taking on additional purposes, and this has led to a more realistic rendering of cars. Mercedes and other luxury cars which are often owned by the owners of the buildings rendered are likely to be utilized elements in perspectives to add a deluxe feeling.

A. アイレベルでの車の表現 How to paint cars at eye level

まず、アイレベルより低く1mぐらいの位置に横長の正台形を描き、進行方向に向って、その台形の一方を広げます。次に、車の後方ガラスとの境の線を決め、右図**a**の幅の1.2倍ぐらいの長さで、後方の車体ラインを決めます。前方の車体ラインは**b**より若干短めに決めます。この時、窓の高さより車体の高さが少し高くなるように車体を決めます。さらに、テールランプをより外側に描き加え、**e**ラインの下方に後輪を、他方、前輪は出来るだけ前方に描き、タイヤやホイール、モール、ドアの取っ手等を描き込むと仕上ります。なお、下図は出来るだけ、フリーハンドで描くようにして下さい。定規を使って下書きすると車の形のバランスがとれないだけでなく、焦点を意識しすぎるようになりうまく描けません。

To begin with, draw a regular trapezoidal form which is extended a bit in the horizontal direction about 1m lower than the eye level and expand one end of the regular trapezoidal form in the direction that the car is moving. Then decide the boundary line with the rear window glass and decide the rear body line of the car so that its length is approximately 1.2 times the width of the illustration **a**. The front line of the car body should be drawn a bit shorter than **a**. At this stage, decide the height of the car body so that it extends a bit higher than the level of the window. Paint the tail lamp outside the line.
d and the rear wheels under the line **e**. Place the front wheels as far forward as possible, and then finish up the rendering of the car by painting in the tires, wheels, molding, door handle, etc Try to draw your preliminary sketches in freehand. If you draw the sketch using a scale it tends to be difficult to express well balanced cars, and the results are often unsatisfactory because you are forced to worry too much about the focus.

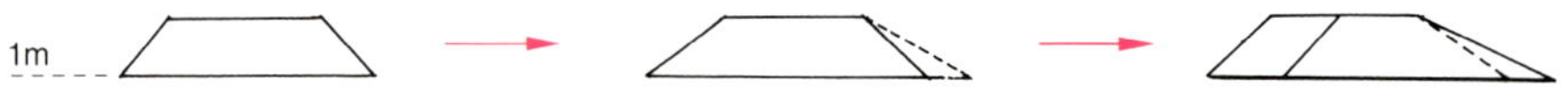

1mぐらいのところに横長の正台形を描きます。
Draw the regular trapezoidal which is a bit extended in the horizontal direction.

進行方向に向かって台形の一方を広げます。
Expand the end of the car in the direction it is moving.

後方ガラスとの境の線を入れます。
Draw the boundary line with the rear window glass.

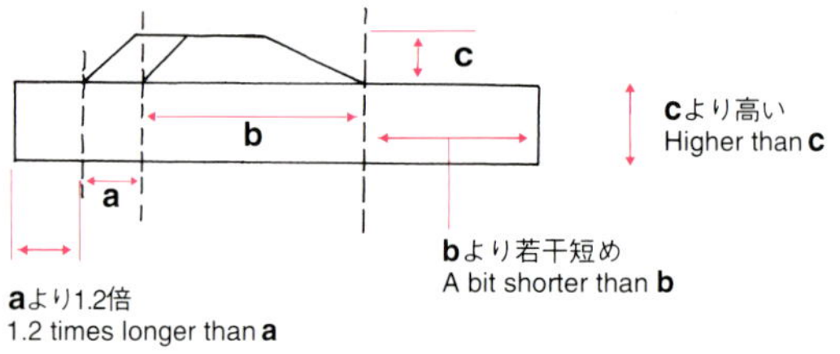

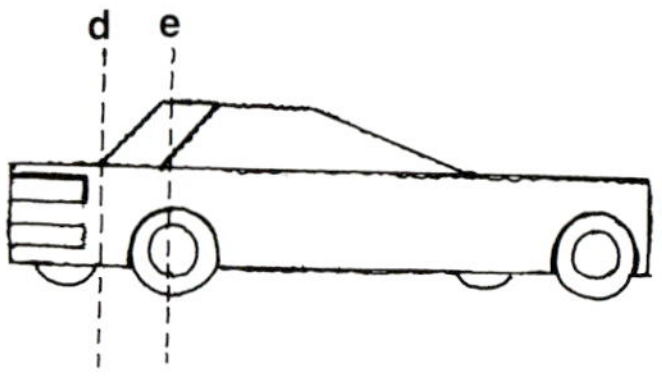

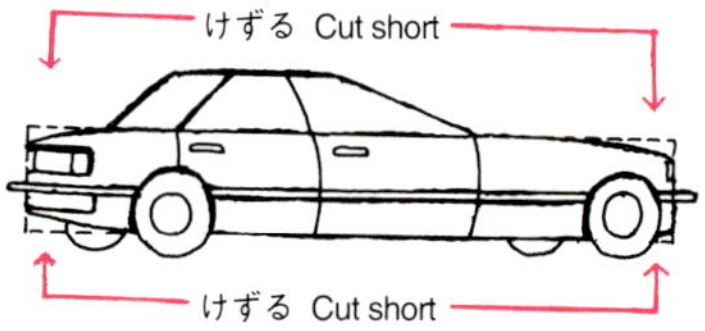

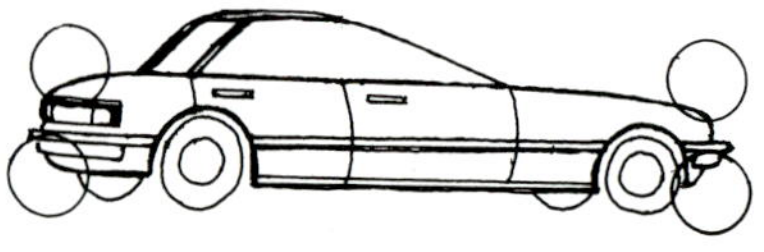

○印のところに丸みをつけます。
Add a round touch around the portions marked by the circle.

車の着色過程
Coloring process for cars

■アイレベルでの車の着色過程
Coloring process for cars at eye level

車の窓とボディを着色します。
Color the window glass and car body.

↓

ボディに明るい色と暗い色を重ね塗りします。
Lay dark and bright colors over the car body.

↓

バックランプを白で描き込み、暗い色で車体の下とバックランプ、バンパーを描き車の窓をはっきりさせます。
Paint the taillight with a white and render the lower portion of the car body,taillight and bumpers in dark colors to enhance the clarity of the windows.

↓

車の影を路面の暗い色で描き、不透明の暗い色でタイヤを着色します。
Use dark colors to paint the shade of the car on the road,and color the tires with opaques.

↓

車体を暗い色で線描して、よりリアルに描き込み、タイヤ・ホイールを描き上げます。
Use clear lines for your rendering of the car bodies so that the cars look more realistic, and then draw the tire wheels.

↓

車体にモールを描き込み、仕上げます。
Finally draw the moldings on the car body.

■鳥瞰での車の着色過程
Coloring process for cars in bird's-eye view perspectives

↓

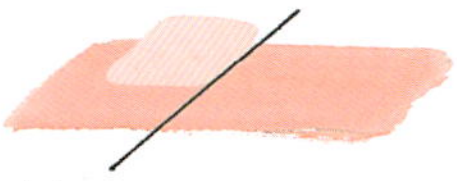

中心
Center

↓

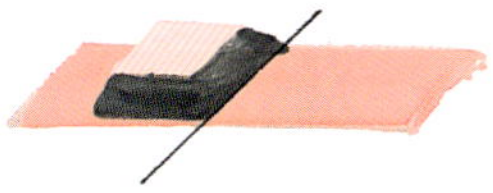

中心
Center

↓

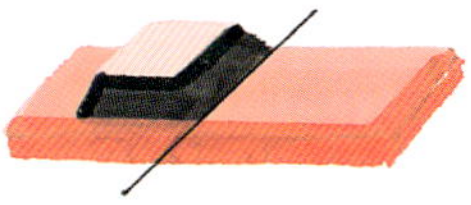

中心
Center

↓

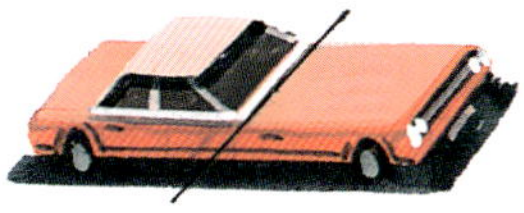

近景 Foreground

中景 Near distance

遠景 Far distance

遠景になる程細かい描写は省く
Omit the small details seen from a distance.

［車の向きの決め方］ How to determine the direction of cars

車の窓ガラスである正台形の一方、つまり後方ガラス面を変化させていけば、下の図のように車の向きが変化します。

If you make a change on the end of the regular trapezoidal forming the window glass of the car, that is, if a change is made in the rear window glass, you can change the direction of car, as shown in the illustration below.

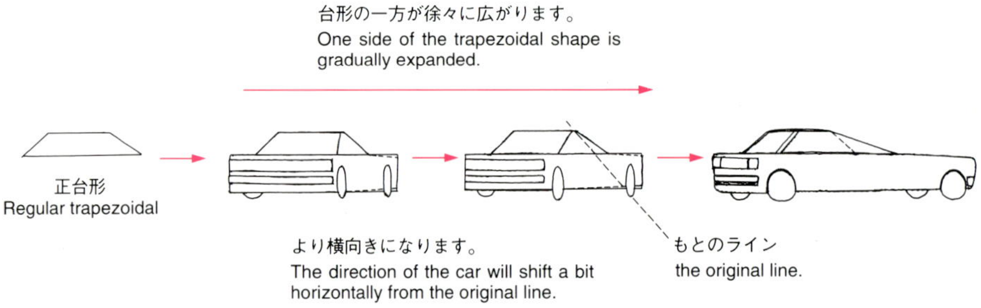

［近景・中景・遠景の車の表現］ Expression of cars in the foreground, near distance and far distance

近景の車はよりリアルに、遠景の車はシルエット程度に、中景の車は簡略した形で描くと、車の遠近感が表現出来ます。

Draw the cars in the foreground more realistically, use simple shapes for the cars in the near distance, and silhouette the cars in the far distance. If you follow this simple procedure, you will successfully express the cars in your perspective.

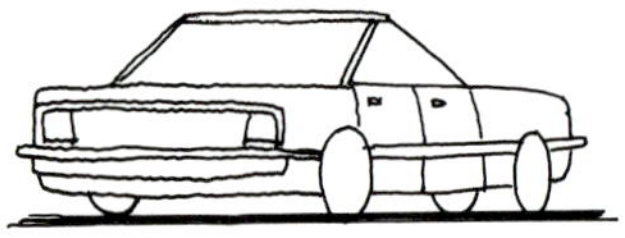

近景 Cars in the near distance

遠景 Cars in the far distance

●遠・中・近景の車の比較
Comparison of cars drawn in the far distance, short distance, and foreground.

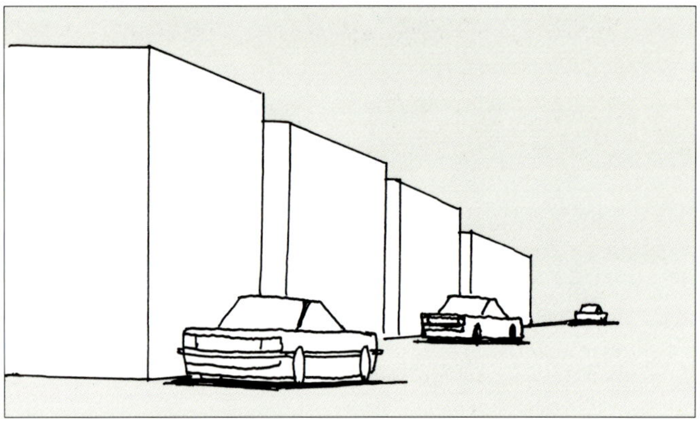

B. 鳥瞰パースでの車の表現 Expression of cars in bird's-eye view perspectives

半鳥瞰での車の表現
How to paint cars in bird's-eye view perspectives

外観パースと同様に描き、それを修正するような方法で、車体の上場や窓ガラスの屋根が見えるように手を加えればよいでしょう。

Use the same techniques applied to painting cars in exterior perspectives. A slight adjustment on the upper portion of the car and roof above the window glass will do.

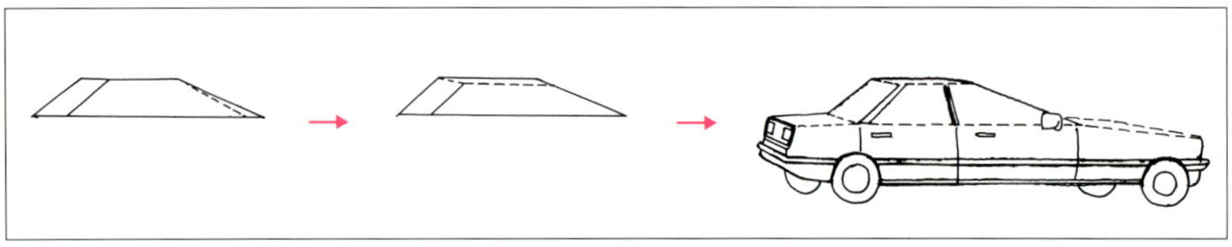

より高い鳥瞰での車の表現
Painting cars from a higher position in bird's-eye view perspectives

まず、車体の大きさを建物の大きさから判断して決めます。車の屋根は、進行方向に向って、中心より少しずらして描き加えます。その後で、窓ガラス面を暗い色で着色してから、車体の立体表現に移ります。車体の立体表現は、車体の下塗りした色よりも暗めの色で、下の図のように着色すればよいでしょう。なお、タイヤ、モール等は、アイレベルと同様に描き入れます。

To begin with, decide the size of the cars in proportion to the size of the building. Shift the roofs of the cars slightly away from the center towards the driving direction. After painting the surface of the windows in dark colors, start expressing the three dimensions of the car's form. To express the three dimensions, follow the example of the illustration below and lay colors a bit darker than the underpainting. Employ the same techniques used for the eye-level perspective to paint the tires, molding etc.

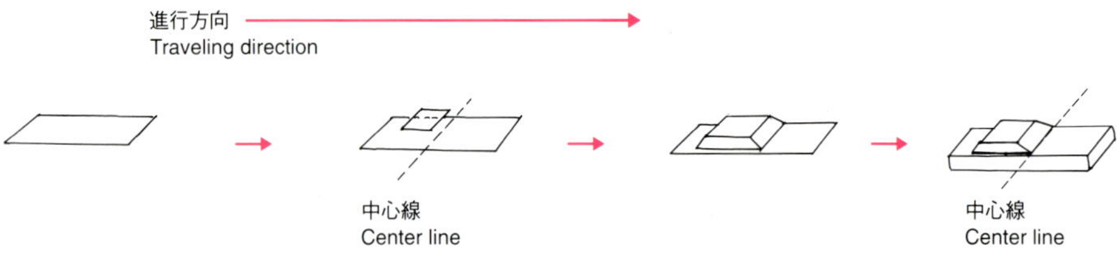

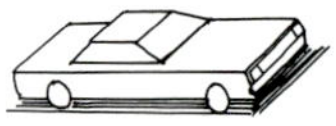

4. 人物の描き方 How to paint human elements

外観パースの人物は、近景・中景・遠景のいずれの場合であっても、目線（HL線）上に頭がそろうように描きます。それらは、ただ、人物の大きさが変わり、それぞれの足元の位置が右の図のように異なるだけです。また、首は、頭と胴体を切り離すことで表現します。

When adding people to exterior perspectives, draw them so that their heads are aligned with the eye level（HL line）regardless of whether they are in the foreground, near distance or long distance. They should differ only in size and the position of their feet, as shown in the illustration below. Their necks can be expressed by separating the head portion from the body portion.

A. 外観パースでの表現 How to paint human elements in exterior perspectives

人物の基本的なシルエットの描き方
How to paint basic silhouettes of people

人物の描き方における、大人と子供の違いは、子供の場合、頭と胴体を大人よりも大きく太く、また、短めに表現する点にあります。

The difference in rendering adults and children in perspectives is that the heads and bodies of the children are rendered larger, broader and shorter than those of adults.

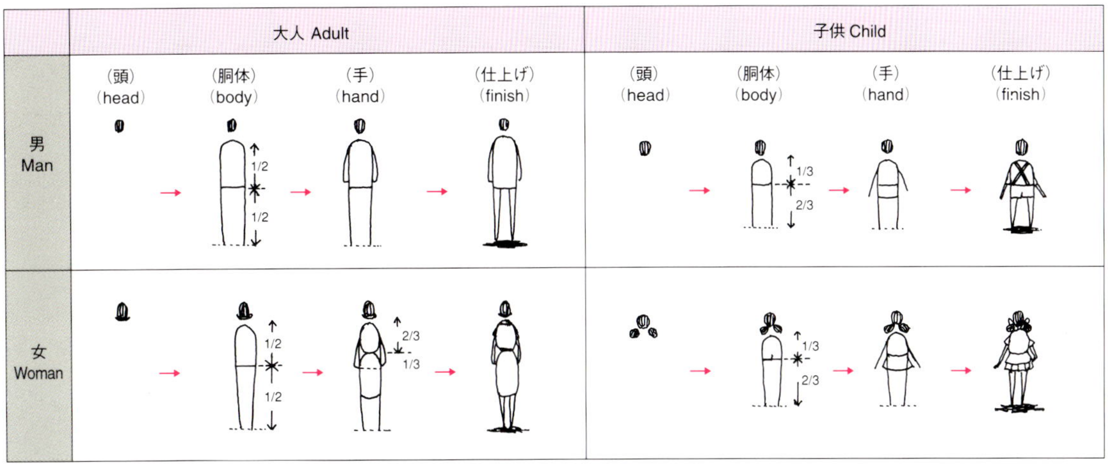

B. 鳥瞰パースでの表現 Expression in bird's-eye view perspectives

鳥瞰パースの人物は、外観パースの場合と異なり、建物の大きさから人物の大きさ（1.5〜1.6m）を割り出し、それに合わせて人物を描きます。また、近景・中景・遠景での大きさの違いは、あまり感じられないので、同じ大きさに描いてもかまいません。ただ、外観パースと違って、頭と胴体をくっ付けて首の表現をしない点に注意して下さい。
特に、目線が高い場合は、点のようなシルエットだけになることもあり、そのような場合でも、黒っぽい色で頭の表現はしておく方がよいでしょう。さらに、にぎやかな感じを表現する場合は、いろいろな明るい色でシルエットを着色すれば、はなやかになります。
また、人物の細かい表現が不可能なことから、鳥瞰パースでのシルエット着色は、白だけでシルエット着色した後に、シルエットの半分下の部分にあざやかな色を重ね塗りして、黒っぽい色で頭を点で描き入れると、人物らしい表現が出来ます。

People are rendered differently in bird's-eye view perspectives than in exterior perspectives: the first step in rendering them is determining their size(1.5-1.6m) in proportion to the size of the building. Since the size of the people can't be conveyed by the difference of distance, it doesn't matter if they are of the same size. The only difference is that their heads and bodies are not separated, as opposed to the case in exterior perspectives.
Especially in the case of higher eye-level perspectives, the people are expressed as silhouettes consisting of many dots. Even when using that type of expression, it is better to render the heads in dark colors. The best way to express a gay atmosphere in the perspective is to use brighter colors for the silhouettes.
Since it is difficult to include the details of the people rendered in bird's-eye view perspectives, begin by coloring their silhouettes only in white. Next, lay the dark colors over the lower half of their bodies, and paint their heads using blackish colors to make them look realistic.

人物の表現
How to paint people

●大人の着色 Coloring adults

(男)(Male)

遠景 far distance　　中景 near distance　　近景 foreground

(女)(Female)

●子供の着色 Coloring children

(男の子)(Male child)

遠景 far distance　　中景 near distance　　近景 foreground

(女の子)(Female child)

●鳥瞰の人物の着色 Coloring people in bird's-eye view perspectives

(男)(Male)　　(女)(Female)

鳥瞰での人物は、小さく描かれることから男と女は色で区別します。

Since people have to be quite small in bird's-eye view perspectives,the males and females are distinguished by the color.

C. リアルな人物の描き方 How to paint people realistically

写真や雑誌等を見て、デッサンするのが最もよい方法ですが、かなり絵心が必要になってきます。
そこで、簡単な方法として、写真や雑誌から選び出した人物の上に、トレーシングペーパーをかぶせて鉛筆でなぞり、それをコピー機を使って必要な大きさに変えて、鉄筆で下図に写し取ると、誰にでもリアルな人物を描くことが出来ます。右の写真は、そうして描き上げた淡彩パースです。

The best way to practice painting people realistically is to sketch the subjects of photographs in magazines. Whatever your approach is, the most important thing is to have a knack for drawing.
One of the simple methods that can be recommended is to use a human subject from a photograph or magazine. After covering it in tracing paper and tracing out the basic form, you can copy it with a copier, adjusting it to the required size with the machine, and then copy it directly onto the sketch. This simple procedure will enable you to draw the human elements in your perspective more realistically. The pictures shown on the LH side are lightly colored examples prepared using this method.

リアルな人物の着色表
Coloring process for realistic rendering of people

5. 空の描き方 How to paint skies

従来のパース画は、空をボードや紙の色（一般的にグレー系が多いようです）を利用し、雲だけを白で表現する方法がとられていました。最近では、パースの用途の変化にともない空も建物同様、よりリアルに表現されるようになり、よく晴れた青空と雲を表現することが一般的になっています。

Traditionally, board or paper colors have been used in rendering the sky in perspectives (in general grayish colors), with the clouds expressed in white. With the recent changes in the purpose of perspectives, however, the sky is often expressed more realistically. Thus, blue skies with scattered clouds are now often seen.

A. 筆塗りによる空の着色 Coloring skies with a paintbrush

まず、空全体を水で湿らせておき、プルシャンブルーとビリジャンに白を加えた空色をつくり、大きな刷毛のような筆にたっぷりつけて、部分的に絵の具を伸ばしながら塗り込み、余白を雲として表現します。この場合、筆にふくめた絵の具をよく伸ばしながらむらなく塗り込まないと、乾いてから白が浮き上がったり色むらが出来ることがあるので、注意して下さい。
特に、空全体を青空の色でくまなく塗り上げた後で、白色を使い雲を表現する場合は、下塗りの青空の段階で、色むらがなくなるまで何度も絵の具を伸ばしてならすことが大切です。他方、白で雲だけを描き入れる場合は、特に、下の図の位置で、雲を描き入れることを初心者の方にすすめます。

Moisten the entire sky area with water, and mix a sky color by adding white to Prussian blue and viridian. Soak the colors sufficiently into a large brush and spread the paint over the sky area, partially extending it, but leaving the clouds unpainted. If the colors haven't been absorbed into the brush or spread well enough, whites can appear on the surface, or the paint may mottle after the colors dry.
When you underpaint the clouds in the sky with white after applying a coat of blue over the entire sky area, it is especially important to thoroughly spread the colors until no color mottling can be found. If only white is being used to express the clouds, however, it's recommendable for beginners to draw in the clouds when they sketch the perspective.

大・中・小の雲を下の図のように配置すると、安定感のある構図になります。
If the clouds are composed in various sizes, as shown in the sample, you will be able to obtain stabilized composition.

●ヨコ長の建物の場合
For the rendering of a building having the width in horizontal direction

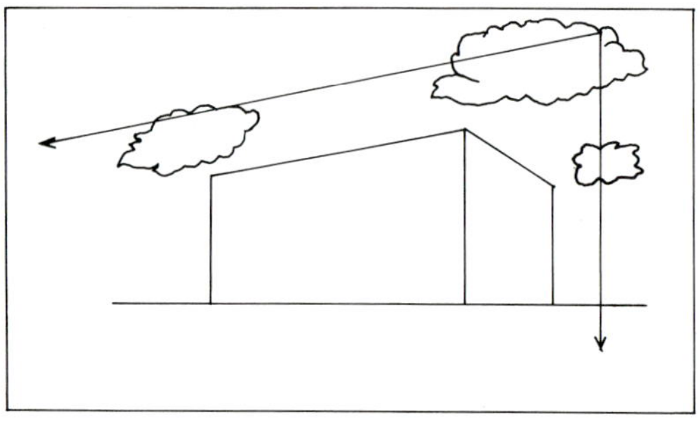

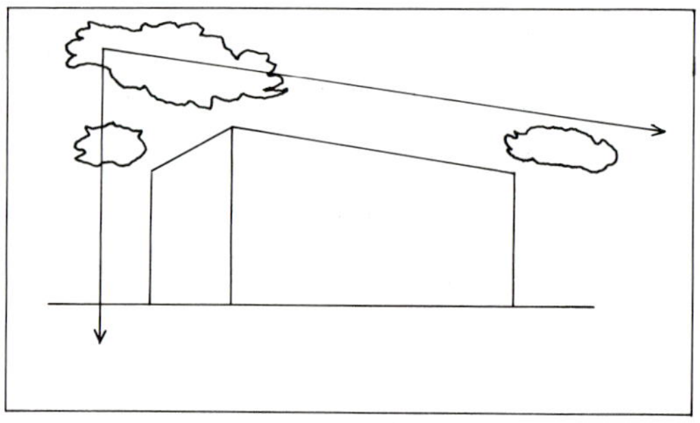

●タテ長の建物の場合
For the rendering of a tallbuilding

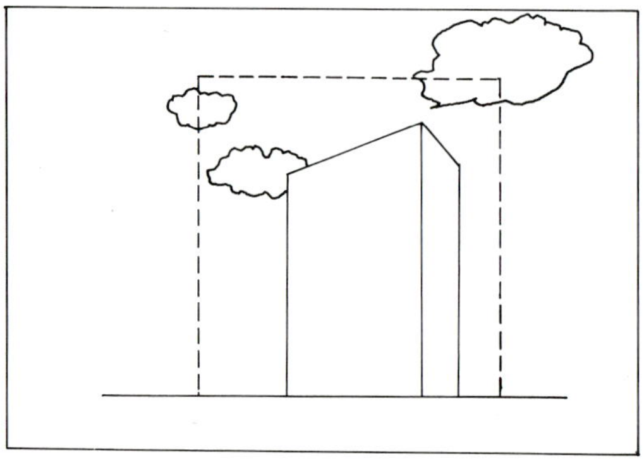

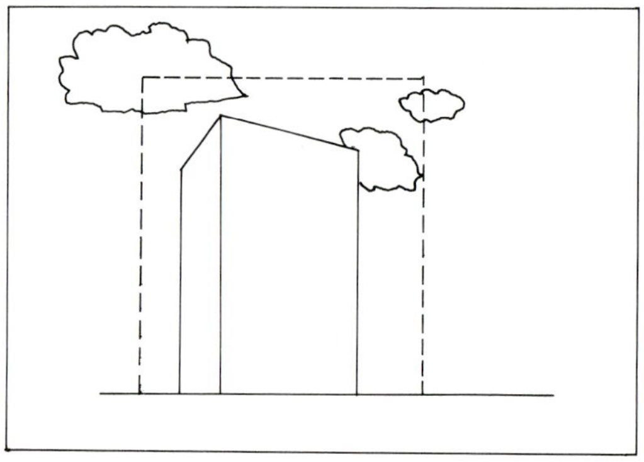

B. エアーブラシによる空の着色 Coloring skies using an airbrush

空色だけで表現する場合は、白い紙に描く場合と、グレー系の紙に描く場合とでは、その絵の具の濃さを変えなければなりません。白い紙では、マンガニーズブルー等の透明水彩絵の具だけで淡く吹き付ける方が発色もよいでしょう。グレー系の紙の場合は、不透明水彩絵の具、つまり、白を混ぜ合わせた色で吹き付けます。また、雲を表現する場合は、全体的に青空の色を吹き付けて、それが乾いてから、白で大・中・小の3種類の雲の形に吹き付けるとよいでしょう。

If you are only using sky color to express the sky, different densities of color should be used for grayish-colored paper and white paper. On white paper, spraying only clear watercolors like manganese blue will help to develop the required color. With grayish color paper, however, it is better to spray on opaques mixed by adding the color white. When expressing the clouds, spray a white on in the shape of clouds after the entire sky has been covered with a bluish color and dried.

空色で下塗りした後、白だけで雲を描き入れたパース画.
Perspective in which clouds are painted with white after the entire sky are has been underpainted.

グレーのボードに白を混ぜた空色を吹き付けた後に、白で雲を吹き付けたパース画.
Perspective in which the clouds are airbrushed on in white after the sky color has been sprayed in advance over a gray board.

画面をあらかじめ湿らせた後に、空色だけで濃淡表現したパース画.
Perspective in which the shade of color is expressed by the sky color after dampening the paper with water in advance.

空色だけで色むらをつけて吹き付けたパース画.
Perspective in which mottling is created by spraying only sky color.

白いボードに空色を先に吹き付けた後に、白で雲を吹き付けたパース画.
Perspective in which the clouds are airbrushed on inwhite after the sky color has been sprayed in advance over a white board

雲はマスキングして、全体的に淡い空色を吹き付けたパース画.
Perspective in which a light sky color is sprayed over the entire sky area after masking the clouds.

6. 屋根や石の描き方 How to paint roofs and stones

A. 屋根の描き方 How to paint roofs

銅板や瓦棒の描き方
How to paint copper slates and batten boards

下地に明暗の変化を入れておきます。
Paint the shade of the color in the sheathing.

細い線で暗い色と明るい色をとなり合わせで描き入れます。
Alternately paint on the fine lines rendered in dark and bright colors.

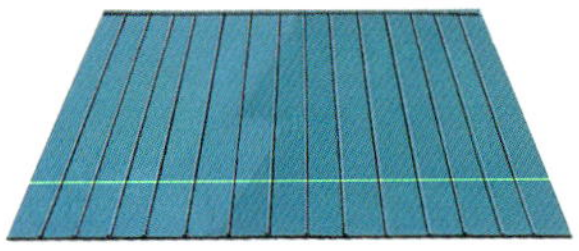

厚みを入れて仕上げます。
Express the thickness.

カラーベスト／シングルの描き方
How to color asbestos shingles

下地に明暗の変化を入れておきます。
Paint the shade of the color in the sheathing.

金網ブラシを使って暗いザラ目と明るいザラ目を入れます。
Use rough scratching brushstrokes for the dark and bright colors using a wire brush.

細かい横線を入れて仕上げます。
Finish the roof by drawing fine horizontal lines.

和瓦の描き方
How to paint Japanese-style roof tiles

下塗り時に明るい部分と暗い部分をつくります。
Paint dark and bright areas during the underpainting process.

暗い色の線は間隔を広めにあけて描き入れ、明るい色の線は暗い色にくっ付けて描き入れます。
Paint the dark lines with wider pitch so that the bright lines come into contact with the dark lines.

瓦の厚みを暗い色で描き加え、瓦の線はゆるやかな曲線で描き入れて下さい。のせ瓦は太く描く方が和瓦らしく見えます。
Paint the thickness of the roof tiles in dark colors, and paint the tile lines with a moderate curve. If the roof tiles placed on the roof are drawn wider, they will look more like Japanese-style roof tiles.

S瓦の描き方
How to paint "S" roof tiles

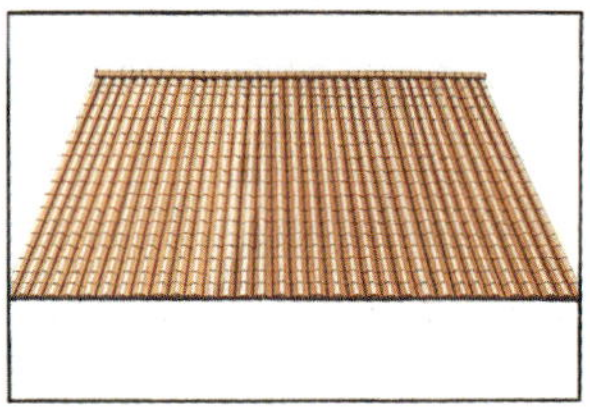

下塗り時に明るい部分と暗い部分をつくります。
Paint dark and bright areas during the underpainting process.

暗い色の線は間隔を小さめにあけて描き入れ、明るい色の線をその暗い線の真中に描くようにします。
Paint the dark lines with a narrower pitch so that the bright-colored lines come between the dark-colored lines.

瓦の厚みは山の連続で描き、瓦の線は曲りの急な曲線で描き入れて下さい。のせ瓦は、あまり太くしない方がいいでしょう。
Paint the thickness of the roof tiles as a continuity with the mountains, and paint the tile lines as a sharp curve. Do not paint the tiles placed on the roof wider.

B. 石の描き方 How to paint stones

玉石・砂利石の描き方
How to paint pebbles and gravel

イエロー・オーカー＋白＋黒＋バーント・アンバーの色で色むらをつくりながら濃淡のある下塗り着色をします。

Spread an undercoat in a shade obtained by mottling yellow ocher, white, black and burnt umber.

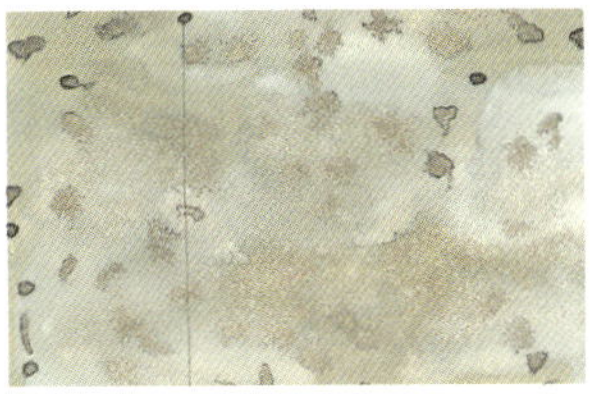

少し暗い色で下塗りの色が乾かないうちに点を描き込みます。

Paint over slightly dark dots before the undercoating is completely dried.

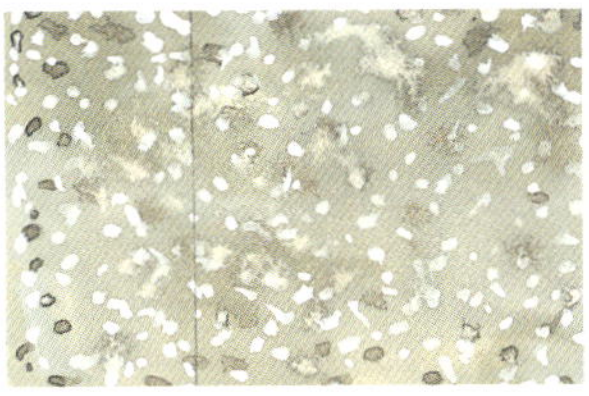

さらに白の多い色で石のハイライトを描き加えます。

Render the highlights on the stones with whitish colors.

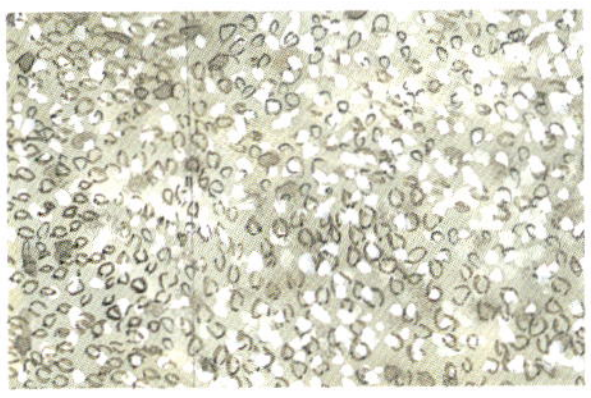

細い丸筆で石の形を部分的に描き込み、さらに細い鉛筆で石の形を描き加えます。

Use a round brush to partially render the details of the stones and drawing their shapes using a fine pencil.

くずれ石の描き方
How to paint broken stones

イエロー・オーカー＋白＋黒＋バーント・アンバーの色で全体的な着色をした後、上部は明るく下部は暗く着色します。

After painting over all of the stones with mixed yellow ochers, white, black and burnt umber, spread brighter colors over the upper portions and darker colors over the lower portions.

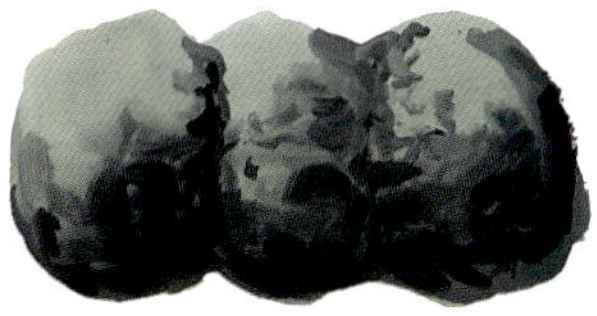

下部の暗い部分にさらに丸筆を使ってより暗い色で立体感を表現します。

Express three dimensions at the lower portion by adding dark colors using a round brush.

上部の部分に白の多く混ざった明るい色で石のハイライトを描き入れてより立体的にします。

Highlight the stones in the upper portion with whitish bright colors to express the three dimensions of the stones more clearly.

細い丸筆で石の表情を描き込みます。

Use a fine round brush to convey the feeling of stones.

御影石の描き方（黒御影石）
How to paint granite black granite）

●ジェット仕上げ及びタタキ仕上げ Jet finishing and bush hammering finishing

イエロー・オーカー＋白＋黒の暗いグレーで全体を着色します。

Paint over all of the stones in a dark gray color produced with yellow ocher, white and black.

その色に、白を加えてラフな明るい面を作ります。

Add more white to that color to create a rough bright surface.

さらに、白を加えてより明るいラフな面を重ね塗りで作ります。もし、色むらがあっても気にする必要はないでしょう。

Add yet more white and lay brighter colors over rough treated surface. It doesn't matter if some mottling occurs at this stage.

金網ブラシを使って暗い色のツブツブを落とします。

Scratch off the fine dark particles using a wire brush.

●ミガキ仕上げ Polish finishing

イエロー・オーカー＋白＋黒の暗いグレーで全体を着色します。

Paint the entire stone area with a dark gray produced with yellow ocher, white and black.

その色に、白を多く加えて光の反射した状態を表現します。ミガキ仕上げであることからメタリックに見えるように直線的に描きます。色むらは気にする必要はありません。

Add white to that color to express the reflection of light. Since polish finishing is required here, render the stones with straight lines so that they look metallic. It is perfectly all right if mottling occurs at this stage.

さらに、ほかの建物の映り込みを黒の多く混ざった色で直線的な面で描き入れます。

Paint the reflection of the building on a straight plane using a blackish color.

金網ブラシを使って鈍黒のブツブツを落とします。

Scratch off the fine particles of dull black using a wire brush.

打放しコンクリートの描き方
How to paint exposed finished concrete

イエロー・オーカー＋白＋黒＋バーント・アンバーで暖色系のグレーをつくり、全体的に着色します。

Apply a layer of warm system gray mixed by adding yellow ocher, white, black and burnt umber over the entire exposed finish of the concrete surface.

下塗りの色に白を加えた明るい色でラフな感じに重ね塗りします。

Lay bright colors produced by adding white to the underpainted color over the underpaint roughly.

白を多く加えた明るい色でさらに明るい部分を作ります。この時、前段階の色の面を残すように重ね塗りします。

Produce the brighter area by applying a color with large amounts of white added. The color of this preliminary painted area should be left without any further additional layers.

細い鉛筆で打放しコンクリートの特徴である木目と点を加えます。

Use a fine pencil to draw the scratch lines and dots that are characteristic of the exposed concrete surface.

大理石の描き方
How to paint marble stones

イエロー・オーカー＋白＋黒で下塗りをします。

Spread an underpainting of colors produced with yellow ocher, white and black.

さらに、白を多く加えた色で明るい面を作ります。

Use a color with a large amount of white added to render a brighter plane.

さらに白っぽい色で重ね塗りして、より明るい面を作ります。

If you would like a much brighter plane, spread the whitish color even further.

下塗りの色に黒とバーント・アンバーを加えた暗い色で大理石の特徴である筋目を入れます。筋目は途中で線を途切れさせたり、太さを変えたりするとよりリアルな表現になります。

Paint stripes to convey the characteristic of the marble material using a dark color mixed by adding black and burnt umber to the underpainted colors. When painting the stripes, cut them off on the way or change their width for a more realistic rendering of the stones.

第5章

うまく描けなかった場合の処理

Chapter 5

How to touch up the perspective

うまく描けなかった場合のチェックポイントと注意

Checkpoints and cautions when touching up

1. 筆塗りパースの着色における問題点 Problems in coloring perspectives with a paintbrush

窓ガラスの着色
Coloring window glasses

❶ 重ね塗りによる透明感がなく、全体的に明るくぼけているか、反対に暗くて重ね塗りによる色の変化がない場合
If the color sense appears subdued due to the overlaying of paint and the entire window glass is brightly shaded off, or if the windows are too dark and no color gradation is expressed, this might be caused by the amount of water added to the colors

絵の具と水の加え方に問題があります。重ね塗りする過程で、淡い色ばかりで重ね塗りしていませんか。反対に、着色しはじめた色から、すでに濃すぎていませんか。
〈絵の具と水加減による濃淡参考図（p.58）〉に自分のつくった色を試し塗りして、合わせながら描いてみて下さい。

Are you laying light colors only when overlaying the paint? Or are you laying excessively dark colors from the very beginning of the coloring process?
Try to spread your color over the shade in the "Reference chart of depth of colors by type of color and amount of water added (p.58)" to compare the shade before laying your colors.

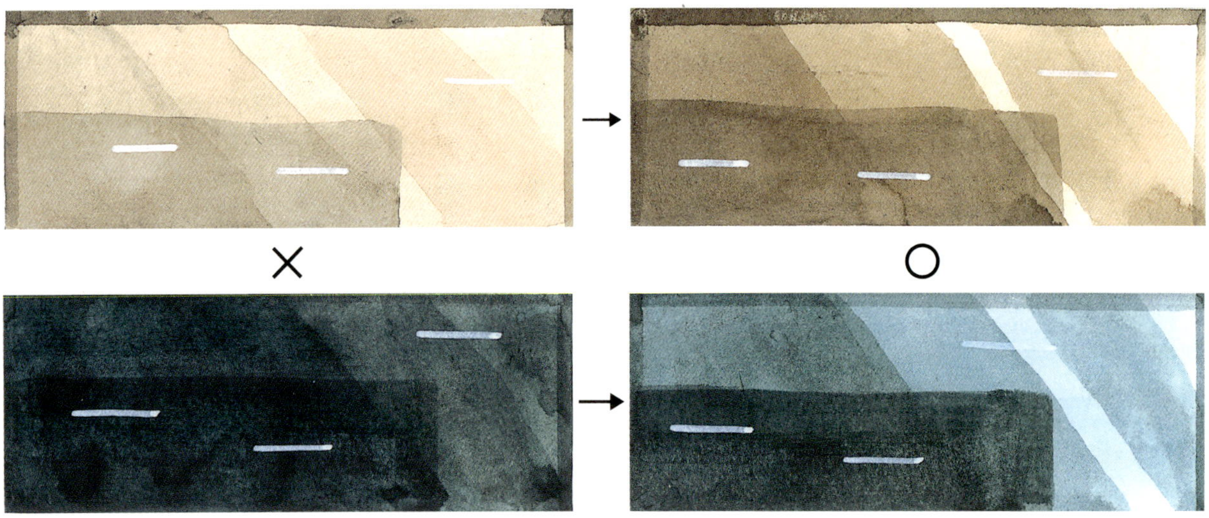

❷窓ガラス面の色がにごって見える場合 If the window glass looks clouded

暖色ニュートラルや寒色ニュートラルを多く加えすぎていませんか。また、淡い色の着色段階で、ニュートラル色を加えていませんか。

Are you adding too much of warm neutral or cold neutral? Or you adding neutral colors when applying light colors?

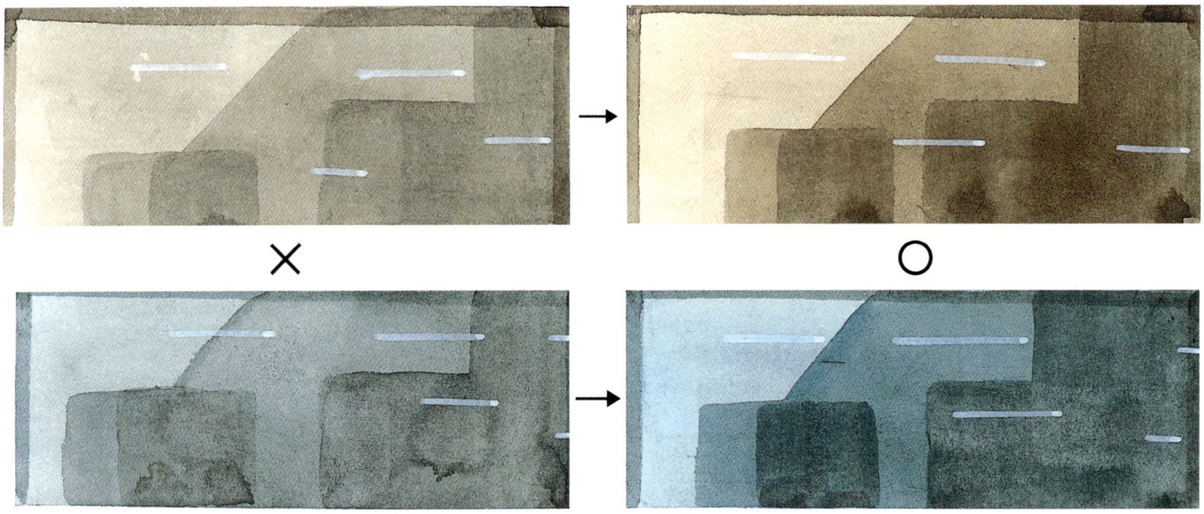

❸ 窓ガラス面がゆがんで見える場合 If the window glass looks distorted

濃い色を重ね塗りしていく過程で、焦点に合った描き込みをしないと、ゆがんで見えます。どんな色を重ね塗りする時も、焦点に合った描き込みをして下さい。

If you fail to align your rendering with the focus when laying dark colors, the window pane will look warped. Never fail to match with the focus while overlaying any colors.

×

→

○

❹ 窓ガラス面に、カスレや色むらが出来る場合 If scratching or mottling appears on the window panes

筆にたっぷりと絵の具をつけて手早く塗れば、カスレません。反対に、余分な絵の具を窓ガラス面に残すと色むらが出来ます。出来るだけ余分な絵の具は外壁面まで引き伸ばせば、色むらがなくなります。

Scratches of color can be avoided if you use quick brushstrokes with ample color soaked in the brush. Leaving excessive colors on the window can result in mottling, however. If you spread as much of the excess color over to the surface of the exterior wall as you can you will be able to eliminate any mottling.

×

→

○

外壁面の着色
Coloring exterior walls

❶こってりとして絵の具むらがある場合 If the colors on the exterior wall look too heavy and some mottling can be seen

絵の具が濃すぎていませんか。化粧品の乳液よりも水っぽくして下さい。また、塗り始めた時、絵の具が盛り上がっていませんか。よく絵の具を伸ばしながら平均的に着色して下さい。この他、筆先にたまった余分な絵の具を取り除いていますか。もし、取り除いていないなら、パレットの角や雑巾で取り除いて下さい。

Aren't the colors too heavy? Dilute them until they become a little more watery than cosmetic milk lotion. Avoid too much color when you begin spreading the paint. Spread the colors well and uniformly. Remove any excess colors remaining in the brush. Make it a habit to remove the excess colors from the brush using the corner of a palette or a duster.

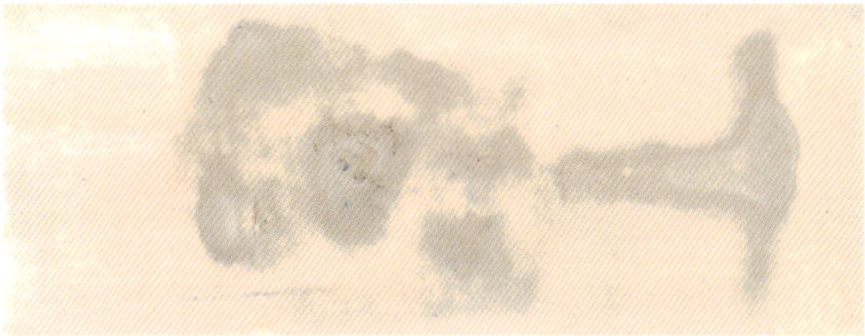

×

→

○

❷ 何度も重ね塗りしても、ガラス面の色が浮き上がってくる場合 If any of the overlaid colors conceal the previously laid colors

絵の具が濃すぎるか、乾ききらないうちに重ね塗りをくり返していませんか。

Are you spreading excessively heavy colors? Are you repeating the overlay of colors before the previously laid color is dried?

×

→

○

❸ 正面壁と側面壁が別の材質に見える場合 If the material in the front exterior wall looks different from that used in the side wall

外壁色の彩度が合っていません。側面壁の暗い色をつくる時に、純色を多く加えて下さい。

The chroma of the color used for the front and side exterior wall doesn't match. When producing the dark color for the side exterior wall, add an ample amount of pure colors.

×

→

○

❹ 影が不自然に見える場合 If the shadow looks unnatural

彩度が合っていません。明るい壁面より影の彩度は低いので、純色を多く加えて下さい。

The chroma of the color doesn't match. Since the chroma in the shade is lower than that on the surface of the bright exterior wall, add an ample amount of pure colors.

×

→

○

❺ 色の変化が不自然に見えたり、絵の具が盛り上がっている場合 If the gradation of color doesn't look natural, or if the colors looks raised

彩度が合っていないので、下地の色とよく見比べて「純色と白・灰・黒の混合による変化」を見ながら彩度を合わせて下さい。絵の具が盛り上がるのは絵の具が濃すぎるか、筆先の余分な絵の具を取り除いていないからです。絵の具を水でうすめるか、雑巾等で余分な絵の具を取り除いて下さい。

Since this is caused when the color chroma does not match, match the color chroma by comparing it with the previously laid colors (color variation made by mixting pure colors with white, gray or black). The rise of colors is caused by excessively heavy colors or excess colors remaining in the brush. Dilute the colors with water, or remove the excess colors in the brush with a dusting cloth.

×

→

○

2. エアーブラシパースの着色における問題点 Problems encountered in coloring when using an airbrush

窓ガラスの吹き付け
Spraying or window glasses

❶ 暗くて色の濃淡がなくなってしまった場合 If the colors are too dark and the color shade is lost

最も暗い部分から吹き付けるようにしていますか。また、明るい部分へと吹き付けていく過程で、吹き付けすぎていませんか。マスキングフィルムが貼り付けてある状態で明るく見えても、フィルムを取り除くとかなり暗く吹き付けられているので注意して下さい。

Are you trying to spray colors from the dark area? Are you spraying too much as you move to the brighter portions? Even if the color looks bright while the canvas is still masked, you will find the colors look darker when the masking film is removed.

×

→

○

❷ 透明感がない場合 If no clear color sense can be felt

着色する色が、筆塗りとは全く逆になるので、筆塗りによるガラス面の着色過程と逆になるように、色も着色も変えなければなりません。

Since the process used to spray the color is a reversal of the processed using an ordinary paintbrush, reverse the colors and coloring sequence used for the coloring of the window panes.

×

→

○

❸ 着色した部分がよごれる場合 If the portion where the color is spread becomes soiled

吹き付けた後、必ず、ドライヤーを使って冷風で乾かして下さい。乾いていない状態でマスキングフィルムを取り外すと、手に絵の具が付いて、画面をよごすおそれがあります。

Never fail to dry the colors with cool air using a dryer after they are sprayed on. If the masking film is removed while the colors are still wet, colors might stick to your hands and soil the perspective.

×

○

外壁面の吹き付け
Spraying on exterior walls

❶思い通りの色が吹き付けられていない場合 If the colors can't be sprayed as required

乾くと絵の具の色が変ります。吹き付ける前に、白い紙の上に試し吹きして色を確かめていますか。また、暗い色であっても水加減で違った色になります。従って、水でうすめる度に必ず試し吹きして下さい。

Colors tends to change when they dry. Spray a bit of the paint on a sheet of white paper and wait until it dries to confirm the color before spraying it onto the perspective. Even the darker colors might change when different amounts of water are added, so it is also important to do trial sprays for them whenever they are diluted.

❷ブツブツが飛びちってくる場合 If the fine particles are scattered

エアーブラシのピースガンがつまっているので、きれいな水で掃除して下さい。

The piece gun of the airbrush is clogged. Clean the piece gun with clean water.

❸水っぽい絵の具が吹き付けられる場合 If watery colors are sprayed

ピースガンがつまっているか、あまり長時間吹き付けすぎていませんか。長時間吹き付けると、水だれが生じたり、不自然な濃さになるので、冷風で乾かしながら吹き付けて下さい。

The piece gun of the airbrush might be clogged or it may have been used for a long period. The use of the piece gun for a long period can sometimes result in water drip, and sometimes the density of the colors starts to look unnatural. To avoid this, keep it dry with cooled air while using it for spraying.

❹色の明暗や濃淡がなくて、暗すぎる場合 If the brightness or shade of colors cannot be expressed, or if the colors are too dark

全体的に吹き付けすぎています。出来るだけ、基準線寄りや、正面壁と側面壁の境目を集中的に吹き付けるようにして下さい。また、濃淡が極端なぐらいに見えるように吹き付けるのがコツです。

Too much spraying as a whole. Try to concentrate the spraying on the area closer to the reference line or boundary between the front and side exterior walls. The trick is to spray so that the shade can be quite distinctly seen.

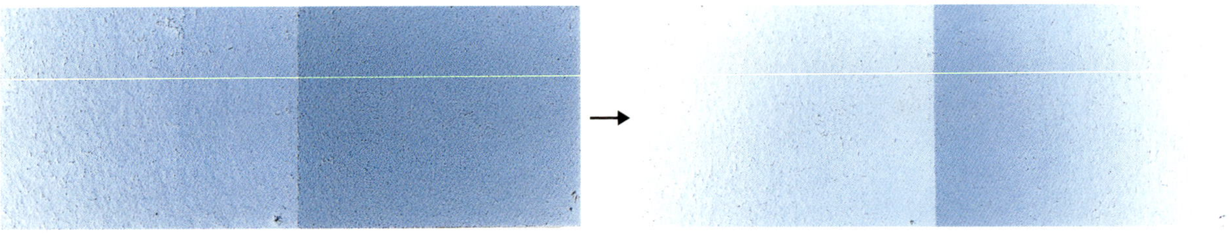

× → ○

❺マスキングフィルムを取り外したら、かなり暗く吹き付けられていた場合

If the color turns out to be too dark when the masking film is removed

マスキングフィルムが被っている状態で、白く明るく見えても、かなり暗い色が吹き付けられていることに注意して、明るめに吹き付けを終えるようにして下さい。コツとしては、吹き付ける度に白い紙を合わせて比較しながら見ると、暗さがわかり易いでしょう。

Even if the colors look white and bright while the perspective is still masked, fairly dark colors have often been sprayed. To avoid this, try to spray coloring that will brighten the finish somewhat. The trick is to perform a trial spray over white paper and compare the colors whenever they are sprayed. This method will enable you to judge the darkness more accurately.

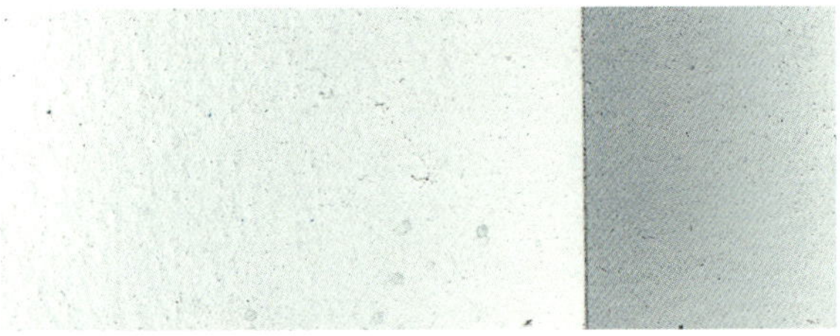

× →

○

❻彩度が合わないで不自然に見える場合 If the color chroma does not match and looks unnatural

影や正面・側面を吹き付ける時、別々の色で吹き付けないで、最も暗い色を中心にして、水加減で明るい色をつくるようにして吹き付けるようにしてみて下さい。

Avoid using different colors when spraying over the shade, front and side exterior walls. Prepare the colors for spraying by adjusting the amount of water added, centering on the darkest color.

3. 淡彩パースの着色における問題点 Problems encountered when finishing perspectives in light colors

❶ けばけばしい色のパースになった場合 If the perspective finished becomes too loud

純色での着色が多くありませんか。出来るだけ「透明水彩絵の具による着色」(p.87)を参照してニュートラル色を加えながら彩度をおさえて下さい。

The colors that you are using may be too pure. Reduce the chroma by adding as many neutral colors as possible referring to the section "Coloring of clear watercolors." (p.87)

× ○

❷ 白っぽい色がつくれない場合 If it is impossible to produce whitish colors

白っぽい色は、白を加えてつくるのではなく、紙の白さを生かす方法で着色するので、水を多く加えて水っぽい色で着色して下さい。参考にp.58の「絵の具と水加減」を再度読んで下さい。

Whitish colors are not necessarily produced by adding white paint. Often, the whiteness of the paper is used. If necessary, therefore, spread watery colors by adding an ample amount of water. For your reference, read the section "Ratio of colors and water "(p.58) again.

× ○

❸ 色むらが出来る場合 If mottling appears in the perspective

広い面を着色する場合は、あらかじめ使用する色を多めに調合して、筆にたっぷり付けて着色します。また、途中で水を加えると色むらの原因になります。絶対に途中で水を加えてはなりません。一度に塗り上げる自信のない時は、部分的に塗り上げるのがコツであると同時に、暗い色で着色する部分は無視して塗り込んでいくと色むらが防げるでしょう。

Before spreading the colors over the large portion, produce an ample amount of the color in advance. Spread the color after it has been sufficiently soaked into the brush. Adding water while the color is being spread causes mottling. Never add water in the middle of coloring. If you are not confident about finishing up the coloring at a stretch, attempt to spread the color partially. If you stay calm and continue spreading the dark colors over the dark finishing areas you will be able to avoid mottling.

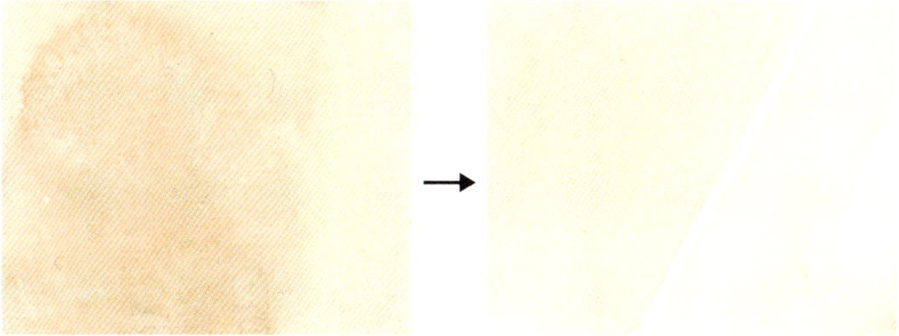

× ○

❹ 急に暗い色になった場合 If the colors suddenly turn dark

同じ濃さの色を乾いた後に重ね塗りして暗くする方法で着色して下さい。乾いていないと色むらの原因になります。

Employ the method to darken the portions by overlaying a color of the same density after the previously laid color has dried. Overlaying color without waiting for the previously laid color to dry results in mottling.

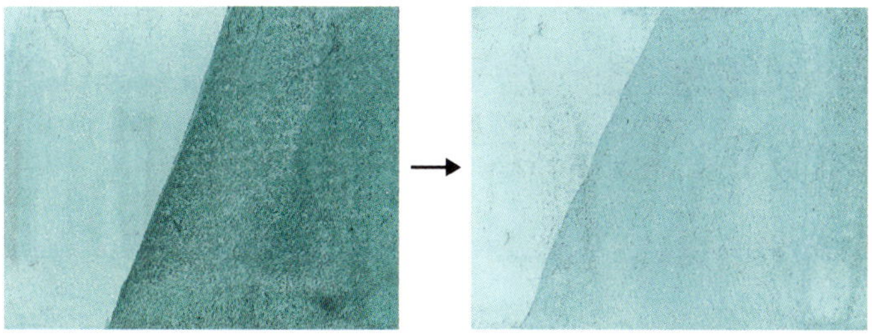

× ○

❺ 着色後、顔料の分離がおきた場合 If the pigments are separated after coloring

塗り始める前に、パレット上で、絵の具と水をよく混ぜ合わせていますか。

Do you thoroughly blend the colors with water on the palette before starting the coloring?

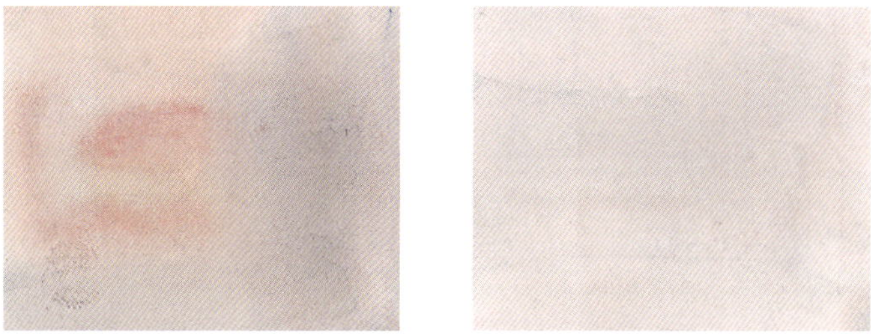

× ○

❻ 形が複雑で塗りにくい場合 If the shapes are too complicated to lay colors

部分的に「すき間」を開けて着色していくようにして下さい。

Try to make a partial "space" while coloring.

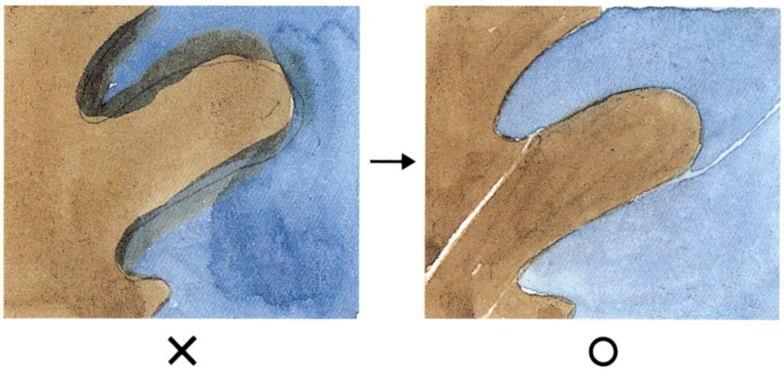

❼ 形が細かくて、塗っていくうちに色むらやシミが出来る場合 If the shapes are too fine and the coloring becomes mottled or smeared

暗い色で着色する部分は無視して、淡い色から着色して下さい。暗い色や、高彩度の色で着色すべき部分は、淡い色がはみ出していても、後から着色されると目立たなくなります。

Ignore the areas colored in darker paints, and start the coloring with the lighter colors. Even if the lighter colors seep out of their areas, they can be later be concealed if they are in areas to be covered with high-chroma or dark colors.

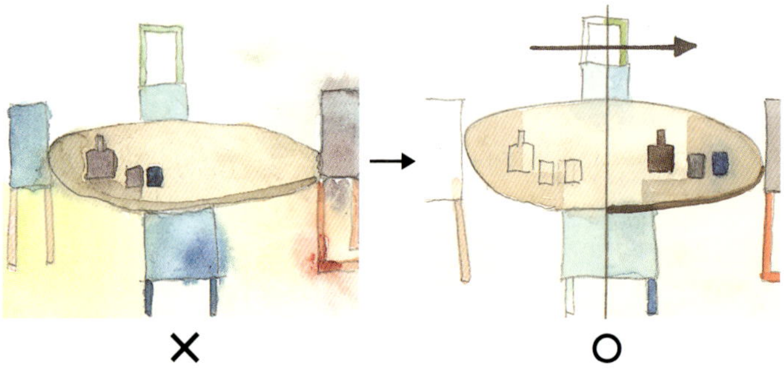

❽ 色がにごって、絵がきたない場合 If the colors become clouded and the perspective gets foul

黒を混ぜたり、白を混ぜたりしていませんか。出来るだけ、白っぽい色は水を多く加えることでつくるようにして、反対に、暗い色はニュートラル色を加えることでつくるように努めて下さい。

Are you adding the black and white colors alternately? Try to produce the whitish colors by adding ample amounts of water, and the dark colors by adding neutral colors.

❾ 絵にメリハリがない場合 If the perspective lacks modulation

小さくて、細かく暗い部分は、出来るだけ濃くて暗い色で着色して下さい。また、全体的に、暗い色で着色していませんか。

Spread heavy and dark colors on the small, fine and dark areas. Are you spreading the dark colors over larger areas in the perspective?

❿ 絵に安定感がない場合 If the perspective lacks stability

インテリアパースでの床は、不透明水彩絵の具で着色すると安定感と質感が表現されやすいでしょう。外観パースの場合は、不透明・透明に限らず、暗く路面を着色すると安定感が出るでしょう。

More stability and massiveness can be expressed in interior perspectives if you use opaque watercolors over the floor. For exterior perspectives, spreading dark colors (either clear or opaque) over the road, will convey a more stabilized feeling.

⓫ 水ぼてが出来る場合 If blemishes are caused in the perspective

着色後、画面上に残る余分な絵の具を、筆で吸い取るようにして下さい。

Try to absorb the excess color on the canvas with the paintbrush after the coloring has been finished.

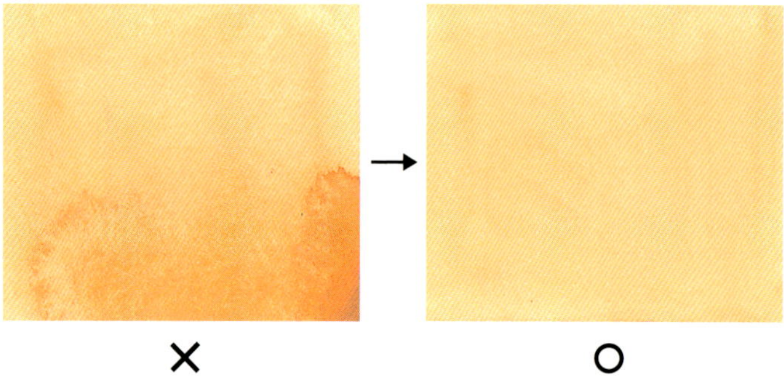

第6章
作品の実際

Chapter 6
Actual Works

1. 筆塗りによる作品 Works prepared using paintbrush

空を白い雲だけで表現し、建物のポイントカラーである赤色を強調した筆塗りパースの作品。
Perspective in which sky is expressed only by the white clouds, with emphasis on the red used as the point color for the building.

木造住宅の木製部分の色調を生かし、外溝や植栽の色調も自然な色で筆塗りされたパース作品。
Perspective in which the color tone of the wooden portions of the wooden house is utilized, with the exterior landscape and plants painted in natural colors.

不透明水彩絵の具で材質感をリアルに表現した筆塗りインテリアパースの作品。
Perspective in which the texture of the construction material is expressed in opaque watercolors using paintbrush.

ガラス面の透明表現が強調された筆塗りパースの作品。
Paintbrush perspective with special emphasis on the clearness of the surfaces of the windows.

2. エアーブラシによる作品 Works finished by airbrush

エアーブラシによって、濃淡表現をきつくしたパースであるが、ソフトな仕上りのパース作品。
Perspectives in which the color shade is stressed using an airbrush, but is finished softly.

エアーブラシ着色によって距離感を強調したパース作品。
Perspective in which the expression of the distance of the building is emphasized by airbrushed coloring.

インキングした下図にエアーブラシのみで吹き付け着色されたパース作品。
Perspective in which the finished colors consist only of airbrushed colors over the inking sketch.

その他効果的に着色された作品
Other finished perspectives using colors effectively

エアーブラシによって、ハーフミラーやプレーンな外壁材を短時間に仕上げた作品。
Perspective in which an air brush is used to complete half mirrors, plain outer wall materials, and other works in a short period of time.

エアーブラシによって、ラスタータイルやハーフミラーガラスを効果的に表現したパース作品。
Perspective in which luster tiles and half mirror glass are effectively colored using an airbrush.

エアーブラシによる吹き付けパースの良さが最も生かされたパース作品。
Perspective in which window glass is naturally expressed.

ガラス面の表現が自然なパース作品。
Perspective in which window glass is naturally expressed.

外壁色のはなやかさを自然な感じにする為に、下塗りエアーブラシ仕上げにしたパース作品。
Perspective underpainted with an airbrushing to express a natural gay color for the exterior wall.

一点透視パースの欠点を色調で補ったパース作品。
Perspective in which the drawback of having only one vanishing point is compensated for by the color tone.

下塗りエアーブラシ仕上げによって、和室の高級感を表現したパース作品。
Perspective in which the luxury feeling of a Japanese-style room is expressed by underpainting with an airbrush.

エアーブラシ着色によるリアルな表現のパース作品。
Perspective in which realistic expression is achieved through airbrush coloring.

インキングした下図にエアーブラシで着色し、点景の小さなものは筆塗り着色したパース作品。
Perspective in which the coloring airbrushed over an inking sketch and tiny incidental elements are colored with a paintbrush.

直吹きエアーブラシパースで、近隣の建物を淡いシルエットで表現し、さらに、植栽のはなやかさで建物を引き立たせたパース作品。
Perspective in which the adjacent buildings are lightly silhouetted with an airbrush and the building is set off with abundant greenery.

建物の金属感を強調した、下塗りエアーブラシ着色のパース作品。
Perspective in which the metallic texture of the building is emphasized by the airbrushed underpainting.

ガラス面の透明感を強調し、大都会感を表現したパース作品。
Perspective in which the clearness of the window panes is emphasized and a big-city feeling is expressed.

筆塗りだけで描き上げたパースで、窓ガラスと点景の表現が重要なパース。
Paintbrush perspective in which the expression of the window glass and incidental elements play an important role.

エアーブラシでドームの立体感を表現し、細かい部分は筆塗りで仕上げた典型的なパース作品。
Representative perspective in which an airbrush is used to express a dome in three dimensions and details finished using a paintbrush.

3. 筆塗り併用エアーブラシパースの作品 Works finished with both paintbrush and airbrush

建物の材質感を下塗りエアーブラシ着色で強調し、画面上に木の葉をあしらったパース作品。
Perspective in which the textures of the building materials are emphasized by the airbrushed underpainting and the tree leaves rendered at the upper corner.

筆塗りとエアーブラシを併用して、大きな面の着色をきれいに仕上げたパース作品。
Perspective in which a large area is clearly finished using a combination of paintbrush and airbrush.

ラスタータイルの表現が自然なパース作品。
Perspective in which luster tiles are naturally expressed.

4. 淡彩による作品 Works prepared in light colors

インキングされた下図で、強調すべき部分を集中して淡彩着色されたパース作品。
Perspectives in which light colors are mainly concentrated on the areas that need to be stressed over the inking sketch.

大まかにインキングされた下図の上に、短時間で仕上げられた淡彩パースの作品。
Perspectives which are quickly finished using light colors over a rough inking sketch.

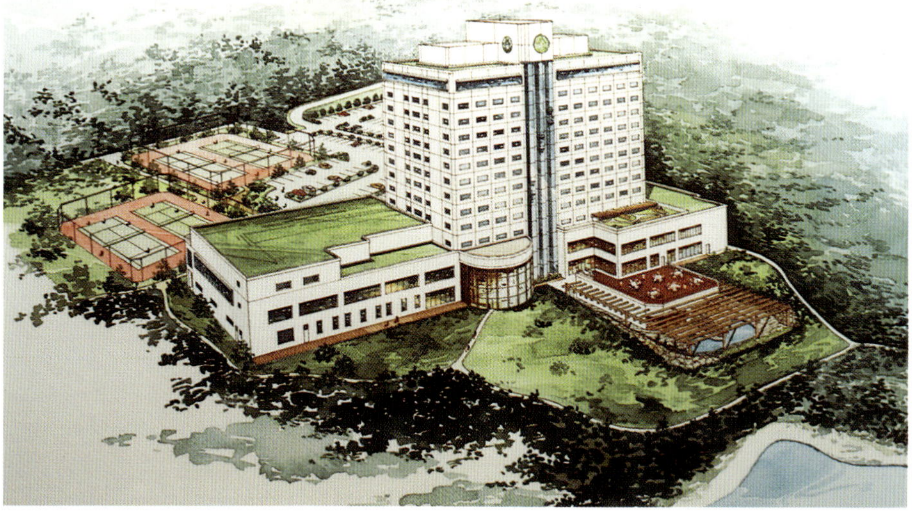

淡彩インテリアパースの作品
Interior perspectives in light color finishes

和風レストランの木製部分を透明水彩絵の具のみで効果的に表現したパース作品。
Perspective in which the wooden portion of a Japanese style restaurant is effectively expressed using clear watercolors.

天井面を淡い色の重ね塗りで表現し、ガラス越しの外部も、淡い色で効果的に着色したパース作品。
Perspective in which ceiling is finished by overlaying light colors, and the exterior seen through the windows is effectively rendered in light colors.

床を除き、比較的淡く着色して仕上げたパース作品。
Perspective in which relatively light colors are used for all portions except the portion of floor.

壁面を淡く水っぽい絵の具で着色したパース作品。
Perspective in which the exterior wall is lightly finished using watery colors.

第7章

実技添削

Chapter 7

Practical skill and postal tuition course

7

応募規定

本書では、著者のご好意により読者の皆様に添削指導も行っております。153頁と154頁にそれぞれ添削用の下図が用意してあります。複写(拡大可)して自分の作品に仕上げて下さい。なお、添削希望の場合は、「仕上げた作品」と「住所氏名を記入し返送できる料金の切手を貼った返信用封筒」、「住所、氏名、年齢、電話番号を明記し、それぞれの下図の角にある「添削シール」(コピー不可)を貼ったA4サイズの用紙」をセットにして下記住所までお送り下さい。

〒102　東京都千代田区九段北1-9-12　谷内ビル
㈱グラフィック社
『建築パース　新戦力マスター』添削係

APPLICATION PROCEDURES

This book features a correction and comment guidance service for readers. On p.153-p.154, you will find drawings for each correction guidance item. For those readers who wish to receive such guidance for their work, copy whichever (or both) drawing is applicable to you, use it as a rough sketch for your own work, then work on the improvements.

When you have completed your work, send it in the following manner to the address provided below. Your corrected work will be returned to you by Federal Express courier service.

HOW TO PROCEED:

1. Contact the Federal Express office nearest to you. Ask for the FEDEX Airway Bill Form, then fill in your name, address, telephone number, and other important items in the space provided on the right for Recipient.
Include this form with your work.
Mailing costs for both sending and returning your work will be defrayed by the reader. For returning the work to you, please indicate in the space provided for TRANSPORTATION CHARGES in the Airway Bill Form (or in a separate piece of paper) whether your payment will be made by credit card or "Bill Sender". Please make sure to specify this or else your work cannot be returned to you.
2. On p.153-p.154, there is also a correction seal (not to be copied) that you can tear off. Attach this on one corner of your work.

Send your work, following the above instructions, by mail or courier to:

MASTERING NEW ARCHITECTURAL
RENDERING TECHNIQUES
c/o Graphic-sha Publishing Co., Ltd.
Yanai Building
1-9-12 Kudan-kita, Chiyoda-ku Tokyo 102 Japan
Phone: 81-3-3263-4318; Fax: 81-3-3263-5297

*Correction service is free-of-charge.

1. 実技添削での注意点 Some considerations in postal tuition service

実践的な練習と復習

今までの過程で、パース画の描き方を説明してきましたが、大切なことは練習することにあります。
そこで、各パターンの下図を挙げておきますので、その下図を使って、この本に従って練習してみましょう。
もし、難しいようであれば、タイル面を吹き付けに変えたり、階高を低くしたり、または、形を簡略したりするとよいでしょう。あるいは、本書の冒頭に示したパースを下図にしてもかまいません。
練習過程で、上手に描けなくても最後まで描き進んで下さい。その後で、上手に描けなかった点を、各項目ごとに再び復習することが大切です。
復習する際に、筆を点検して下さい。例えば、筆を濡らして先をそろえた時に余分な毛が出ていたりして、筆先がきれいにそろっていないなら、カッターナイフで、余分な毛を切ったり筆先をそろえましょう。
また、細い線が引けなかったり、まっ直ぐな線が引けないなら、溝引き定規の使い方を何回も練習する必要があります。出来るだけ、腕全体でスピーディに引く練習をすると同時に、線の始まりと終わりを仮引きして下さい。つまり、実際には線を引かずに、少し筆を浮かして仮引きした上で、下図の線と仮引きが合えば、本引きしてもよいでしょう。
次に問題になるのが色づくりだと思います。色づくりについては、外壁色の色づくりや窓ガラスの色づくりをよく復習して、実際につくってみましょう。この本書で説明した色づくりは、色数も少なく、パース画に必要な色だけを扱っていますので、練習すれば必ず出来るはずです。また、絵の具の濃さについても、「絵の具と水加減」(p.58)の説明を参考にして、実際に練習をくり返して下さい。
最も難しいのは筆使いでしょう。筆使いにしても練習以外に解決方法はないので、何度も練習することです。なお、本書では、筆塗りパースの項で、筆運びの欠点を補う要領を説明してありますので、再度確認して覚えておくとよいでしょう。

Pratical exerases and review

We have introduced some of the basic requirements for painting perspectives. The secret to mastering the skill of preparing perspectives is practice. Practice makes perfect.
Though some rough sketches of each pattern are shown here, also make it a habit to refer to your own practice perspectives in accordance with the instructions given in this tuition manual.
If the utilization of rough sketches seems difficult for you, you can switch from a paintbrush to an airbrush for the coloring of tiled surfaces, you can shorten the height of the floor, or you can simplify the shape. You can also use the perspectives shown in the first chapter of this manual as your practice sketches.
Even if you are disappointed or dissatisfied with your practice perspectives, its important to keep practicing, and to carry on until the perspectives are finished. After finishing a perspective, review the points that you cannot express to your satisfaction and practice redoing them while referring to the respective instructions given in this manual.
Inspect your brushes before starting coloring. When you find that the tips of your brushes are uneven after water is squeezed out of them, cut the tips off with a cutter to make them even again.
When you find that you cannot paint fine or straight lines satisfactorily, practice using a scale. Make sure that the beginning and finishing points are drawn in advance, and practice painting the lines in rapid strokes, making use of your whole arm. Instead of painting final lines, make them temporary, floating the brush slightly above the surface of the canvas and trying to match the lines of the sketches. If the lines are successfully matched, then you can start painting the final lines.
The next point you have to master is how to produce the colors. When practicing color production, concentrate especially on the colors for exterior walls and window glass, -- mix the actual colors and try them out. This manual only provides instructions on how to produce a limited number of colors. Since only the colors required for perspectives are explained, you will never fail to produce them after certain amount of practice. For the density of colors, refer to the explanation given in "Ratio of colors and water" (p.58) and practice.
One of the most difficult challenges for you may be how to handle your brushes. Since there is no better way to address this problem than actually practicing handling brushes, that's exactly what you need to. Tricks to rectify poor brush handling are described in the chapter on preparation of paintbrush perspectives. It is essential that you review these tricks and until you master them.

2. 住宅——エアーブラシ着色 Residential houses — coloring with airbrush

●ボード　クレセントボード／白／310番
(Board) Crescent board/white/No.310

❶屋根の吹き付けのポイント
Basic points in spraying colors over the roofs

エアーブラシによる吹き付けだけでの着色なので、最も暗い屋根から着色し始めます。ただし、吹き付けは、極端なぐらい明暗をつけるようにしないと、マスキングフィルムを取り外した時に色の変化が感じられない場合があります。

Since only an airbrush is used for the coloring, it should be started from the darkest portion of the roof. Take note that the change in colors cannot often be felt when the masking film is removed unless you make a deliberate attempt to overdo the shades of the colors.

❷窓ガラス面の吹き付けのポイント
Basic points in spraying colors over window glass

窓ガラス面に、「住宅の窓ガラス着色」で述べたような下図を入れておき、マスキングした後で、デザインカッターを使って切り込みを入れます。その後、最も暗く着色する部分からフィルムを取り外しながら吹き付けていき、最後にマンガニーズブルーで空の色を吹き付けます。色は、筆塗りの場合と反対で、暖色ニュートラルから始め、バーント・アンバー、マンガニーズブルーへと変えていけばよいでしょう。もう一度、窓ガラスの着色実例の「住宅の窓ガラスの着色手順」とエアーブラシでの吹き付け例を参照して下さい。

Draw the sketch over the portion of window glass as shown in the chapter on "Coloring process for windows in residential houses," mask, and cut the masking away with a design cutter as you progress.After that, start spraying colors by removing the masking film and spray a final coat of manganese blue over the sky portion. The coloring sequence is a reversal of that employed with a brush. Start by spraying warm system colors and then shift to burnt umber and manganese blue. Refer to the window glass coloring examples in "Coloring process for windows in residential houses " and the color spraying examples.

❸外壁面の吹き付けのポイント
Basic points in spraying colors over exterior walls

外壁で最も暗い部分から吹き付けますが、まず、マスキングした後、屋根以外の下図に、全て切り込みを入れます。吹き付け順序は、側面の影→正面の影→軒裏→側面壁→正面壁へと進めて下さい。

Starting spraying over the darkest portions in the exterior wall and proceed to the lighter portions in sequence. Make sure that the masking is completed before you begin, and cut the masking for the entire sketch except the roof portion. The spraying sequence is: Shade in the side exterior - shade in the front - eaves - side exterior wall - front exterior wall.

❹建物の仕上げのポイント
Basic points in finishing building perspectives

最後に、シャッター、丸杭、玄関床、打ち放しの塀へと吹き付けた後、目地やハイライトを入れて建物を仕上げて下さい。

After spraying the shutters, round piles, porch floor and exposed finished fence, render the joints and highlights to finish the perspective of building.

❺点景の描き込みのポイント
Basic points in drawing incidental elements

点景は、エアーブラシで吹き付けてもよいのですが、筆塗りの方が速いでしょう。

You can spray incidental elements with an airbrush if you like, but ordinary paintbrushes are better suited for finishing the perspective quickly.

3. 集合住宅——エアーブラシ着色 Condominium — coloring with airbrush

●ボード　クレセントボード／白／310番
（Board） Crescent board / white / No.310

❶ 建物の吹き付けのポイント
Basic points in spraying colors over the condominium

窓ガラス面から吹き付けてもよいのですが、最も暗い屋根を含め、建物全体が一色だけなので、窓ガラスを後廻しにした方が速いでしょう。吹き付け順序は、屋根→側面壁の影→正面壁の影→軒裏→側面壁→正面壁へと進めます。

You can start spraying from the window glass if you like, but since the entire condominium including the darkest roof portion is sprayed in a single color, it's better to wait until a later stage to do this. The spraying sequence is: Roof - shade in side exterior wall - shade in front exterior wall - eaves - side exterior wall - front exterior wall.

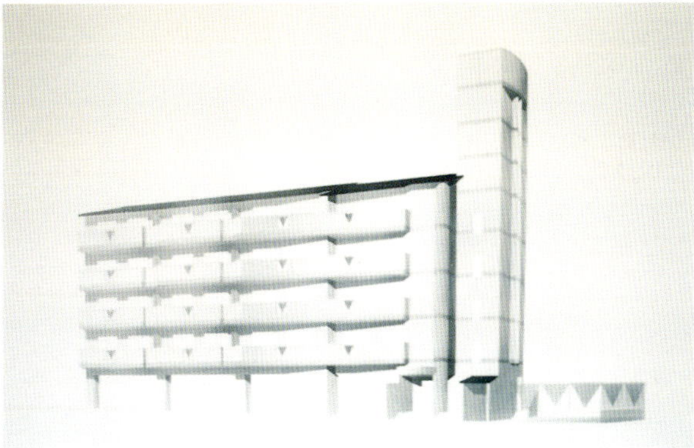

❷ 窓ガラスと空の吹き付けのポイント
Basic points in spraying colors over window glass and sky portions

まず、窓ガラス面を、「マンションの窓ガラスの着色手順」(p.66)で述べたような下図を入れてからマスキングをします。窓ガラスの吹き付けが終ったら、雲の形を残して空の部分を吹き付け、窓ガラス面にも空の色を吹き付けます。なお、１階部分と２階以上の窓ガラスの色が違うので、２階以上の吹き付けが終ったら、その部分を紙で被ってから１階部分の吹き付けをして下さい。この反対でも同じです。最後に雲を取り外して、軽く空の色を吹き付けるとなおよいでしょう。この見本では、１階の窓ガラス面と路面が同系色なので、１階の窓ガラスの吹き付け時に、同時に路面も仕上げてありますが、別々にしてもかまいません。

To begin with, sketch the window as described in the chapter on "Coloring process for windows of condominiums." (p.66) After spraying over the window pane, spray the sky portion leaving areas for the clouds to be painted in later. Since the color of the window glass on the ground floor differs from that on the first floor, begin by spraying the colors over the first floor, waiting until the portions to be colored are entirely covered before moving to the ground floor. The procedures is similar In the reverse sequence. It's generally better to leave portions for the clouds when spraying over the sky portion. Since the window panes on the ground floor and the road surface are in the same color system, you can spray the colors over the windows on the ground floor and the surface of the road either simultaneously or separately.

❸窓ガラス面の仕上げ
Finishing the Window glass

1階店舗のガラス面に暗い人物や明るい人物のシルエットを入れ、さらに照明を入れて下さい。その後、サッシの影からサッシへと、筆で着色して描き入れます。サッシの影は少し太めに描き入れた方が、サッシが描きやすいでしょう。

Silhouetle the dark and bright images of the people in the windows of the shops on the ground floor, and then paint the lighting . Color from the sash to the sashes with brush. Drawing the shade of the sash a bit wider will make it easier to draw the sashes themselves.

❹建物の仕上げ
Finishing the building

建物の目地を入れて建物を仕上げます。

Paint the joins in the building to finish the perspective.

❺点影の描き込み
Painting the incidental elements

構図的に間がぬけやすい建物なので、車を描き入れる時は、必ず建物の両端部分に重なるように車を描き入れて下さい。

Since this perspective can easily look silly when certain compositions are used,try to draw the cars on both sides of building so that they are superimposed with part of building.

実技添削用下図❶
Sketch used for practical training in correspondence course ❶

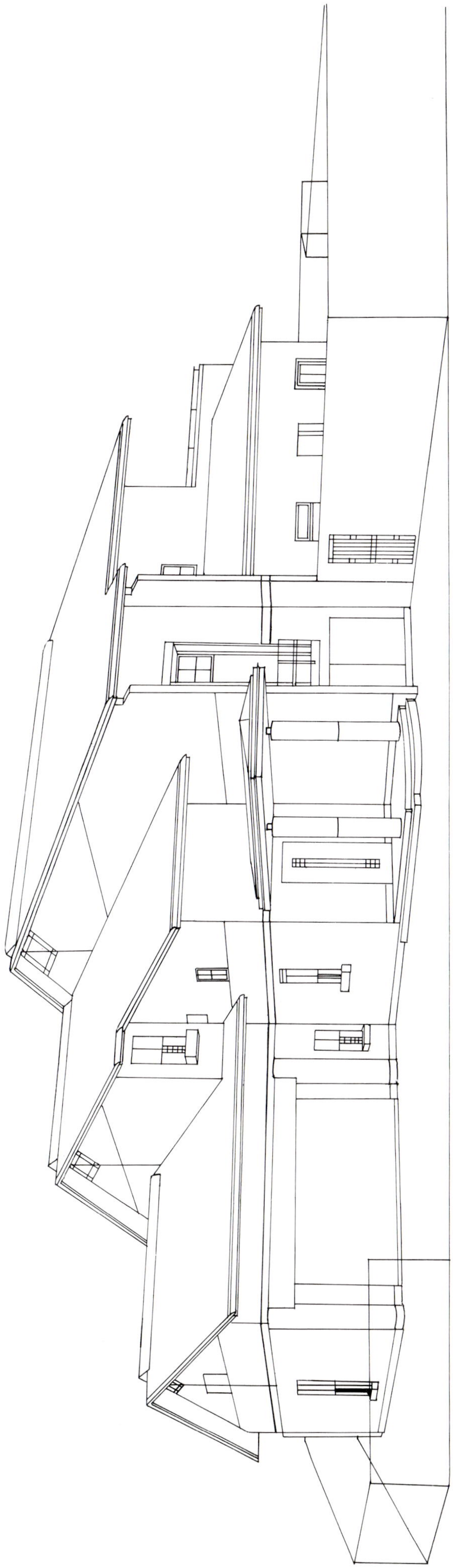

添削シール❶
Correction Seal

実技添削用下図 ❷
Sketch used for practical training in correspondence course ❷

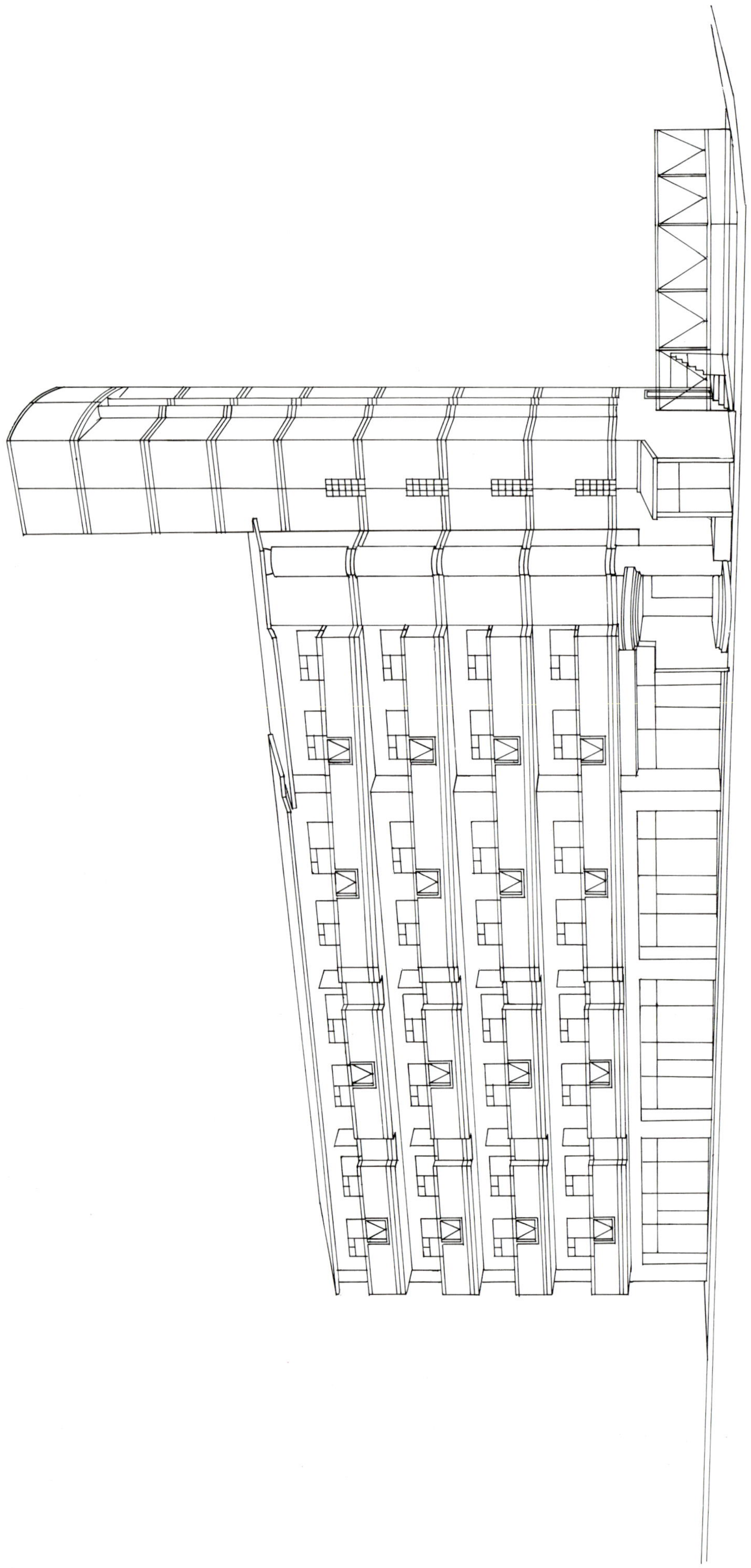

自由に使える下図 Sketch for free personal use

車の下図
Sketches of cars

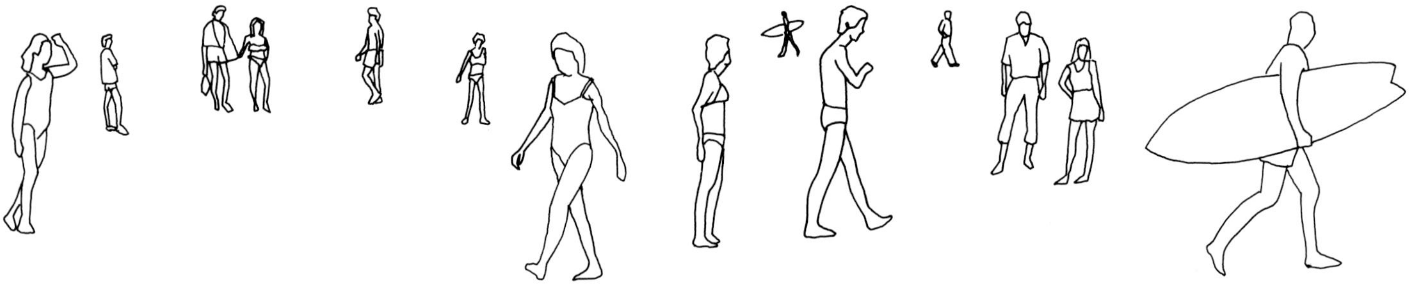

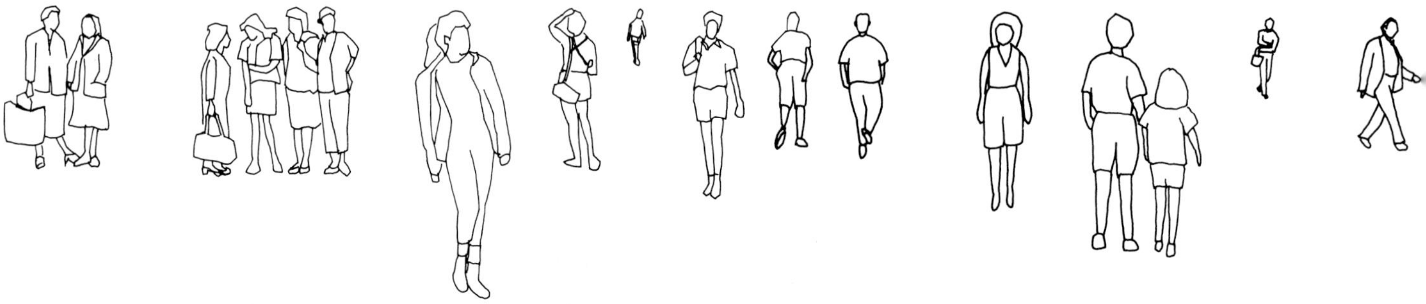

Afterword

あとがき

本書は、色を使ったことの少ない初心者にも理解していただけるように、できるだけ色数を少なく限定して、パース着色が進められるようにまとめあげたほか、基礎的な絵画上の注意事項まで付け加えました。理解できるまで、何度も読み返し練習することをすすめます。
執筆にあたり、あれもこれも説明したい気持で一杯になりましたが、何しろ書籍としての限界があり不十分な点も少なくありません。私の誠意を示す意味から、読者への添削でそれを補いたいと考えておりますので、147頁の応募規定を参照のうえ、質問文や作品をどしどし送ってください。必ず、ご希望にそえるように努力いたします。
終えるにあたって、本書の出版が、私の熱意を汲み取っていただいたグラフィック社編集部の大田悟氏の並々ならぬ助言と協力によって実現できたことに、心から感謝の念を表すと共に、より多くの読者の手助けになることを心から願っております。

1996年7月

松原弘晃デザインルーム:松原弘晃／作画協力者:熊尾武久

In the interest of achieving clear understanding among beginners who have not used colors extensively, this book limits the number of colors to the greatest possible degree, to allow the learning of perspective coloring techniques to be advanced in a smooth and coherent fashion. Also included have been basic cautionary items concerning the drawings. It is highly recommended that the book's drills be repeated again and again, until attaining a solid working grasp of the process.
In compiling this book, we were faced with the urge to furnish explanations on a truly unlimited number of areas. However, there are naturally limitations as to what can be communicated through the written medium, and there are many areas which may prove inadequate. As testimony to the sincerity of the authors, we wish to help compensate for such deficiencies by providing a correction service. In short, readers are encouraged to forward us a steady stream of questions, drawings and other items, while we ask only that return-use stamps and the proper stickers be included. We pledge make every effort in our capacity to address individual needs and desires.
Finally, I wish to express my most profound gratitude to Satoru Ota of the Editorial Division of Graphic-sha Publishing Company, who was so appreciative of my enthusiasm in this project, and so instrumental in channeling that largely unstructured passion into the publication of this volume. In this same spirit, it is my hope that this book will be of assistance and support for readers interested in pursuing ever higher levels of excellence in this fascinating field.

Jul y 1996

Hiroaki Matsubara Design Room : Hiroaki Matsubara
Drawing Production Associates : Takehisa Kumao

Author Profile
著者紹介

松原弘晃（まつばらひろあき）
Hiroaki Matsubara

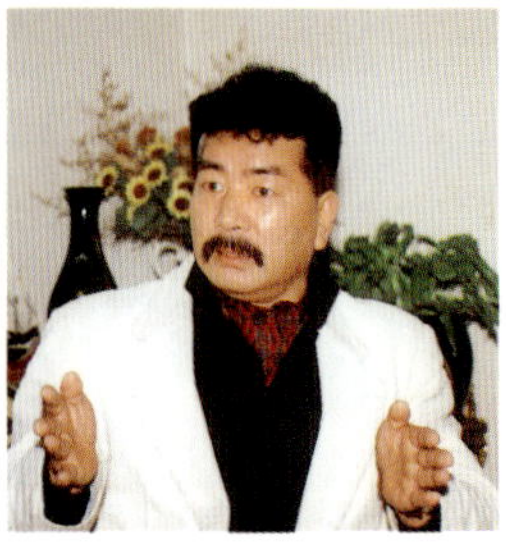

1948年：大阪に生まれる。
大阪市立美術研究所にてデッサンを学び、大学進学と同時に建築パースを描き始め、パースデザイナーとしての道を歩みながら伊東敬氏、高橋靖夫氏に師事する。
大学卒業後、色彩論と絵画学の研究のため米国に留学。
帰国後、1974年、大阪にて松原弘晃デザインルームを設立すると同時に、プロ養成の松原パース・スクールを併設し今日に至る。
著書「父の背中」（共著）ほか。

Born in Osaka in 1948, and studied design at Osaka Municipal Art Research Institute. Matsubara took up the discipline of drawing architectural perspectives upon entering university, pursuing his dream of becoming a perspective designer while serving under Takashi Itoh and Yasuo Kobayashi. Upon graduation he traveled to the United States to research the theory of color and pictorial art, and after returning to Japan established the adjacent facilities of the Hiroaki Matsubara Art Room and Matsubara Perspective School in Osaka.
（Main Writings）
"My Father's Back"（joint work, 1974）, etc.

建築パース　新戦力マスター
Mastering New Architectural Rendering Techniques

描き方がダイレクトに伝わる実技指導添削付き
includes a guidance material on evaluating your rendering style

発行　1996年8月25日 初版第1刷発行

著者　松原弘晃（© Hiroaki Matsubara）
本文DTP　滝沢英典
企画編集　大田 悟
翻訳　バベルインターナショナル
校正　アレフ

発行者　久世利郎
発行所　株式会社 グラフィック社
〒102 東京都千代田区九段北1-9-12 谷内ビル
Tel. 03-3263-4318　Fax. 03-3263-5297
振替・00130-6-114345
印刷・製本　錦明印刷株式会社

乱丁・落丁はお取り替え致します。

ISBN4-7661-0820-5 C3052